SSL Remote Access VPNs

Jazib Frahim, CCIE No. 5459
Qiang Huang, CCIE No. 4937

Cisco Press

Cisco Press
800 East 96th Street
Indianapolis, IN 46240 USA

SSL Remote Access VPNs

Jazib Frahim, Qiang Huang

Copyright© 2008 Cisco Systems, Inc.

Published by:
Cisco Press
800 East 96th Street
Indianapolis, IN 46240 USA

Printed in the United States of America

First Printing June 2008

Library of Congress Catalog Card Number: 2005923483

ISBN-13: 978-1-58705-242-2

ISBN-10: 1-58705-242-3

Warning and Disclaimer

This book is designed to provide information about the Secure Socket Layer (SSL) Virtual Private Network (VPN) technology on Cisco products. Every effort has been made to make this book as complete and as accurate as possible, but no warranty or fitness is implied.

The information is provided on an "as is" basis. The authors, Cisco Press, and Cisco Systems, Inc. shall have neither liability nor responsibility to any person or entity with respect to any loss or damages arising from the information contained in this book or from the use of the discs or programs that may accompany it.

The opinions expressed in this book belong to the author and are not necessarily those of Cisco Systems, Inc.

Trademark Acknowledgments

All terms mentioned in this book that are known to be trademarks or service marks have been appropriately capitalized. Cisco Press or Cisco Systems, Inc., cannot attest to the accuracy of this information. Use of a term in this book should not be regarded as affecting the validity of any trademark or service mark.

Corporate and Government Sales

The publisher offers excellent discounts on this book when ordered in quantity for bulk purchases or special sales, which may include electronic versions and/or custom covers and content particular to your business, training goals, marketing focus, and branding interests. For more information, please contact: **U.S. Corporate and Government Sales** 1-800-382-3419 corpsales@pearsontechgroup.com

For sales outside the United States, please contact: **International Sales** international@pearsoned.com

Feedback Information

At Cisco Press, our goal is to create in-depth technical books of the highest quality and value. Each book is crafted with care and precision, undergoing rigorous development that involves the unique expertise of members from the professional technical community.

Readers' feedback is a natural continuation of this process. If you have any comments regarding how we could improve the quality of this book, or otherwise alter it to better suit your needs, you can contact us through e-mail at feedback@ciscopress.com. Please make sure to include the book title and ISBN in your message.

We greatly appreciate your assistance.

Publisher	Paul Boger
Associate Publisher	Dave Dusthimer
Cisco Press Program Manager	Jeff Brady
Executive Editor	Brett Bartow
Managing Editor	Patrick Kanouse
Development Editor	Betsey Henkels
Senior Project Editor	Tonya Simpson
Copy Editor	Written Elegance, Inc.
Technical Editors	Pete Davis, Dave Garneau
Editorial Assistant	Vanessa Evans
Book Designer	Louisa Adair
Composition	Mark Shirar
Indexer	Heather McNeil
Proofreader	Sheri Cain

Americas Headquarters	Asia Pacific Headquarters	Europe Headquarters
Cisco Systems, Inc.	Cisco Systems, Inc.	Cisco Systems International BV
170 West Tasman Drive	168 Robinson Road	Haarlerbergpark
San Jose, CA 95134-1706	#28-01 Capital Tower	Haarlerbergweg 13-19
USA	Singapore 068912	1101 CH Amsterdam
www.cisco.com	www.cisco.com	The Netherlands
Tel: 408 526-4000	Tel: +65 6317 7777	www-europe.cisco.com
800 553-NETS (6387)	Fax: +65 6317 7799	Tel: +31 0 800 020 0791
Fax: 408 527-0883		Fax: +31 0 20 357 1100

Cisco has more than 200 offices worldwide. Addresses, phone numbers, and fax numbers are listed on the Cisco Website at **www.cisco.com/go/offices.**

About the Authors

Jazib Frahim, CCIE No. 5459, has been with Cisco for more than nine years. Having a bachelor's degree in computer engineering from Illinois Institute of Technology, he started out as a TAC engineer in the LAN Switching team. He then moved to the TAC Security team, where he acted as a technical leader for the security products. He led a team of 20 engineers in resolving complicated security and VPN technologies. He is currently working as a technical leader in the Worldwide Security Services Practice of Advanced Services for Network Security. He is responsible for guiding customers in the design and implementation of their networks with a focus on network security. He holds two CCIEs, one in routing and switching and the other in security. He has written numerous Cisco online technical documents and has been an active member on the Cisco online forum NetPro. He has presented at Networkers on multiple occasions and has taught many on-site and online courses to Cisco customers, partners, and employees.

He has recently received his master of business administration (MBA) degree from North Carolina State University. He is also an author of the following Cisco Press books: *Cisco Network Admission Control, Volume II: NAC Deployment and Troubleshooting,* and *Cisco ASA: All-in-One Firewall, IPS, and VPN Adaptive Security Appliance.*

Qiang Huang, CCIE No. 4937, is a product manager in the Cisco Systems Campus Switch System Technology Group, focusing on driving the security and intelligent services roadmap for Cisco market-leading modular Ethernet switching platforms. He has been with Cisco for almost ten years. During his time at Cisco, Qiang played an important role in a number of technology groups including the following: technical lead in the Cisco TAC security and VPN team, where he was responsible for troubleshooting complicated customer deployments in security and VPN solutions; a security consulting engineer in the Cisco Advanced Service Group, providing security posture assessment and consulting services to customers; a technical marketing engineer focusing on competitive analysis and market intelligence in network security with specialization in the emerging SSL VPN technology. Qiang has extensive knowledge of security and VPN technologies and experience in real-life customer deployments. Qiang holds CCIE certifications in routing and switching, security, and ISP dial. He is also one of the contributing authors of *Internetworking Technologies Handbook,* Fourth Edition. Qiang received a master's degree in electrical engineering from Colorado State University.

About the Technical Reviewers

Pete Davis has been working with computers and networks since he was able to walk. By age 15, he was one of the youngest professional network engineers and one of the first employees at an Internet service provider. Pete implemented and maintained the systems and networks behind New England's largest consumer Internet service provider, TIAC (The Internet Access Company). In 1997, Pete joined Shiva Corporation as a product specialist. Since 1998, Pete has been with Altiga Networks, a VPN concentrator manufacturer in Franklin, Massachusetts, that was acquired by Cisco on March 29, 2000. As product line manager, Pete is responsible for driving new VPN-related products and features.

Dave Garneau is principal consultant and senior technical instructor at The Radix Group, Ltd., a consulting and training company based in Henderson, Nevada, and focusing on network security. As a consultant, he specializes in Cisco network security (including IronPort, now part of Cisco) and VPN technologies (both IPsec and SSL VPN). As an instructor, he has trained more than 2500 people in eight countries to earn certifications throughout the Cisco and IronPort certification programs. He has written lab guides used worldwide by authorized Cisco Learning Partners, as well as publishing papers related to network security. Dave holds the following certifications: CCSP, CCNP, CCDP, CCSI, CCNA, CCDA, ICSP, ICSI, and CNE.

Dedications

Jazib Frahim:

I would like to dedicate this book to my lovely wife, Sadaf, who has patiently put up with me during the writing process.

I would also like to dedicate this book to my parents, Frahim and Perveen, who support and encourage me in all my endeavors.

Finally, I would like to thank my siblings, including my brother Shazib and sisters Erum and Sana, sister-in-law Asiya, my cute nephew Shayan, and my adorable nieces Shiza and Alisha. Thank you for your patience and understanding during the development of this book.

Qiang Huang:

I would like to dedicate this book to my parents, who always taught me to make better use of my free time, and to my wife for her patience and support of this project.

Acknowledgments

We would like to thank the technical editors, Pete Davis and David Garneau, for their time and technical expertise. They verified our work and provided recommendations on how to improve the quality of this manuscript. We would also like to thank Vincent Shan, Andy Qin, James Fu, and Awair Waheed from the Cisco Security Technical Group for their help and guidance. We also recognize Saddat Malik for providing content source for several figures in Chapter 2. Special thanks go to Scott Enicke and Aun Raza for reviewing this book prior to final editing.

We would like to thank the Cisco Press team, especially Brett Bartow and Betsey Henkels, for their patience, guidance, and consideration. Their efforts are greatly appreciated.

Many thanks to our managers, Ken Cavanagh, Raj Gulani, and Hasan Siraj, for their continuous support throughout this project.

Finally, we would like to acknowledge the Cisco TAC. Some of the best and brightest minds in the networking industry work there, supporting our Cisco customers often under very stressful conditions and working miracles daily. They are truly unsung heroes, and we are all honored to have had the privilege of working side by side with them in the trenches of the TAC.

This Book Is Safari Enabled

The Safari® Enabled icon on the cover of your favorite technology book means the book is available through Safari Bookshelf. When you buy this book, you get free access to the online edition for 45 days.

Safari Bookshelf is an electronic reference library that lets you easily search thousands of technical books, find code samples, download chapters, and access technical information whenever and wherever you need it.

To gain 45-day Safari Enabled access to this book:

- Go to http://www.ciscopress.com/safarienabled.
- Complete the brief registration form.
- Enter the coupon code QRGS-BHHI-3H9M-M3I3-G2KE.

If you have difficulty registering on Safari Bookshelf or accessing the online edition, please e-mail customer-service@safaribooksonline.com.

Contents at a Glance

Introduction   xviii

Chapter 1   Introduction to Remote Access VPN Technologies   3

Chapter 2   SSL VPN Technology   17

Chapter 3   SSL VPN Design Considerations   63

Chapter 4   Cisco SSL VPN Family of Products   85

Chapter 5   SSL VPNs on Cisco ASA   93

Chapter 6   SSL VPNs on Cisco IOS Routers   223

Chapter 7   Management of SSL VPNs   313

Index   332

Contents

Introduction   xviii

Chapter 1   Introduction to Remote Access VPN Technologies   3

Remote Access Technologies 5

IPsec 5
   Software-Based VPN Clients 7
   Hardware-Based VPN Clients 7

SSL VPN 7

L2TP 9

L2TP over IPsec   11

PPTP   13

Summary   14

Chapter 2   SSL VPN Technology   17

Cryptographic Building Blocks of SSL VPNs   17
   Hashing and Message Integrity Authentication   17
      Hashing   18
      Message Authentication Code   18
   Encryption   20
      RC4   21
      DES and 3DES   22
      AES   22
      Diffie-Hellman   23
      RSA and DSA   24
   Digital Signatures and Digital Certification   24
      Digital Signatures   24
      Public Key Infrastructure, Digital Certificates, and Certification   25

SSL and TLS   30
   SSL and TLS History   30
   SSL Protocols Overview   31
      OSI Layer Placement and TCP/IP Protocol Support   31
      SSL Record Protocol and Handshake Protocols   33
      SSL Connection Setup   34
      Application Data   42
      Case Study: SSL Connection Setup   43
   DTLS   48

SSL VPN   49

  Reverse Proxy Technology   50

    URL Mangling   52

    Content Rewriting   53

  Port-Forwarding Technology   55

  Terminal Services   58

  SSL VPN Tunnel Client   58

Summary   59

References   60

Chapter 3   SSL VPN Design Considerations   63

Not All Resource Access Methods Are Equal   63

User Authentication and Access Privilege Management   65

  User Authentication   66

  Choice of Authentication Servers   66

  AAA Server Scalability and High Availability   67

    AAA Server Scalability   67

    AAA Server High Availability and Resiliency   68

    Resource Access Privilege Management   68

Security Considerations   70

  Security Threats   71

    Lack of Security on Unmanaged Computers   71

    Data Theft   71

    Man-in-the-Middle Attacks   72

    Web Application Attack   73

    Spread of Viruses, Worms, and Trojans from Remote Computers to the Internal
      Network   73

    Split Tunneling   73

    Password Attacks   74

  Security Risk Mitigation   74

    Strong User Authentication and Password Policy   75

    Choose Strong Cryptographic Algorithms   75

    Session Timeout and Persistent Sessions   75

    Endpoint Security Posture Assessment and Validation   75

    VPN Session Data Protection   76

    Techniques to Prevent Data Theft   76

    Web Application Firewalls, Intrusion Prevention Systems, and Antivirus and
      Network Admission Control Technologies   77

Device Placement   78

Platform Options   79

Virtualization   79

High Availability   80

Performance and Scalability   81

Summary   82

References   82

Chapter 4   Cisco SSL VPN Family of Products   85

Overview of Cisco SSL VPN Product Portfolio   85

Cisco ASA 5500 Series   87
   SSL VPN History on Cisco ASA   87
   SSL VPN Specifications on Cisco ASA   88
   SSL VPN Licenses on Cisco ASA   89

Cisco IOS Routers   90
   SSL VPN History on Cisco IOS Routers   90
   SSL VPN Licenses on Cisco IOS Routers   90

Summary   91

Chapter 5   SSL VPNs on Cisco ASA   93

SSL VPN Design Considerations   93

SSL VPN Prerequisites   95
   SSL VPN Licenses   95
   Client Operating System and Browser and Software Requirements   96
   Infrastructure Requirements   97

Pre-SSL VPN Configuration Guide   97
   Enrolling Digital Certificates (Recommended)   98
      Step 1: Configuring a Trustpoint   98
      Step 2: Obtaining a CA Certificate   99
      Step 3: Obtaining an Identity Certificate   100
   Setting Up ASDM   101
      Uploading ASDM   102
      Setting Up the Appliance   103
   Accessing ASDM   104
   Setting Up Tunnel and Group Policies   106
      Configuring Group-Policies   107
      Configuring a Tunnel Group   110
   Setting Up User Authentication   110

Clientless SSL VPN Configuration Guide   114
   Enabling Clientless SSL VPN on an Interface   116

Configuring SSL VPN Portal Customization   117
    Logon Page   118
    Portal Page   123
    Logout Page   125
    Portal Customization and User Group   126
    Full Customization   129
Configuring Bookmarks   134
    Configuring Websites   135
    Configuring File Servers   137
    Applying a Bookmark List to a Group Policy   139
    Single Sign-On   140
Configuring Web-Type ACLs   141
Configuring Application Access   144
    Configuring Port Forwarding   144
    Configuring Smart Tunnels   147
Configuring Client-Server Plug-Ins   150

AnyConnect VPN Client Configuration Guide   152
    Loading the SVC Package   154
    Defining AnyConnect VPN Client Attributes   155
        Enabling AnyConnect VPN Client Functionality   155
        Defining a Pool of Addresses   156
        Configuring Traffic Filters   159
        Configuring a Tunnel Group   159
    Advanced Full Tunnel Features   159
        Split Tunneling   159
        DNS and WINS Assignment   161
        Keeping the SSL VPN Client Installed   162
        Configuring DTLS   163

Cisco Secure Desktop   164
    CSD Components   165
        Secure Desktop Manager   165
        Secure Desktop   165
        Cache Cleaner   166
    CSD Requirements   166
        Supported Operating Systems   166
        User Privileges   167
        Supported Internet Browsers   167
        Internet Browser Settings   167
    CSD Architecture   168
    Configuring CSD   169
        Loading the CSD Package   169
        Defining Prelogin Sequences   170

Host Scan   182

Host Scan Modules   183

Basic Host Scan   183

Endpoint Assessment   183

Advanced Endpoint Assessment   184

Configuring Host Scan   184

Setting Up Basic Host Scan   184

Enabling Endpoint Host Scan   186

Setting Up an Advanced Endpoint Host Scan   187

Dynamic Access Policies   189

DAP Architecture   190

DAP Records   191

DAP Selection Rules   191

DAP Configuration File   191

DAP Sequence of Events   191

Configuring DAP   192

Selecting a AAA Attribute   193

Selecting Endpoint Attributes   195

Defining Access Policies   197

Deployment Scenarios   205

AnyConnect Client with CSD and External Authentication   206

Step 1: Set Up CSD   207

Step 2: Set Up RADIUS for Authentication   207

Step 3: Configure AnyConnect SSL VPN   208

Clientless Connections with DAP   209

Step 1: Define Clientless Connections   210

Step 2: Configuring DAP   211

Monitoring and Troubleshooting SSL VPN   212

Monitoring SSL VPN   212

Troubleshooting SSL VPN   215

Troubleshooting SSL Negotiations   215

Troubleshooting AnyConnect Client Issues   215

Troubleshooting Clientless Issues   217

Troubleshooting CSD   219

Troubleshooting DAP   219

Summary   220

Chapter 6   SSL VPNs on Cisco IOS Routers   223

SSL VPN Design Considerations   223

IOS SSL VPN Prerequisites   225

IOS SSL VPN Configuration Guide   226
    Configuring Pre-SSL VPN Setup   226
        Setting Up User Authentication   226
        Enrolling Digital Certificates (Recommended)   229
        Loading SDM (Recommended)   232
    Initial SSL VPN Configuration   235
        Step 1: Setting Up an SSL VPN Gateway   237
        Step 2: Setting Up an SSL VPN Context   239
        Step 3: Configuring SSL VPN Look and Feel   241
        Step 4: Configuring SSL VPN Group Policies   245

Advanced SSL VPN Features   247
    Configuring Clientless SSL VPNs   247
    Windows File Sharing   253
    Configuring Application ACL   257
    Thin Client SSL VPNs   259
        Step 1: Defining Port-Forwarding Lists   261
        Step 2: Mapping Port-Forwarding Lists to a Group Policy   262
    AnyConnect SSL VPN Client   264
        Step 1: Loading the AnyConnect Package   264
        Step 2: Defining AnyConnect VPN Client Attributes   266

Cisco Secure Desktop   276
    CSD Components   277
        Secure Desktop Manager   277
        Secure Desktop   277
        Cache Cleaner   278
    CSD Requirements   278
        Supported Operating Systems   278
        User Privileges   279
        Supported Internet Browsers   279
        Internet Browser Settings   279
    CSD Architecture   280
    Configuring CSD   281
        Step 1: Loading the CSD Package   282
        Step 2: Launching the CSD Package   283
        Step 3: Defining Policies for Windows-Based Clients   283
        Defining Policies for Windows CE   298
        Defining Policies for the Mac and Linux Cache Cleaner   298

Deployment Scenarios   301
    Clientless Connections with CSD   301
        Step 1: User Authentication and DNS   302
        Step 2: Set Up CSD   303
        Step 3: Define Clientless Connections   303

AnyConnect Client and External Authentication   304
Step 1: Set Up RADIUS for Authentication   305
Step 2: Install the AnyConnect SSL VPN   306
Step 3: Configure AnyConnect SSL VPN Properties   306

Monitoring an SSL VPN in Cisco IOS   307

Summary   311

Chapter 7   Management of SSL VPNs   313

Multidevice Policy Provisioning   314
Device View and Policy View   314
Device View   314
Policy View   318
Use of Common Objects for Multidevice Management   320

Workflow Control and Role-Based Access Control   322
Workflow Control   323
Workflow Mode   324
Role-Based Administration   326
Native Mode   326
Cisco Secure ACS Integration Mode   327

Summary   331

References   331

Index   332

Icons Used in This Book

Command Syntax Conventions

The conventions used to present command syntax in this book are the same conventions used in the IOS Command Reference. The Command Reference describes these conventions as follows:

- **Boldface** indicates commands and keywords that are entered literally as shown. In actual configuration examples and output (not general command syntax), boldface indicates commands that are manually input by the user (such as a **show** command).
- *Italics* indicate arguments for which you supply actual values.
- Vertical bars (|) separate alternative, mutually exclusive elements.
- Square brackets [ ] indicate optional elements.
- Braces { } indicate a required choice.
- Braces within brackets [{ }] indicate a required choice within an optional element.

Introduction

This book provides a complete guide to the SSL VPN technology and discusses its implementation on Cisco SSL VPN–capable devices. Design guidance is provided to assist you in implementing SSL VPNs in an existing network infrastructure. This includes examining existing hardware and software to determine whether they are SSL VPN capable, providing design recommendations, and guiding you on setting up the Cisco SSL VPN devices.

Toward the end of Chapters 5 and 6, common deployment scenarios are covered to assist you in deploying an SSL VPN in your network.

Who Should Read This Book?

This book serves as a guide for network professionals who want to implement the Cisco SSL VPN remote access solution in their network to allow users to access the corporate resources easily and safely. The book systematically walks you through the product or solution architecture, installation, configuration, deployment, monitoring, and troubleshooting the SSL VPN solution. Any network professional should be able to use this book as a guide to successfully deploy SSL VPN remote access solutions in their network. Requirements include a basic knowledge of TCP/IP and networking, familiarity with Cisco routers/firewalls and their command-line interface (CLI), and a general understanding of the overall SSL VPN solution.

How This Book Is Organized

Part I of this book includes Chapters 1 and 2, which provide an overview of the remote access VPN technologies and introduce the SSL VPN technology. The remainder of the book is divided into two parts.

Part II encompasses Chapters 3 and 4 and introduces the Cisco SSL VPN product lines, with guidance on different design considerations.

Part III encompasses Chapters 5 through 7 and covers the installation, configuration, deployment, and troubleshooting of the individual components that make up the SSL VPN solution.

- Part I, "Introduction and Technology Overview," includes the following chapters:

    Chapter 1, "Introduction to Remote Access VPN Technologies": This chapter covers the remote access Virtual Private Network (VPN) technologies in detail. Protocols, such as the Point-to-Point Tunneling Protocol (PPTP), Internet Protocol Security (IPsec), Layer 2 Forwarding (L2F), Layer 2 Tunneling Protocol (L2TP) over IPsec, and SSL VPN, are discussed to provide readers with an overview of the available remote access VPN technologies.

    Chapter 2, "SSL VPN Technology": This chapter provides a technology overview of the building blocks of SSL VPNs, including cryptographic algorithms, SSL and Transport Layer Security (TLS), and common SSL VPN technologies.

- Part II, "SSL VPN Design Considerations and Cisco Solution Overview," includes the following chapters:

  Chapter 3, "SSL VPN Design Considerations": This chapter discusses the common design best practices for planning and designing an SSL VPN solution.

  Chapter 4, "Cisco SSL VPN Family of Products": This chapter discusses the SSL VPN functionality on Cisco Adaptive Security Appliance (ASA) and Cisco IOS routers and provides product specifications that are focused on SSL VPNs.

- Part III, "Deploying Cisco SSL VPN Solutions," includes the following chapters:

  Chapter 5, "SSL VPNs on Cisco ASA": This chapter provides details about the SSL VPN functionality in Cisco ASA. This chapter discusses clientless and full tunnel SSL VPN client implementations and focuses on Cisco Secure Desktop (CSD). This chapter also discusses the Host Scan feature that is used to collect posture information about end workstations. The dynamic access policy (DAP) feature, its usage, and detailed configuration examples are also provided. To reinforce learning, many different deployment scenarios are presented along with their configurations.

  Chapter 6, "SSL VPNs on Cisco IOS Routers": This chapter provides details about the SSL VPN functionality in Cisco IOS routers. It begins by offering design guidance and then discusses the configuration of SSL VPNs in greater detail. The configurations of clientless, thin client, and AnyConnect Client modes are discussed. The second half of the chapter focuses on Cisco Secure Desktop (CSD) and offers guidance in setting up CSD features. To reinforce learning, two different deployment scenarios are presented along with their configurations. Toward the end of this chapter, SSL VPN monitoring through SDM is also discussed.

  Chapter 7, "Management of SSL VPNs": This chapter discusses the central management of SSL VPN devices using Cisco Security Manager.

This chapter covers the following topics:

- IPsec
- SSL VPN
- L2TP
- L2TP over IPsec
- PPTP

CHAPTER 1

Introduction to Remote Access VPN Technologies

Since the advent of the Internet, network administrators have looked for ways to leverage this low-cost, widespread medium to transport data while protecting data integrity and confidentiality. They looked for ways to protect the information within the data packets while providing transparency to the end user. This spawned the concept of Virtual Private Networks (VPN). Subsequently, the Internet Engineering Task Force (IETF) was engaged to craft standard protocols and procedures to be used by all vendors of VPNs for data protection and confidentiality.

The IETF defined a number of VPN protocols, including Point-to-Point Tunneling Protocol (PPTP), Layer 2 Forwarding (L2F) Protocol, Layer 2 Tunneling Protocol (L2TP), Generic Routing Encapsulation (GRE) Protocol, Multiprotocol Label Switching (MPLS) VPN, Internet Protocol Security (IPsec), and Secure Socket Layer VPN (SSL VPN).

VPN protocols can be categorized into two distinct groups:

- Site-to-site protocols
- Remote access protocols

Site-to-site protocols allow an organization to establish secure connections between two or more offices so that it can send traffic back and forth using a shared medium such as the Internet. These connections can also be used to connect the private or semiprivate networks of an organization with the private or semiprivate networks of a different organization over the shared medium. This eliminates the need for dedicated leased lines to connect the remote offices to the organization's network. IPsec, GRE, and MPLS VPN are commonly used site-to-site VPN protocols.

Figure 1-1 shows a simple IPsec VPN topology that SecureMe (a fictitious company) is planning to deploy. SecureMe wants to ensure that the two locations (Chicago and London) can communicate over the Internet without risking the integrity of their data. In this network diagram, host A resides on the private network of the Chicago router and sends a packet to host B that exists on the private network of the London router. When the Chicago router receives the clear-text packet, it encrypts the datagram based on the negotiated security policies and then forwards the encrypted datagram to the other end of the VPN tunnel. The London router receives and decrypts the datagram and eventually forwards it to the destination host B. Without access to the negotiated security policies (or keys) required to decrypt the packet, the information enclosed within the packet remains secure while the packet traverses the public Internet.

Figure 1-1   *IPsec Site-to-Site VPN Tunnel*

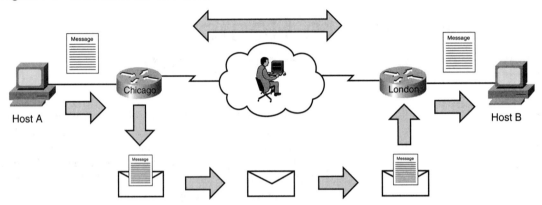

The remote access protocols benefit an organization by allowing mobile users to work from remote locations such as home, hotels, airport internet kiosks and Internet cafes as if they were directly connected to their organization's network. Organizations do not need to maintain a huge pool of modems and access servers to accommodate remote users. Additionally, they save money by not having to pay for the toll-free numbers and long-distance phone charges. Some commonly used remote access VPN protocols are SSL VPN, IPsec, L2TP, L2TP over IPsec, and PPTP.

Figure 1-2 shows a deployment model in which different types of remote users are using the remote access VPN technologies. The figure illustrates a mobile user, a home-office user, and a number of small branch office users accessing corporate resources using the remote access protocols.

Figure 1-2   *Remote Access Deployment*

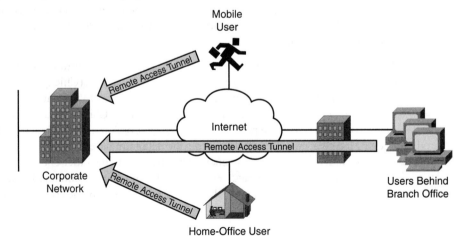

Many enterprises prefer to use IPsec because it can be used as either a site-to-site or remote access protocol. Additionally, IPsec is an obvious choice for a number of vendors because of its robust feature set and security characteristics, including data integrity and packet and data encryption. However, other VPN methods are commonly used as well, depending on the requirements and infrastructure of an organization. SSL VPN is becoming a preferred choice for many organizations because of its benefits. In many cases, it allows remote access VPN users to access corporate resources without needing to install additional software on the shared workstations.

Remote Access Technologies

Organizations are constantly under pressure to reduce costs by leveraging newer technology in their existing network infrastructure. With the growth of the Internet and greater focus on globalization, organizations are required to provide their employees with 24/7 access to organizational resources. The increasing number of mobile workers and telecommuters is a major factor in the exponential growth of remote access technologies. These users require the traditional LAN-based applications, such as data, voice, and video, to work seamlessly, thereby giving users the illusion of being directly connected to the corporate LAN. This chapter discusses a number of remote access technologies, including the following:

- IPsec
- SSL VPN
- L2TP
- L2TP over IPsec
- PPTP

The sections that follow discuss all these technologies.

IPsec

IPsec is the most widely used VPN technology. Because it provides protection at the IP level (Layer 3), it can be deployed to secure communication between a pair of gateways, a pair of host computers, or even between a gateway and a host computer. It offers the security features that are required in the enterprise and service provider infrastructures. IPsec was designed to provide data integrity to ensure that packets have not been modified during transmission, packet authentication to make sure that packets are coming from a valid source, and data encryption to assure confidentiality of the content.

NOTE   A number of RFCs provide the framework for IPsec. They include RFC 2401–2412, 2104, 1829, and 1851.

Internet Key Exchange (IKE) uses the framework provided by the Internet Security Association and Key Management Protocol (ISAKMP) and parts of two other key management protocols, namely Oakley and Secure Key Exchange Mechanism (SKEME). The purpose of IKE, as defined in RFC 2409, "The Internet Key Exchange," is to negotiate different security associations (SA) by using the available key management protocols.

ISAKMP negotiates using two phases. In Phase 1, ISAKMP creates a secure and authentic communication channel between the peers. By using this bidirectional channel, the VPN peers can agree on how the further negotiation should be handled by sending protected messages to one another. Phase 2 negotiations then create two unidirectional channels that are used to secure and authenticate the actual data packets.

The Cisco IPsec remote access solution introduces two additional sets of negotiations to successfully negotiate an IPsec tunnel. These negotiations, also referred to as Phase 1.5, include extended authentication (X-AUTH) and mode configuration (mode config) to provide additional security enhancements. Figure 1-3 illustrates these different phases. During X-AUTH, the VPN client is prompted to provide user credentials for authentication. After successful authentication, the IPsec gateway pushes a number of configuration parameters and security policies to the end-user connection in mode config.

Figure 1-3   *IPsec Phases in Cisco Devices*

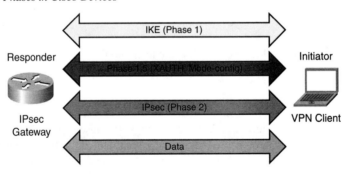

The Cisco IPsec remote access solution comes in two different flavors:

- Software-based VPN clients
- Hardware-based VPN clients

Software-Based VPN Clients

The software-based IPsec remote access solution in Cisco products requires you to install a software-based VPN client on the workstations. In organizations where installation of a third-party application is not allowed, administrators can explore other technologies, such as L2TP over IPsec, which is discussed later in this chapter. The software-based VPN client runs on a variety of operating systems, such as Windows, Solaris, Linux, and Mac OS X. It can be downloaded from Cisco.com free of charge as long as the Cisco IPsec gateway is under a valid service contract.

Hardware-Based VPN Clients

The Cisco hardware-based VPN clients implement the same functionality as discussed in the earlier section using the dedicated Cisco hardware devices. The hardware-based VPN is supported on the following platforms:

- Cisco IOS router
- Cisco PIX firewall
- Cisco ASA 5505
- Cisco VPN 3002 hardware client

A Cisco small office, home office (SOHO) router can act as a VPN client and initiate a VPN tunnel on behalf of the hosts residing on the private subnet. When the IPsec gateway receives interesting traffic destined to its protected network, it determines the IP address of the hardware client by checking the configuration.

SSL VPN

Secure Socket Layer (SSL) VPN is the emerging remote access technology that provides secure connectivity to the internal corporate resources through a web browser or a dedicated client. It sits between the transport and application layers of the OSI model. The SSL protocol was developed by Netscape to promote e-commerce sites that required data encryption and user authentication. With online banking, for example, the user session is securely established by using this protocol. Even though it was originally designed to provide secure web access, organizations are increasingly leveraging this protocol to provide secure access to commonly used applications, such as Simple Mail Transfer Protocol (SMTP), Post Office Protocol version 3 (POP3), and Internet Message Access Protocol (IMAP).

The greatest strength of SSL VPN comes from the fact that SSL is a mature protocol and is readily available in virtually all web browsers. Using SSL VPN, you can securely navigate your internal web server, or even check your e-mails, from a kiosk or Internet café. You can customize the SSL VPN solution to meet any business requirement. This includes not only providing access to corporate resources without loading a VPN client but also providing strong data confidentially while using a cost-effective and flexible method. The Cisco solution enhances the SSL VPN functionality to provide many deployment modes that include the following:

- **Clientless mode:** Provides secure access to corporate resources, specifically web and e-mail servers, without loading any applets or other clients.

- **Thin client mode:** Provides access to most of the TCP-based protocols, such as SMTP, POP, Secure Shell (SSH), Terminal, and Telnet by loading a Java applet on the client machine.

- **Full tunnel mode:** Provides full access to corporate resources as if you were connected directly to the network. This mode requires you to use a dynamically downloadable SSL VPN client before access is granted.

NOTE   To learn more about SSL VPN and the three deployment modes, consult Chapter 2, "SSL VPN Technology."

SSL VPN offers the advantage that it is platform independent. Using any browser that supports SSL, you can access resources without worrying about the underlying operating system. Secondly, you do not have to troubleshoot a third-party VPN client, should the connection not work as expected. Additionally, SSL VPN solves the network traversal problem, as many organizations restrict most forms of VPN traffic, such as IPsec and PPTP, to pass through their networks.

One major difference between SSL VPN and other remote access technologies is in the implementation of user sessions. With the remote access technologies discussed in this chapter, the VPN client initiates a direct connection to the servers residing on the protected network. However, in the clientless mode of SSL VPN, the SSL VPN gateway acts as a proxy between the VPN client and the internal resources. As shown in Figure 1-4, if a user wants to access the internal website, intranet.securemeinc.com, the SSL VPN session is terminated on the gateway, and then the gateway initiates a new session to the internal server on behalf of the client.

Figure 1-4   *SSL VPN Gateway and Connection Proxy*

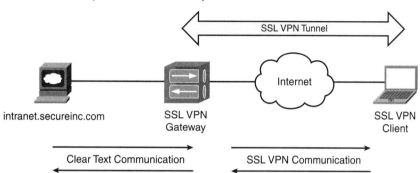

L2TP

Layer 2 Tunneling Protocol (L2TP), documented in RFC 2661, combines features from Layer 2 Forwarding (L2F) from Cisco Systems and PPTP from Microsoft. Documented in RFC 3931, enhancements were made in version 3 to add security features and improved encapsulation that meet the emerging industry requirements. It packages data within Point-to-Point Protocol (PPP) and uses registered User Datagram Protocol (UDP) port 1701 for both tunnel negotiations and data encapsulation.

L2TP can replace remote access deployments that currently use PPTP and L2F technologies. L2TP is usually deployed in two remote access models:

- **Voluntary tunnel model:** This model works in a manner similar to PPTP, because the tunnel is initiated by an L2TP-enabled client and is terminated on an L2TP-enabled server. Consequently, the L2TP tunnel is established between the client and the server, and the Internet service provider (ISP) does not need to have L2TP enabled in its infrastructure. Part (a) of Figure 1-5 illustrates this model.

- **Compulsory tunnel incoming call model:** This model works in a manner similar to L2F, where a PPP session is established between the end workstation and the ISP gateway. Based on user authentication, the L2TP session is initiated by the ISP L2TP access concentrator (LAC) to the L2TP network server (LNS) that is owned by the organization. Therefore, the end user does not even know that the L2TP tunnel exists between the ISP LAC and the corporate LNS, as depicted in part (b) of Figure 1-5.

Figure 1-5   *L2TP Deployment Models*

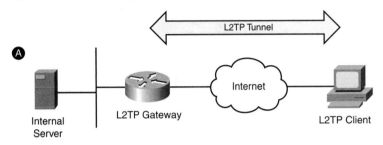

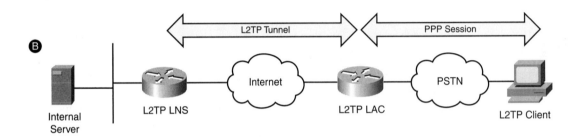

NOTE   L2TP uses UDP port 1701 for both tunnel negotiations and data encapsulation. Therefore, if you have a firewall between the client and the server, you need to allow only this protocol.

Most newer versions of Microsoft Windows, including Windows 2000 and Windows XP, have native support for L2TP as a remote access protocol. L2TP can use a number of authentication protocols for user authentication such as

- Password Authentication Protocol (PAP)
- Challenge-Handshake Authentication Protocol (CHAP)
- Microsoft CHAP (MS-CHAP)

Support for smart cards is also available when using Extensible Authentication Protocol (EAP). Data confidentiality is provided through 40-bit or 128-bit encryption by using Microsoft Point-to-Point Encryption (MPPE). However, it is highly recommended to add IPsec encryption to L2TP implementations. This way, IPsec can provide confidentiality, authentication, and integrity to the data wrapped within L2TP encapsulation. Integrating IPsec with L2TP is commonly referred to as L2TP over IPsec, and discussed in the next section.

L2TP over IPsec

Organizations that prefer to use a built-in remote access client in the Windows-based operating systems can use L2TP. However, L2TP fails to provide strong data confidentiality. Therefore, most of the L2TP implementations use IPsec to provide data security. This methodology is commonly referred to as L2TP over IPsec and is documented in RFC 3139.

In an L2TP over IPsec implementation, the client workstation and the home gateway device go through seven steps, as depicted in Figure 1-6 and described in the corresponding list that follows.

Figure 1-6   *L2TP over IPsec Negotiations*

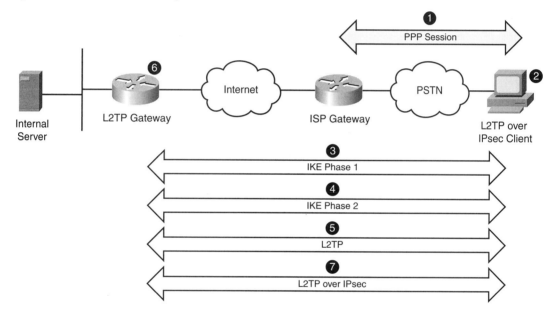

1   The user establishes a PPP session to the service provider access router and receives a dynamic public IP address. This step is optional if the workstation already has an IP address and can send traffic to the Internet.

2   The user launches the L2TP client that is configured to use IPsec for data security.

3   The client workstation initiates a session and negotiates a secure channel for exchanging keys (Phase 1 negotiations of IKE).

4   After successfully establishing Phase 1, the client establishes two secure channels for data encryption and authentication (Phase 2 negotiations of IKE). The data channels are set up to encrypt L2TP traffic that is destined to UDP port 1701.

5 After IPsec is established, the client initiates an L2TP session within IPsec.

6 The user-specified authentication credentials are used to validate the L2TP session. Any PPP or L2TP attributes are negotiated after successfully authenticating the user.

7 After the L2TP session is established, the user workstation sends data traffic that is encapsulated within L2TP. The L2TP packets are encrypted by IPsec and then sent out to the other end of the tunnel over the Internet.

NOTE   If you have a firewall between the L2TP over IPsec client and home gateway, you need to allow IP protocol 50 (ESP) and UDP port 500 to pass through. L2TP packets (UDP port 1701) are encapsulated within ESP. Some L2TP over IPsec vendors allow NAT transparency (NAT-T) by encapsulating traffic into UDP port 4500.

Figure 1-7 shows an L2TP over IPsec packet format after all the headers and encapsulations have been added to the original packet.

Figure 1-7   *L2TP over IPsec Packet Format*

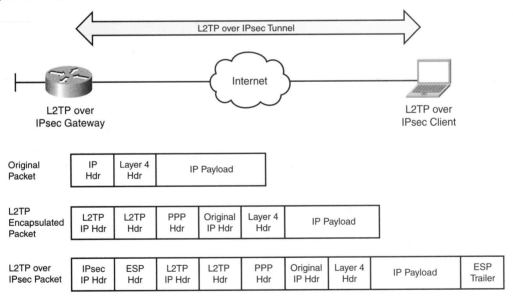

PPTP

Point-to-Point Tunneling Protocol (PPTP) is a client-server network protocol that allows remote users to access network resources over the Internet. PPTP was developed by Microsoft and is documented in RFC 2637. PPTP packages data within Point-to-Point Protocol (PPP) and then wraps the data within IP packets. PPTP uses an extended version of Generic Routing Encapsulation (GRE) Protocol as the encapsulating mechanism to make the IP packets routable.

With PPTP, the client uses TCP port 1723 to initiate the connection to the PPTP gateway. The gateway prompts the user for authentication credentials. After successfully authenticating the user and negotiating other parameters, such as compression and encryption, the client encapsulates data packets in GRE and transmits them to the gateway over an insecure connection. The gateway de-encapsulates the packets and places them on the private network. Figure 1-8 illustrates the communication and transport channels of PPTP.

Figure 1-8   *PPTP Connection Negotiations*

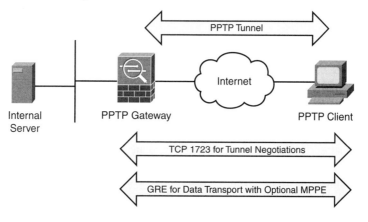

NOTE   GRE is Internet Protocol 47. If you have a firewall between the client and the server, make sure that you allow TCP port 1723 and GRE protocol to pass through it.

The data confidentiality is provided through 40-bit or 128-bit encryption using Microsoft Point-to-Point Encryption (MPPE), similar to L2TP.

PPTP functionality is freely available in most versions of Microsoft Windows operating systems. Consequently, it is the preferred choice for organizations that do not want to load a third-party VPN client and use solely Windows-based operating systems. However, PPTP is not a widely deployed remote access technology because of security flaws in its protocol implementation.

Remote access technologies can be selected depending on the security policy set by your enterprise. Table 1-1 summarizes the remote access technologies that were discussed in this chapter.

Table 1-1 *Remote Access VPN Technologies Summary*

Functionality	PPTP	IPsec	L2TP	L2TP over IPsec	SSL VPN
VPN client	Built in to most Windows OSs	Requires a third-party client	Built into newer Windows OSs	Built into newer Windows OSs	VPN client is optional
Encryption	MPPE	DES, 3DES, AES	MPPE	DES, 3DES, AES	DES, 3DES, RC4-128, RC4-40, AES
Deployment	Rarely used	Extensively used	Rarely used	Limited use	Steady growth

Summary

Remote access VPN services provide a way to connect home and mobile users to the corporate network. Until only a decade ago, the only way to provide this service was through dialup connections using analog modems. Organizations had to maintain a pool of modems and access servers to accommodate remote users. Additionally, they were billed for providing toll-free and long-distance phone services. With the rapid growth of the Internet technologies, more and more dialup mobile users are migrating to broadband digital subscriber line (DSL) and cable-modem connections. As a result, corporations are in the process of moving these dialup users to remote access VPNs for faster communication. To help you select a remote access VPN technology that meets the needs and requirements of your organization, this chapter provides an overview of the different technologies. The remote access VPN technologies discussed included IPsec, SSL VPN, L2TP, L2TP over IPsec, and PPTP.

This chapter describes the following topics:

- Background
- SSL and TLS
- SSL VPN

SSL VPN Technology

As Secure Socket Layer (SSL) Virtual Private Network (VPN) technology has become more mature and has rapidly been deployed over recent years, it has gained the attention of network and IT administrators who are looking for remote access VPN solutions that provide ubiquitous access and low-cost deployment and management. At present, no official standards exist for SSL VPN technologies; various vendors use different implementations. This chapter takes a close look at the evolution of the SSL VPN technology to help you understand how this technology works.

Cryptographic Building Blocks of SSL VPNs

A VPN carries private traffic over public networks. A secure VPN meets the following basic requirements:

- **Authentication** guarantees that the VPN entity communicates with the intended party. The authentication can apply to either a VPN device or a VPN user. For example, in a remote access VPN, the VPN head-end device can authenticate the user PC to make sure that it is indeed the PC that owns the IP address that it uses to connect to the concentrator. The concentrator can also authenticate the end user who is using the PC to properly assign user privileges based on the user's information.

- **Confidentiality** ensures the data's privacy by encrypting the data.

- **Message integrity** guarantees that the data's content has not been modified during the transmission.

The following sections examine how these requirements are fulfilled through the use of various cryptographic algorithms. Readers who are already familiar with these cryptographic algorithms can skip these sections and move directly to the SSL section.

Hashing and Message Integrity Authentication

The following sections describe hashing and its use in cryptography.

Hashing

Hashing plays an important role in a security system by ensuring the integrity of the transmitted message. A hashing algorithm converts a variable-length text field into a fixed-size string. Hashing algorithms used in a security system have the following two properties:

- **One-way hashing mechanism:** This means that given the hash output, it is difficult to invert the hashing function to get the original message.

- **Collision-free output:** This means that for a hashing algorithm, it is computationally infeasible to find any two messages that have the same hash output.

Because of these properties, a hash is also known as a message digest or digital fingerprint. People can generate a small hash output from a large document and use the hash output as the digital fingerprint of the document. This digital fingerprint can then be used to ensure that the message has not been tampered with during its transmission over an insecure channel. In addition, from the digital fingerprint, it is impossible to reveal the content of the original message.

Up to now, the most commonly used cryptographic hash algorithms have been message digest algorithm 5 (MD5) and Secure Hash Algorithm 1 (SHA-1). Both of these have been considered one-way and strongly collision-free hashing algorithms. MD5 provides 128-bit output, and SHA-1 provides 160-bit output. Because of its larger size, SHA-1 is normally considered more secure, but computationally more expensive, than MD5. With hardware and software implementation in today's networks, the performance difference is usually not a concern. Therefore, SHA-1 is the preferred hashing algorithm for use in a VPN deployment.

Message Authentication Code

Message authentication code (MAC) is a cryptographic checksum that is used to ensure the integrity of the message during transmission. To generate a MAC, you can use either an encryption algorithm, such as Data Encryption Standard (DES), or a hashing algorithm. Hashing is generally much faster than encryption algorithms, so the hash-based MAC (HMAC) is the most popular way. HMAC is a keyed hash function. Here is how it works: To generate an HMAC of a message M, you need to pick two system parameters, a hashing function H (normally MD5 or SHA-1) and a key K. The HMAC of the message is calculated as follows:

$$HMAC(K,M) = H(K \text{ XOR } opad, H (K \text{ XOR } ipad, M))$$

where opad is the string 0X5c and ipad is the string 0x36.

In a crypto system, the key K used here is normally generated during the key negotiation and establishment process between the two peers. Note that the two-level hash makes an HMAC function much more secure than a simple keyed hash function.

Figure 2-1 illustrates how HMAC functions between the sender and recipient of the message.

Figure 2-1   *HMAC*

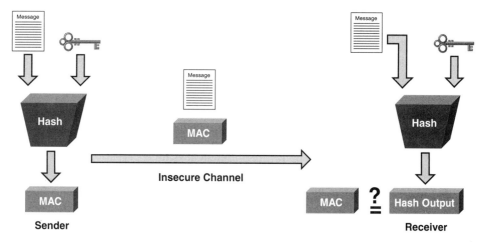

The Security of MD5 and SHA-1

Recent research conducted by a group of Chinese cryptographers, including Xiaoyun Wang, has shown that MD5 and SHA-1 are not collision free, and algorithms have been developed to find collisions faster than using brute force. For example, SHA-1 has a 160-bit output, so if you hash 2^{80} random messages, you will find one pair of messages that have the same hash output. Three Chinese cryptographers proved that they can find collisions in SHA-1 with 2^{69} operations, which is 2000 times faster than using brute force.

The implications of these findings are described by Bruce Schneier at his web blog (http://www.schneier.com/blog/archives/2005/02/cryptanalysis_o.html) and by Eric Rescorla at http://www.rtfm.com/movabletype/archives/2004_08.html#001059.

Here is a brief summary:

- The attack threatens the nonrepudiation property provided by hashing algorithms in digital certificates.
- It is believed that HMAC is still secure against this attack.
- The current attack is on the far edge of feasibility with current technology.

These findings push industry toward developing more secure hash algorithms such as SHA-256 or other crypto methods. More details on SHA-2 can be found at http://en.wikipedia.org/wiki/SHA-2.

Encryption

Encryption algorithms transfer plain text into cipher text. Different from hashing, encryption algorithms require keys for encryption and decryption. Two main types of encryption algorithms exist:

- **Symmetric encryption:** Uses the same key for encryption and decryption. It is also known as secret-key cryptography. The symmetric algorithms are normally used to encrypt the content of a message. Two main types of symmetric encryption algorithms exist:

    — Stream ciphers, such as RC4

    — Block ciphers, such as DES, Triple DES (3DES), and Advanced Encryption Standard (AES)

- **Asymmetric encryption:** Uses different keys for encryption and decryption. Asymmetric encryption is also known as public-key cryptography. An asymmetric encryption system consists of two computationally associated keys. One, known to the public domain, is called the public key; the other is known only to the owner of the key pair. Depending on the use of the public and private key pairs, asymmetric algorithms can be used for either encryption or authentication purposes. Figure 2-2 illustrates the usage of asymmetric algorithms. Consider the example of Alice and Bob, who want to use asymmetric algorithms for secure communications. For encryption purposes, Alice would encrypt the message using Bob's public key and send the cipher text to Bob. Upon receiving the cipher text, Bob, who is the only owner of the corresponding private key, can then decrypt the message with his private key. For authentication purposes, Alice would encrypt (or sign) the message using her own private key. Other people such as Bob can then verify the authenticity of the message by using Alice's public key, which is the only key that matches the signing private key. The real-world use of asymmetric algorithms in crypto systems involves other components. We discuss them in the next few sections.

Because symmetric algorithms are much faster than asymmetric algorithms, digital certification or key management is more commonly used for data encryption than asymmetric algorithms. The popular examples of asymmetric algorithms are Diffie-Hellman (DH) algorithms and Rivest, Shamir, and Adelman (RSA).

Figure 2-2 *Applications of Asymmetric Algorithms*

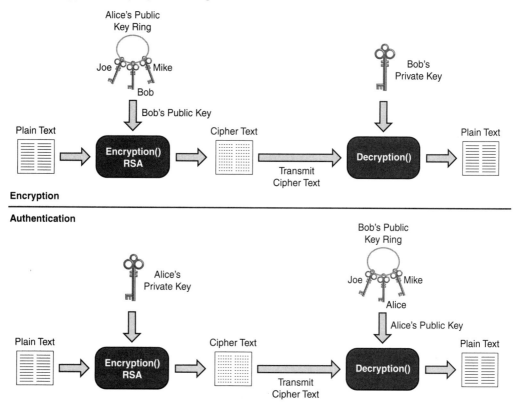

RC4

Designed by Ron Rivest in 1987 for RSA Security, RC4 is the mostly widely used stream cipher. Because of its speed and simplicity, RC4 has been deployed in many applications, such as the SSL Protocol and the Wired Equivalent Privacy (WEP) Protocol, which are used to secure wireless network traffic.

As a stream cipher, RC4 works on bits of plain-text data and encrypts them one at a time by XORing the keystream with the plain text. The keystream is generated by passing the encryption key and initialization vector (IV) through a pseudorandom number generator.

For SSL, most web browsers support RC4 encryption with two different key sizes: RC4-40bit and RC4-128bit. Newer browsers, such as Internet Explorer 7.0 and Firefox, have started to support stronger ciphers such as AES.

DES and 3DES

Data Encryption Standard (DES) is by far the most widely used symmetric encryption algorithm. DES is a 64-bit block cipher that works on an 8-byte data block. The output cipher block has the same 8-byte length. At the decryption side, the same algorithm is applied in reverse with the same key. Due to the requirement of having parity bits, the effective key strength of DES is 56 bits.

To encrypt a message that exceeds the DES block size, the individual cipher blocks are chained using a certain mode of operations. There are various modes of operations, such as Electric Code Book (ECB), cipher block chaining (CBC), and so on. The CBC mode is the commonly used mode of operation in commercial implementations. In CBC mode, each block of cipher text is XORed with the next plain-text block to be encrypted, thus making all the blocks dependent on all the previous blocks. The first block of data is XORed with the IV. The CBC mode adds more security compared to the ECB mode because of its extra XOR steps.

Since its design by IBM in 1970s, the DES algorithm has withheld aggressive cryptoanalysis over the years. However, its 56-bit key length is too short, and it has become weak over the years with the rapidly increasing computational power of consumer-grade systems.

3DES addresses DES's insufficient key length problem. 3DES performs DES three times with three sets of keys for a total of a 168-bit key length. To perform 3DES, the popular operation is to Encrypt-Decrypt-Encrypt (EDE). That is, DES encrypts the message using key 1, decrypts the message using key 2, and finally, encrypts the message using key 3.

AES is one of the cipher options for SSL v3 and Transport Layer Security (TLS).

AES

To replace the aging DES standard, the National Institute of Standards and Technology (NIST) called for the submission of an Advanced Encryption Standard (AES) in 1997. Out of several candidates such as MARS, Twofish, Serpent, Rijndael, and RC6, Rijndael was chosen as the final standard.

AES is also a block cipher that works on a 128-bit data block and has a key size of 128, 192, and 256 bits. More information on AES can be found at: http://en.wikipedia.org/wiki/Advanced_Encryption_Standard.

As a new federal standard and one that is less computationally intensive and cryptographically stronger than 3DES, AES has been rapidly added in vendors' implementations and deployed in VPN networks. Currently, many vendors also support AES hardware acceleration. AES is one of the cipher options for SSL v3 and TLS.

Diffie-Hellman

Published in 1976, Diffie-Hellman (DH) was the first published public-key algorithm. Diffie-Hellman is a key agreement protocol that enables communication parties to agree on a shared secret without any prior-known secrets. Diffie-Hellman is often used in key exchange and during the establishment phase of a VPN tunnel. The Diffie-Hellman algorithm works as follows:

1 The communication parties agree on two system parameters: a large prime p and a generator g. These are chosen such that for any value $V < p$, there exists a value w so that $g^w \bmod p = V$. With this requirement, g can be used to generate all the numbers from 1 to $p{-}1$.

2 Each communication party, say X and Y, generates a private key, x and y, each of which is a random number smaller than p. To calculate the corresponding public keys, X_x and Y_y, the following formulas are used:

— Public key for party X: $X_x = g^x \bmod p$

— Public key for party Y: $Y_y = g^y \bmod p$

3 The two communication parties then exchange the public key over the insecure channel. Upon receiving the other side's DH public key, each party calculates the shared secret (SS) using the following formulas:

Party X: SS = $(Y_y)^x \bmod p = g^{yx} \bmod p$
Party Y: SS = $(X_x)^y \bmod p = g^{xy} \bmod p$

Both parties come up with the same common secret.

The DH parties must share the system parameters p and g, which are called DH group parameters. The following are several common DH groups with a different p:

• Group 1: 768-bit modulus

• Group 2: 1024-bit modulus

• Group 5: 1536-bit modulus

Note that during the DH public key exchange process, no authentication process is defined. This ensures that the communication parties are getting the right public key from the intended party. Thus, DH is vulnerable to a man-in-the-middle attack, in which an attacker can intercept the communication channel and spoof the identity of the communication parties to perform DH exchange with party X and Y, respectively. Thus, the attacker establishes two shared secrets with X and Y separately, and can use these shared secrets to intercept further communication between the two communication parties protected by the DH secrets. An authenticated DH exchange mitigates this vulnerability.

Well-known uses of DH algorithms are key exchange and perfect forward secrecy in the Internet Key Exchange (IKE) Protocol, the key exchange protocol for IPsec VPN and the key exchange in the TLS protocol.

RSA and DSA

RSA and DSA are the two most common public key algorithms used in digital signature applications. RSA was designed by Ron Rivest, Adi Shamir, and Len Adelman (hence RSA) in 1977. Different from the Diffie-Hellman algorithm, the RSA algorithm is based on the fact that no efficient way exists to factor very large numbers. The common key size is 512-bit, 1024-bit, and 2048-bit. The performance of RSA is much slower than secret key algorithms such as DES. So RSA is normally not used for bulk data encryption. It is used mainly in digital signatures to "sign" the digital signature or in digital enveloping to encrypt a secret key that is used to encrypt the data.

In 1991, NIST proposed that the Digital Signature Algorithm (DSA) be used for applications that require digital signatures. It was standardized as the Digital Signature Standard (DSS) by the United States federal government standard for digital signatures.

Digital Signatures and Digital Certification

Authentication and integrity are important properties for secure VPNs. These include entity authentication, data origin authentication, integrity, and nonrepudiation. Digital signatures and certificates provide a scalable trust system. The following sections describe the digital signatures that provide the security properties and digital certification described in the preceding section.

Digital Signatures

In a secure communication, you must often ensure that a message comes from an authentic sender, not from malicious parties who spoof and claim that they are the intended sender. On the flip side, you might also require that the sender of the message cannot later deny being the source of the message (this is known as *nonrepudiation*). People sign paper documents and use the signatures as proof of authenticity and nonrepudiation. In the digital world, digital signatures (through digital signing) are designed for exactly the same purpose.

Digital signing refers to the action of encrypting the hash of the message by using the sender's own private keys. The output is called a digital signature. From the knowledge you have gained in the previous sections, it is not hard to see why the term *digital signature* is used: The hash of the message generates an easy-to-calculate, one-way digital fingerprint of the message. Signing using a private key guarantees the authenticity of the source of the message, because only the person who signs the message has the private key. The signature can be easily verified by using the corresponding public key that is posted in the public domain.

Figure 2-3 illustrates the signature verification process. Essentially, the recipient of the message with the corresponding signature performs two calculations: decryption of the received signatures using the sender's public key to get the hash and calculation of the hash using the received message. After these two actions are completed, the recipient compares the two outputs. If they are the same, the recipient verifies the signatures to be authentic.

Figure 2-3 *Digital Signature Verification*

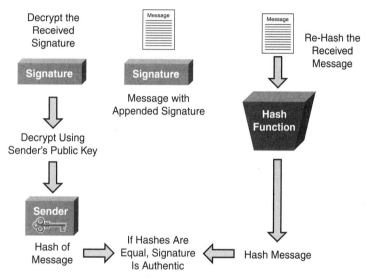

The common digital signature algorithms are RSA with MD5 or SHA-1 and DSS with SHA-1.

Public Key Infrastructure, Digital Certificates, and Certification

The preceding section showed how you can use digital signatures to achieve important security requirements, such as entity authentication, nonrepudiation, and data origin authentication. You might have noticed that one piece is still missing in the picture. To verify the digital signature, you need to have the sender's public key. This public key should be distributed not only to the public in a scalable way but also be trusted as the true public key of the sender. (For example, Bob can post his public key and claim it is Alice's public key.) In essence, you need to establish a trust system that provides a third-party vetting of, and vouching for, user identities. A public-key infrastructure (PKI) consists of protocols, standards, and services that establish and support the applications of such a trust system.

PKI allows users to authenticate each other use digital certificates that are issued by certificate authorities. The following are the building blocks of a PKI system:

- **X.509:** An ITU-T standard for PKI that defines the standard formats for public key certificates.

- **Public-Key Infrastructure X.509 (PKIX):** An IETF workgroup that defines the use of digital certificates.

- **Public key cryptography standards (PKCS):** Refers to a group of public key cryptography standards devised and published by RSA laboratories. PKCS is the cryptographic foundation of the PKI. Well known standards include the following:

  — PKCS 1 defines the RSA cryptography standard.

  — PKCS 7 defines the Cryptographic Message Syntax Standard, which specifies the signing and encrypting of a message under a PKI.

  — PKCS 10 defines the Certification Request Standard, which specifies the format of messages sent to a certification authority to request certification of a key pair.

The sections that follow examine digital certificates and certification, which are key components of a PKI system.

Digital Certificates

A digital certificate is essentially a binding between a user's identity and its public key. The digital certificates are issued by a third-party entity called a certification authority (CA) to ensure trust in and authenticity of the certificate. The section that follows discusses CAs in the context of the certification process.

Figure 2-4 shows the contents of a digital certificate.

Figure 2-4 *X.509 Digital Certificates*

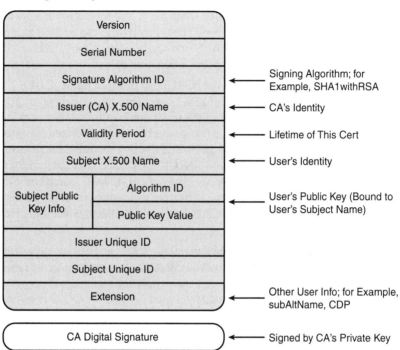

The VPN deployment fields shown in Figure 2-4 are as follows:

- **Signature algorithm ID:** Specifies the signing algorithm (for example, RSA with SHA-1 or DSS with SHA-1).

- **Issuer (CA) X.500 name:** The CA server's identity. Basically, this field specifies who issued this certificate.

- **Validity period:** Specifies the lifetime of this certificate. It is a good security practice to set a reasonable lifetime for a certificate. During the certification validation process, the VPN gateway will check the validity period to make sure that the received certificate is still valid.

- **Subject name:** Contains the user's identity with the X.500 directory format. For example, cn=vpnuser1, ou=Marketing department, and o=Cisco Systems, Inc.

- **Subject public key:** Contains the public key of the user, which is bound to the user's identity.

- **Extension**: A placeholder for useful options.
  - **SubAltName:** This is used when the X.500 format is not a good way to represent the user's identity. The SubAltName can be used to represent a user's identity. The SubAltName can be a user's e-mail address or FQDN (fully qualified domain name, often used by networking devices).
  - **Certificate revocation list (CRL) distribution point (CDP):** The CDP is an essential component of a PKI system because it makes the CRL scalable. The CRL contains a list of the serial numbers of revoked certificates. A certificate can be revoked for various reasons, such as ceasing operation and a compromise of private keys. The CA is responsible for revoking certificates and maintaining the CRL. CDP specifies the location (normally a Lightweight Directory Access Protocol [LDAP] search string) where the CRL is stored. During the certificate validation process, VPN devices retrieve CRLs from the CDP and check whether the received certificate has been revoked.

    In a large-scale PKI deployment, the CRL can become large. The Online Certificate Status Protocol (OCSP) is a new Internet protocol designed to provide a more scalable solution to manage the certification revocation status of the X.509 digital certificates. OCSP does not require VPN devices to retrieve the CRL and store and parse it locally.

    With OCSP, the VPN device queries the CA about the certificate revocation status of a digital certificate under its validation. The CA server processes the query and replies with the certificate revocation status. The communication between the VPN devices and the CA server are digitally signed and cryptographically verifiable between the two parties.
- **CA digital signature:** This field is the hash of the content of the digital certificate that is signed by the CA server.

Certification

Certification is the process of the certification authority (CA) issuing digital certificates. CA is the basis of trust for the entire PKI system and is responsible for verifying users' identity, issuing certificates, revoking certificates, and publishing CRLs. Figure 2-5 illustrates the digital certification and basic certificate validation process.

Figure 2-5 *Digital Certification*

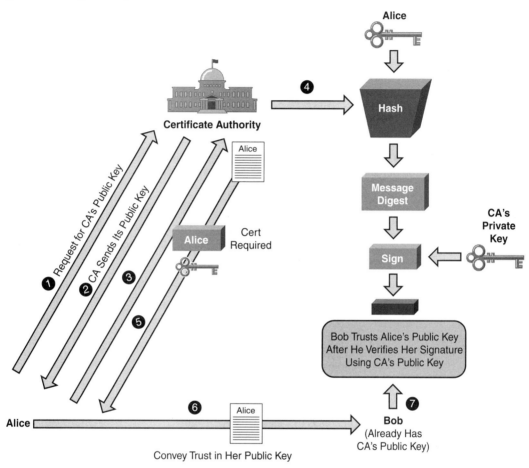

Convey Trust in Her Public Key

Alice wants to convey trust to Bob using a digital certificate. First she needs to enroll to the CA server to get her identity certificate. Alice follows these steps:

1 Alice first requests the root certificate, that is, the certificate of the CA server.

2 The CA server replies with its root certificate to Alice. Because this is the first communication between Alice and the CA server, no mechanism is predefined to protect this communication. So an out-of-band authentication is required after Alice gets the CA certificate to ensure that no man-in-the-middle attack occurs.

3 Alice generates a certificate request that has Alice's identity information and her public key. Alice signs the certificate request using the CA's public key that is inside the CA root certificate.

4   The CA server gets the certificate request, verifies Alice's identity, and generates a digital certificate for Alice, binding her identity and her public key. This identity certificate is signed by the CA, which provides another binding between Alice's identity and the CA's identity.

5   The CA server issues the certificate to Alice.

6   Upon receiving her identity certificate, Alice presents it to Bob to convey trust.

7   Bob follows the digital signature verification process just described to validate Alice's certificate and subsequently establishes trust to Alice's public key.

As you can see, by trusting the CA (its public and private keys), people exchanging information demonstrate trust in the authenticity of the other party using the digital certification process described previously.

Sometimes, the CA delegates some of the tasks previously described to an entity known as a registration authority (RA). The RA provides an interface between the user and the CA server. For example, the interface could be a CGI script on the web server that receives the user's certificate request.

Large scalable PKI systems can have a hierarchical structure that consists of multiple layers of CAs, a root CA, and many subordinate CAs that form certification chaining. During the certification validation process, an end user might want to go up the certification chain to validate the user certificate and all the subordinate certificates up to the root CA.

SSL and TLS

The following sections provide a brief overview of the SSL and TLS protocols. First, the evolution of these protocols is discussed. This is followed by protocol details to show how SSL and TLS employ the cryptographic building blocks that have just been described to provide secure communication. A short case study follows to show the protocol in action.

SSL and TLS History

The Secure Socket Layer (SSL) was originally developed in the 1990s by Netscape Communications to allow communications to occur securely in the World Wide Web (WWW) environment, which accommodates e-commerce applications such as online shopping. Such applications required secure communications. The design goal was to provide confidentiality, message integrity, identity authentication (server authentication and optional client authentication), and application transparency (to allow SSL to be used to secure other communication protocols such as mail and news).

After the initial publicly released version of SSL v2 in 1994, SSL became popular and a de facto standard. Over the years, the protocol has undergone several improvements and standardizations and is still evolving support for newer technologies and applications.

SSL v2 was released by Netscape Communications in 1994 and deployed on Netscape Navigator browsers. In 1995, Netscape strengthened the cryptographic algorithms of SSL with the release of SSL v3. It addressed several security problems in SSL v2 such as

- **Downgrade attacks:** SSL v2 allows attackers to force the selections of weaker ciphers. The release of SSL v3 authenticated the handshake messages, thereby solving this issue.v

- **Truncation attacks:** SSL v2 depends on the TCP connection closing to signal the end of transmission. This allows attackers to launch a denial of service attack by forging TCP connection closure. Adding the finished message in SSL v3 solved this problem.

- **Weak MACs:** In SSL v2, MAC relies on MD5 only.

NOTE   SSL v3 also added several new ciphers, such as DSS, DH, and FORTEZZA.

In 1996, the Internet Engineering Task Force (IETF) established the Transport Layer Security (TLS) working group in an effort to standardize SSL protocols from different vendors, mainly Netscape and Microsoft, which developed Private Communication Technology (PCT) and Secure Transport Layer Protocol (STLP). Finally, the standard protocol TLS was published as RFC 2246 in 1999. Overall, TLS is similar to SSL v3 with a few changes and additions.

Two new variants of TLS exist: Wireless TLS (WTLS) and Datagram TLS (DTLS). WTLS is designed to support wireless applications, and DTLS is designed to work over datagram transports such as UDP.

SSL Protocols Overview

The following sections give a brief overview of a number of protocols: OSI Layer Placement and TCP/IP Protocol Support, SSL Record Protocol and Handshake Protocols, SSL Connection Setup, and 27Application Data. The sections end with a case study to demonstrate how SSL Connection Setup works.

OSI Layer Placement and TCP/IP Protocol Support

SSL is a platform-independent and application-independent protocol that is used to secure TCP-based applications. It sits on top of the TCP layer, below the application layer, and acts like sockets connected by TCP connections. Figure 2-6 shows the SSL placement in the protocol stack.

Figure 2-6 *SSL and TCP/IP*

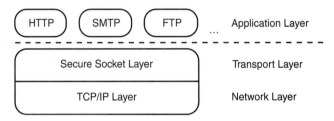

SSL assumes reliable underlying packet delivery; thus, it always runs only on top of TCP, not over UDP or directly over IP. Although SSL should work with any static client-server TCP application in an ideal situation, in reality, it is not as easy as simply replacing the TCP socket calls with SSL calls. For the most popular applications defined in the TCP/IP suite, such as HTTP and Simple Mail Transfer Protocol (SMTP), standards have been defined for all the technical details to be used for SSL to secure the communications. The following are two well-known examples:

- **HTTP over SSL:** Securing the web was the main initial drive for designing SSL, and HTTP is the first application-layer protocol secured by SSL.

  When Netscape first implemented HTTP over SSL in its Navigator, it used https:// for the pages that are fetched using HTTP over SSL to differentiate them from the standard pages that are fetched using HTTP with http://. HTTP over SSL then became known as HTTPS, which stands for HTTP over SSL. HTTPS later was standardized in RFC 2818. HTTPS operates on TCP port 443, while HTTP operates on TCP port 80 by default.

  People have much the same user experience using HTTPS and HTTP. After the users enter **https://***URL* in the browser, the browser, as a client, makes a connection to the server and negotiates an SSL connection. After the SSL connection is established, the HTTP data is transmitted over the SSL tunnel.

- **Email over SSL:** Similar to HTTP over SSL, e-mail protocols such as SMTP, Post Office Protocol 3 (POP3), and Internet Message Access Protocol (IMAP) can be supported by SSL.

  The standard for SMTP over TLS was documented in RFC 2487.

  The standard for POP3 and IMAP over TLS was documented in RFC 2595.

Later, we discuss how to use an SSL VPN to secure Microsoft Exchange Protocol.

SSL Record Protocol and Handshake Protocols

This section describes the SSL protocol operation, including SSL connection negotiation, key derivation, and secure data transfer. The section explains how the various cryptographic elements described earlier are used in SSL to build a secure communication.

An SSL connection is established in two main phases. The handshake phase (phase 1) negotiates cryptographic algorithms, authenticates the server, and establishes keys for data encryption and MAC. The secure data transfer phase (phase 2) is under the protection of an established SSL connection. This chapter describes each phase in detail, but we first look at the structure of the SSL protocol.

SSL is a layered protocol. At the lowest layer is the SSL record protocol. The record protocol consists of several message types or protocols carrying out different tasks. Figure 2-7 shows the SSL protocol structure.

Figure 2-7   *SSL/TLS Protocol Structure*

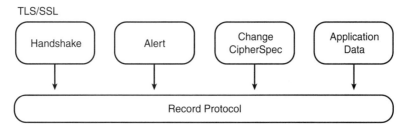

The following list describes the primary functions of each protocol defined in SSL/TLS:

- **Record protocol** is mainly an encapsulation protocol. It transmits various higher-level protocols and application data. The record protocol takes messages to be transmitted from upper-client protocols; performs the necessary tasks such as fragmentation, compression, applying MAC, and encryption; and then transmits the final data. It also performs the reverse actions   decryption, verification, decompression, and reassembly—to the receiving data. The record protocol consists of four upper-layer client protocols: Handshake Protocol, Alerts Protocol, Change Cipher Spec Protocol, and Application Data Protocol.

- **Handshake protocols** are responsible for establishing and resuming SSL sessions. Three subprotocols exist:

  — **Handshake Protocol** negotiates the security attributes of an SSL session.

  — **Alerts Protocol** is a housekeeping protocol that is used to convey alert messages between the SSL peers. The alert messages contain errors, exception conditions such as a bad MAC or decryption failure, or notification such as a closure of the session.

— **Change Cipher Spec Protocol** is used to signal transitions in cipher strategies in the subsequent records.

- **Application Data Protocol** handles the transmission of upper-layer application data.

Note that the TLS record protocol was designed as a framework, and new client protocols can be easily added in the future. The client protocols previously described are those that are used in SSL connections.

SSL Connection Setup

This section looks at the messages and operations necessary to establish an SSL connection. Using a simple-mode SSL negotiation as an example should help you understand how the different pieces discussed so far (cryptographic algorithms and SSL protocols) work together to bring up an SSL connection.

Because you are mainly an SSL VPN user rather than an implementer, the focus is on explaining the big picture, not the implementation details.

Handshake protocols are used for the SSL client and server to establish the connection. The main tasks of this process are as follows:

- **Negotiate security capabilities:** This handles protocol version and cipher suites.
- **Authentication:** The client authenticates the server. Optionally, the server can also authenticate the clients.
- **Key exchange:** Two parties exchange keys or information that is needed to generate the master keys.
- **Key derivation:** The two parties derive the master secret that is later used to generate keys used for bulk data encryption and MAC.

Figure 2-8 shows the flow and messages of a typical SSL connection setup. Each block has a few SSL handshake messages with the format of <protocol:message_type> and each represents one or more (if fragmentation exists) TCP frame sent by the client or the server.

To help you understand the steps that take place during a handshake, the sections that follow break messages down into a few logical phases, each of which accomplishes one of the main tasks described in the preceding bulleted list.

Figure 2-8   *TLS Handshake*

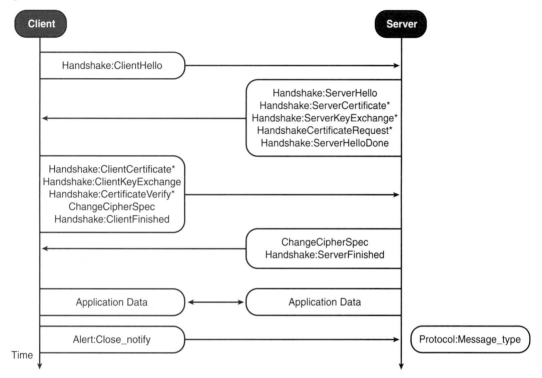

Hello Phase

During this phase, the client and the server start the logical connection and negotiate the basic security attributes of the SSL session, such as SSL protocol versions and cipher suites. The client initiates the connection, first by sending a ClientHello message that is defined as follows:

```
struct {
    ProtocolVersion client_version;
    Random random;
    SessionID session_id;
    CipherSuite cipher_suites<2..2^16-1>;
    CompressionMethod compression_methods<1..2^8-1>;
} ClientHello;
    struct {
        ProtocolVersion client_version;
        Random random;
        SessionID session_id;
        CipherSuite cipher_suites<2..2^16-1>;
        CompressionMethod compression_methods<1..2^8-1>;
    } ClientHello;
```

From the preceding definition, you can see that the ClientHello message contains the following:

- **Protocol version:** The protocol version field defines the highest SSL version that the client supports. It is defined in the format of <major version.minor version>. For example, for SSL v3, the major version is 3 and the minor version is 0. So the protocol version is 3.0. For TLS, the protocol version is 3.1.

- **Client random:** This is a client-generated random structure that has both temporal information and randomly generated data. It contains the client's date and time plus a 28-byte pseudorandom number. This client random is later used to calculate the master secret and to prevent replay attacks.

- **Session ID (optional):** A session ID identifies an active or resumable session state. An empty session ID indicates that the client wants to establish a new SSL connection or session, while a nonzero session ID indicates that the client wants to resume a previous session.

- **Client CipherSuite:** This is the list of cipher suites that are supported by the client. The cipher suite defines a set of cryptographic algorithms that are used throughout the SSL connection, such as authentication and key exchange methods, data encryption algorithms, and message digest algorithms. For example, TLS_RSA_WITH_RC4_128_SHA means that it supports TLS and uses RSA for authentication and key exchange, RC4 with a 128-bit key for data encryption algorithms, and SHA-1 for message digest algorithms used in MAC.

- **Compression method:** Defines the compression methods supported by the client.

Upon receiving the ClientHello message, the sever replies with the ServerHello as part of the reply message. The ServerHello has the same structure as the ClientHello:

```
struct {
    ProtocolVersion server_version;
    Random random;
    SessionID session_id;
    CipherSuite cipher_suite;
    CompressionMethod compression_method;
} ServerHello;
struct {
    ProtocolVersion server_version;
    Random random;
    SessionID session_id;
    CipherSuite cipher_suite;
    CompressionMethod compression_method;
} ServerHello;
```

The server sends back the highest protocol version that is supported by the client and the server. The client and server will use this version throughout the connection. The server also generates its own server random that will later be used to generate the master secret.

CipherSuite is the single cipher suite selected by the server out of the cipher suites proposed by the client. For the session ID, the following two scenarios exist:

- **New session ID:** If the client sends an empty session ID to initiate a new session, the server generates a new session ID. Or, if the client sends a nonzero session ID asking to resume a session, but the server cannot or will not resume the session, the server also generates a new session ID.

- **Resumed session ID:** The server uses the same session ID that is sent by the client who asks to resume a previous session.

Finally, the server also replies by using the selected compression method in the ServerHello.

In summary, after the hello phase, the client and server have initiated a logical connection, and negotiated security attributes such as protocol version, cipher suites, compression methods, and session ID. They have also generated nonce (client random and server random) that will be used later for master key generation.

Authentication and Key Exchange

After the hello exchange, the client and server use the negotiated security attributes to move on to perform authentication and key exchange. In this phase, the client and server need to come up with an authenticated shared secret, called a pre_master secret, which is later converted into a master secret.

SSL v3 and TLS support several authentication and key exchange methods. The exact payloads in SSL exchange messages 2 and 3 shown in Figure 2-9, depending on the methods used during the exchange. The following are the main key exchange methods supported by SSL v3 and TLS:

- **RSA:** This is the most common authentication and key exchange method. In this mode, the client generates a random secret as the pre_master secret and sends the encrypted pre_master secret to the server in the ClientKeyExchange message. The pre_master secret is encrypted by the server's RSA public key that is authenticated by the server's certificate, which is sent by the server in the Certificate message.

  Ephemeral RSA, also known as RSA-export in cipher spec, is used to support the scenario in which an exported client with 512-bit RSA keys (because of crypto export regulations) needs to communicate with a domestic server with strong 1024-bit or higher RSA keys. In this case, the server generates a temporary 512-bit RSA key and sends it to the client through a ServerKeyExchange message that is signed by the server's strong key. The client then uses this temporary 512-bit key to encrypt the pre_master secret.

- **Diffie-Hellman:** The client and server perform a DH exchange and use the calculated DH common secret as the pre_master secret. Three types of Diffie-Hellman key exchange methods exist: fixed Diffie-Hellman, ephemeral Diffie-Hellman, and anonymous Diffie-Hellman. The anonymous DH does not have authentication. Hence, it is vulnerable to man-in-the-middle attacks, as mentioned earlier in the discussion of the DH algorithm.

The next section features the most commonly used RSA key exchange method as an example to explain exchange messages during this phase.

After the ServerHello message, the server sends the Certificate message and the ServerHelloDone message. The Certificate message contains the public key certificate of the server. The ServerHelloDone message is a simple message that indicates that the server has sent all the messages it needs to send in this phase.

When an RSA key exchange is used, the client needs to generate the pre_master secret and send it using a ClientKeyExchange message. The pre_master secret and the ClientKeyExchange message are defined as follows:

```
select (KeyExchangeAlgorithm) {
    case rsa: EncryptedPreMasterSecret;
    case diffie_hellman: ClientDiffieHellmanPublic;
    case fortezza_kea: FortezzaKeys;
} exchange_keys;
} ClientKeyExchange;

struct {
    ProtocolVersion client_version;
    opaque random[46];
} PreMasterSecret;

struct {
    public-key-encrypted PreMasterSecret pre_master_secret;
} EncryptedPreMasterSecret;
struct {
    select (KeyExchangeAlgorithm) {
        case rsa: EncryptedPreMasterSecret;
        case diffie_hellman: ClientDiffieHellmanPublic;
        case fortezza_kea: FortezzaKeys;
    } exchange_keys;
} ClientKeyExchange;

struct {
    ProtocolVersion client_version;
    opaque random[46];
} PreMasterSecret;

struct {
    public-key-encrypted PreMasterSecret pre_master_secret;
} EncryptedPreMasterSecret;
```

As you can see from the preceding definition, the pre_master secret has two pieces: the client's offered protocol version and a random number. The protocol version was designed to protect against rollback attacks. The client encrypted the pre_master secret using the server's public key that is retrieved from the server's certificate.

If client authentication is required, the server sends a CertificateRequest message to request that the client send its certificate. The client replies with two messages: the ClientCertificate and CertificateVerify. The ClientCertificate contains the client's certificate, and the CertificateVerify message does the client authentication job. It contains a hash of all the handshake messages so far signed by the client's public key. As discussed earlier in the section on public key algorithms, to authenticate the client, the server retrieves the client's public key from the ClientCertificate, uses the public key to decrypt the received signature, and finally compares the decrypted hash with the hash locally calculated by the server with its own copy of the handshake messages. If they match, the client's identity is authenticated.

In summary, after this phase, the client and server go through an authenticated key exchange process so that they have a shared common secret pre_master secret. After that, the client and server have all the necessary pieces to derive the master secret.

Key Derivation

In this section, you learn how the SSL client and server use the data that is securely exchanged during the previous phases to create a master secret. The master secret is never exchanged, but rather created by the client and server individually. Several keys are then derived from the master secret for message encryption and integrity authentication. We will not get into the details of key derivation, but rather show the key conceptual steps so that you get a feel for this important phase. The SSL client and server use the following previously exchanged data to generate the master secret:

- Pre-master secret
- The client random and the server random

The key derivation algorithms of SSL v2, SSL v3, and TLS are different. Here you see the key generation of the SSL v3 and TLS protocols.

As defined in the SSL v3 protocol specification (SSL v3 draft 2), SSL v3 generates the master key using the following:

```
master_secret =
      MD5(pre_master_secret + SHA('A' + pre_master_secret +
          ClientHello.random + ServerHello.random)) +
      MD5(pre_master_secret + SHA('BB' + pre_master_secret +
          ClientHello.random + ServerHello.random)) +
      MD5(pre_master_secret + SHA('CCC' + pre_master_secret +
          ClientHello.random + ServerHello.random));
master_secret =
      MD5(pre_master_secret + SHA('A' + pre_master_secret +
          ClientHello.random + ServerHello.random)) +
      MD5(pre_master_secret + SHA('BB' + pre_master_secret +
          ClientHello.random + ServerHello.random)) +
      MD5(pre_master_secret + SHA('CCC' + pre_master_secret +
          ClientHello.random + ServerHello.random));
```

The master secret is then used as an entropy source to derive sufficient keying material, which is eventually partitioned into the message encryption and authentication keys. Computing the following generates the key_block:

```
key_block =
        MD5(master_secret + SHA('A' + master_secret +
                                ServerHello.random +
                                ClientHello.random)) +
        MD5(master_secret + SHA('BB' + master_secret +
                                ServerHello.random +
                                ClientHello.random)) +
        MD5(master_secret + SHA('CCC' + master_secret +
                                ServerHello.random +
                                ClientHello.random)) + [...];
key_block =
        MD5(master_secret + SHA('A' + master_secret +
                                ServerHello.random +
                                ClientHello.random)) +
        MD5(master_secret + SHA('BB' + master_secret +
                                ServerHello.random +
                                ClientHello.random)) +
        MD5(master_secret + SHA('CCC' + master_secret +
                                ServerHello.random +
                                ClientHello.random)) + [...];
```

From the key_block, the following keys are generated:

- **Client write key:** The client uses this key to encrypt the data, and the server uses this key to decrypt client messages.

- **Server write key:** The server uses this key to encrypt the data, and the client uses this key to decrypt server messages.

- **Client write MAC secret:** The client uses this key to generate the MAC that is used for data integrity protection. The server uses this key to authenticate client messages.

- **Server write MAC secret:** The server uses this key to generate the MAC that is used for data integrity protection. The client uses this key to authenticate server messages.

TLS uses a master key derivation that is similar to SSL v3. The master key is calculated as follows:

```
master_secret = PRF(pre_master_secret, "master secret",
                        ClientHello.random + ServerHello.random)[0..47];
master_secret = PRF(pre_master_secret, "master secret",
                        ClientHello.random + ServerHello.random)[0..47];
```

Compared to SSL v3, a PRF function replaces the MD5 hashing function. The PRF function is defined as follows:

```
PRF(secret, label, seed) = P_MD5(S1, label + seed) XOR P_SHA-1(S2, label + seed)
PRF(secret, label, seed) = P_MD5(S1, label + seed) XOR P_SHA-1(S2, label + seed)
```

where P_hash is mainly an HMAC function using MD5 or SHA-1, and S1 and S2 are the first and second halves of the input secret.

Using both MD5 and SHA-1 in TLS makes it a bit more secure than SSL v3. This is one of the reasons why TLS is FIPS (Federal Information Processing Standard) certified, whereas SSL v3 is not. More information about FIPS can be found at http://en.wikipedia.org/wiki/Federal_Information_Processing_Standard.

The corresponding key_block for TLS is generated by computing the following:

```
key_block = PRF(SecurityParameters.master_secret,
                "key expansion",
                SecurityParameters.server_random +
                SecurityParameters.client_random);

key_block = PRF(SecurityParameters.master_secret,
                "key expansion",
                SecurityParameters.server_random +
                SecurityParameters.client_random);
```

Finishing Handshake

After the key derivation, the SSL VPN client and server are ready to finish the handshake and send the application data using the established secure connection. To signal readiness, the client and the server send the ChangeCipherSpec message to signal the other side that it is ready to use the negotiated security algorithms and keys. The ChangeCipherSpec message is then followed by the Finished message, which is protected by the newly negotiated security algorithms, keys, and secret.

The Finished message is basically a hash of the entire handshake message and Master Secret. The validation of the Finished message proves the success of the authentication and key exchange process. The following shows the structure of the Finished message.

For SSL v3:

```
struct {
        opaque md5_hash[16];
        opaque sha_hash[20];
    } Finished;

    md5_hash        MD5(master_secret + pad2 +
                        MD5(handshake_messages + Sender +
                            master_secret + pad1));
    sha_hash        SHA(master_secret + pad2 +
                        SHA(handshake_messages + Sender +
                            master_secret + pad1));

    handshake_messages    All of the data from all handshake messages
                          up to but not including this message.  This
                          is only data visible at the handshake layer
                          and does not include record layer headers.
struct {
        opaque md5_hash[16];
        opaque sha_hash[20];
    } Finished;

    md5_hash        MD5(master_secret + pad2 +
                        MD5(handshake_messages + Sender +
                            master_secret + pad1));
```

```
        sha_hash         SHA(master_secret + pad2 +
                             SHA(handshake_messages + Sender +
                                 master_secret + pad1));

    handshake_messages   All of the data from all handshake messages
                         up to but not including this message.  This
                         is only data visible at the handshake layer
                         and does not include record layer headers.
```

For TLS v1:

```
struct {
    opaque verify_data[12];
} Finished;

verify_data
    PRF(master_secret, finished_label, MD5(handshake_messages) +
    SHA-1(handshake_messages)) [0..11];

finished_label
    For Finished messages sent by the client, the string "client
    finished". For Finished messages sent by the server, the
    string "server finished".

handshake_messages
    All of the data from all handshake messages up to but not
    including this message. This is only data visible at the
    handshake layer and does not include record layer headers.
struct {
    opaque verify_data[12];
} Finished;

verify_data
    PRF(master_secret, finished_label, MD5(handshake_messages) +
    SHA-1(handshake_messages)) [0..11];

finished_label
    For Finished messages sent by the client, the string "client
    finished". For Finished messages sent by the server, the
    string "server finished".

handshake_messages
    All of the data from all handshake messages up to but not
    including this message. This is only data visible at the
    handshake layer and does not include record layer headers.
```

After this phase, the SSL client and server start to transfer application data.

Application Data

After the handshake phase, the application can begin to communicate under the protection of the newly established secure SSL connection. The record protocol is responsible for fragmenting, compressing, hashing, and encrypting all the application data at the sending side, as well as decrypting, verifying, decompressing, and reassembling messages at the receiving end.

Figure 2-9 shows the SSL record layer operation.

Figure 2-9 *SSL/TLS Record Protocol Operation*

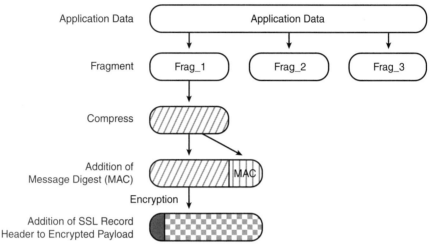

Case Study: SSL Connection Setup

The section examines the setup of an SSL connection as a case study of the workings and implementations of the concepts we have discussed so far. The section examines the communications from both the SSL session level and lower TCP/IP packet level using tools such as ssldump and ethereal.

The SSL connection used in this case study is fairly simple. A user at IP address 10.1.1.200 browses to a website at IP address 66.94.230.34 using HTTPS, views the page, and then closes the connection. First, look at Example 2-1. This shows the client-server exchanges that are captured by using ssldump, which is installed on the user's PC. The ssldump is a tool written by Eric Rescorla to analyze SSL exchanges.

Example 2-1 *SSL Session Dump*

```
[root@playground ~]# ssldump -A

New TCP connection #1: 10.1.1.200(46882) <-> p3.www.scd.yahoo.com(443)
1 1  0.0172 (0.0172)  C>S SSLv2 compatible client hello
  Version 3.1
  cipher suites
  Unknown value 0x39
  Unknown value 0x38
  Unknown value 0x35
  Unknown value 0x33
  Unknown value 0x32
  TLS_RSA_WITH_RC4_128_MD5
  TLS_RSA_WITH_RC4_128_SHA
  Unknown value 0x2f
```

continues

Example 2-1 *SSL Session Dump (Continued)*

```
          TLS_DHE_RSA_WITH_3DES_EDE_CBC_SHA
          TLS_DHE_DSS_WITH_3DES_EDE_CBC_SHA
          Unknown value 0xfeff
          TLS_RSA_WITH_3DES_EDE_CBC_SHA
          TLS_DHE_RSA_WITH_DES_CBC_SHA
          TLS_DHE_DSS_WITH_DES_CBC_SHA
          Unknown value 0xfefe
          TLS_RSA_WITH_DES_CBC_SHA
          TLS_RSA_EXPORT1024_WITH_RC4_56_SHA
          TLS_RSA_EXPORT1024_WITH_DES_CBC_SHA
          TLS_RSA_EXPORT_WITH_RC4_40_MD5
          TLS_RSA_EXPORT_WITH_RC2_CBC_40_MD5
1 2  0.0486 (0.0313)  S>CV3.1(74)   Handshake
          ServerHello
            Version 3.1
            random[32]=
                43 c0 b8 c4 3a a0 fc b6 9c cf 96 49 c9 8e 40 67
                be 68 7e 1a 2f 7d 89 c0 5e 13 3c 0a eb a9 4f cb
            session_id[32]=
                b4 b3 a4 ac 89 46 4a db b9 04 08 65 d0 c8 16 1a
                ab 68 25 91 2e 0e 31 39 1e 33 df 49 79 13 35 2d
            cipherSuite            TLS_RSA_WITH_RC4_128_MD5
            compressionMethod                    NULL
1 3  0.0486 (0.0000)  S>CV3.1(761)  Handshake
          Certificate
1 4  0.0486 (0.0000)  S>CV3.1(4)    Handshake
          ServerHelloDone
1 5  0.0554 (0.0067)  C>SV3.1(134)  Handshake
          ClientKeyExchange

          EncryptedPreMasterSecret[128]=
                24 24 35 f6 e5 5f 80 d6 a0 fd 93 96 6f 09 9d dd
                aa 96 d0 f5 21 40 2c f9 a8 60 f6 9b 33 8b 87 96
                68 3c 7b c3 15 d1 a7 c6 99 a8 29 fd 56 fe de 65
                13 d4 77 42 3c e9 50 77 73 b1 1a 18 5b f1 00 16
                0c 51 3c 04 c7 fa 83 e1 ed 4d 9f ac 55 24 1c 0f
                90 28 9a 25 b9 7a 80 6b 97 d1 17 56 44 c0 c1 b8
                1f 6f 86 fb 04 bb 4a c2 97 c1 40 3a 4f 72 fe bc
                e2 6a a0 5b ba 9a 82 79 5c e3 71 d8 44 b0 c5 4b
1 6  0.0554 (0.0000)  C>SV3.1(1)    ChangeCipherSpec
1 7  0.0554 (0.0000)  C>SV3.1(32)   Handshake
1 8  0.0848 (0.0293)  S>CV3.1(1)    ChangeCipherSpec
1 9  0.0848 (0.0000)  S>CV3.1(32)   Handshake
1 10 0.0856 (0.0008)  C>SV3.1(629)  application_data
1 11 0.1248 (0.0391)  S>CV3.1(364)  application_data
1 12 0.1254 (0.0006)  S>CV3.1(18)   Alert
1 13 0.1259 (0.0004)  C>SV3.1(18)   Alert
1    0.1263 (0.0004)  S>C   TCP FIN
1    0.1267 (0.0003)  C>S   TCP RST
[root@playground ~]# ssldump -A
```

Example 2-1 *SSL Session Dump (Continued)*

```
New TCP connection #1: 10.1.1.200(46882) <-> p3.www.scd.yahoo.com(443)
1 1  0.0172 (0.0172)  C>S SSLv2 compatible client hello
  Version 3.1
  cipher suites
  Unknown value 0x39
  Unknown value 0x38
  Unknown value 0x35
  Unknown value 0x33
  Unknown value 0x32
  TLS_RSA_WITH_RC4_128_MD5
  TLS_RSA_WITH_RC4_128_SHA
  Unknown value 0x2f
  TLS_DHE_RSA_WITH_3DES_EDE_CBC_SHA
  TLS_DHE_DSS_WITH_3DES_EDE_CBC_SHA
  Unknown value 0xfeff
  TLS_RSA_WITH_3DES_EDE_CBC_SHA
  TLS_DHE_RSA_WITH_DES_CBC_SHA
  TLS_DHE_DSS_WITH_DES_CBC_SHA
  Unknown value 0xfefe
  TLS_RSA_WITH_DES_CBC_SHA
  TLS_RSA_EXPORT1024_WITH_RC4_56_SHA
  TLS_RSA_EXPORT1024_WITH_DES_CBC_SHA
  TLS_RSA_EXPORT_WITH_RC4_40_MD5
  TLS_RSA_EXPORT_WITH_RC2_CBC_40_MD5
1 2  0.0486 (0.0313)  S>CV3.1(74)  Handshake
      ServerHello
        Version 3.1
        random[32]=
          43 c0 b8 c4 3a a0 fc b6 9c cf 96 49 c9 8e 40 67
          be 68 7e 1a 2f 7d 89 c0 5e 13 3c 0a eb a9 4f cb
        session_id[32]=
          b4 b3 a4 ac 89 46 4a db b9 04 08 65 d0 c8 16 1a
          ab 68 25 91 2e 0e 31 39 1e 33 df 49 79 13 35 2d
        cipherSuite          TLS_RSA_WITH_RC4_128_MD5
        compressionMethod                     NULL
1 3  0.0486 (0.0000)  S>CV3.1(761)  Handshake
      Certificate

1 4  0.0486 (0.0000)  S>CV3.1(4)  Handshake
      ServerHelloDone
1 5  0.0554 (0.0067)  C>SV3.1(134)  Handshake
      ClientKeyExchange
        EncryptedPreMasterSecret[128]=
          24 24 35 f6 e5 5f 80 d6 a0 fd 93 96 6f 09 9d dd
          aa 96 d0 f5 21 40 2c f9 a8 60 f6 9b 33 8b 87 96
          68 3c 7b c3 15 d1 a7 c6 99 a8 29 fd 56 fe de 65
          13 d4 77 42 3c e9 50 77 73 b1 1a 18 5b f1 00 16
          0c 51 3c 04 c7 fa 83 e1 ed 4d 9f ac 55 24 1c 0f
          90 28 9a 25 b9 7a 80 6b 97 d1 17 56 44 c0 c1 b8
          1f 6f 86 fb 04 bb 4a c2 97 c1 40 3a 4f 72 fe bc
          e2 6a a0 5b ba 9a 82 79 5c e3 71 d8 44 b0 c5 4b
1 6  0.0554 (0.0000)  C>SV3.1(1)  ChangeCipherSpec
```

continues

Example 2-1 *SSL Session Dump (Continued)*

```
1 7  0.0554 (0.0000)  C>SV3.1(32)   Handshake
1 8  0.0848 (0.0293)  S>CV3.1(1)    ChangeCipherSpec
1 9  0.0848 (0.0000)  S>CV3.1(32)   Handshake
1 10 0.0856 (0.0008)  C>SV3.1(629)  application_data
1 11 0.1248 (0.0391)  S>CV3.1(364)  application_data
1 12 0.1254 (0.0006)  S>CV3.1(18)   Alert
1 13 0.1259 (0.0004)  C>SV3.1(18)   Alert
1    0.1263 (0.0004)  S>C  TCP FIN
1    0.1267 (0.0003)  C>S  TCP RST
```

As you can see, the exchange took place exactly as the steps described in Figure 2-9, with one minor exception. Although the client browser was configured to use SSL v3 or TLS, the browser still sends an SSL v2 ClientHello to the server for backward compatibility. Note that the SSL v2 ClientHello message has a slightly different structure from that of SSL v3 and TLS. The server that usually used SSL v3 or TLS continued the exchange using TLS by sending back a TLS ServerHello. Also the server "translated" the fields in the SSL v2 ClientHello message to get TLS values, such as client.random. From the output of the ssldump, you can see that the server chose TLS as the protocol, RSA as the key exchange and authentication method, MD5 as the hashing algorithm, and 128-bit RC4 as the encryption algorithm. The client and server then went through the key exchange to establish the SSL connection after frame 9. Frames 10 and 11 are application data corresponding to an HTTP request from the client and HTTP response from the server replying to the web page. Then the client and server sent the Alert message to close the connection.

We look at this once again at the TCP/IP packet level to see the full exchange and the layout of SSL records inside TCP packets. Figure 2-10 displays the packet capture of an SSL connection.

First, frames 1 to 3 show the TCP three-way handshake that is made to establish the TCP connection over port 443 (HTTPS). From frame 4, the client (10.1.1.200) and the server (66.94.230.34) started the SSL session negotiation:

- In frame 4, the client sent the backward-compatible SSL v2 ClientHello.

- In frame 5, the server replied with three messages (ServerHello, Certificate, and ServerHelloDone) all in one packet.

- In frame 7, the client sent ClientKeyExchange, ChangeCipherSpec, and ClientFinished messages in one packet. Note that as previously stated, just after the ChangeCipherSpec is sent, the subsequent data will be encrypted using the negotiated CipherSpec. That is why the ClientFinished message was shown as "Encrypted Handshake Message" in the packet capture.

Figure 2-10 *Packet Capture of an SSL Connection*

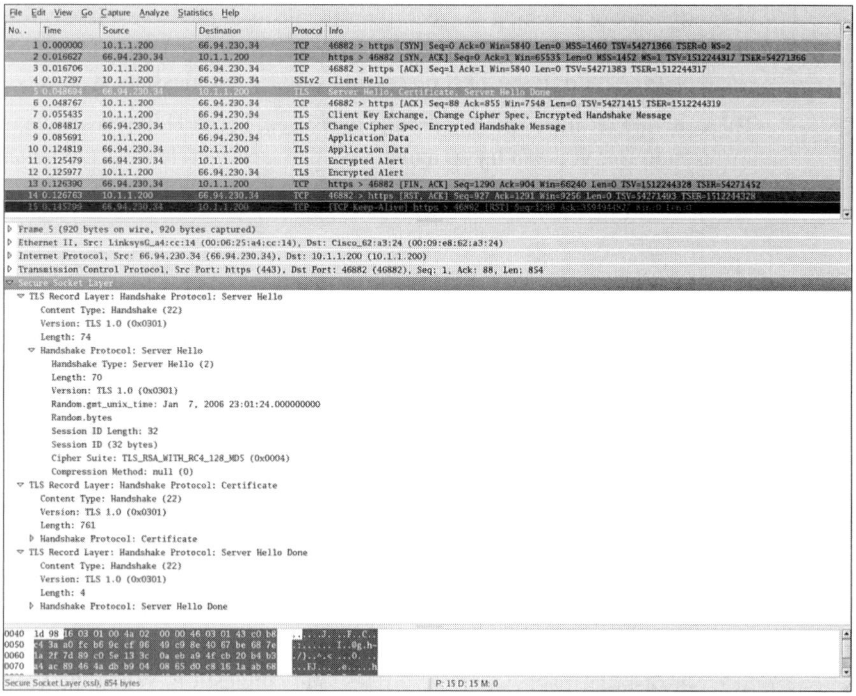

- In frame 8, the server sent ChangeCipherSpec and ServerFinished encrypted with the newly negotiated keys.

- In frames 9 and 10, the client and server exchange application data under the protection of the SSL session.

- In frames 11 and 12, the client and the server used an Alert message to indicate the close of the SSL connection.

- In frames 13 to 15, the client and server went through the TCP connection close phase to tear down the TCP connection.

As you just saw, the SSL client and server can send multiple records in one packet. The middle pane of Figure 2-11 provides an example of message encapsulation of SSL handshake messages, SSL records, and finally TCP/IP packets. For frame 5, in which the server replied ServerHello, Certificate, and ServerHelloDone to the client, take note of the following:

- This example clearly shows the SSL/TLS protocol structure and its position in TCP/IP stack. The handshake protocols are at the top. Then come the SSL/TLS record protocol as the payload of the TCP, and finally you see the IP layer and Layer 2 Ethernet frame.

- Three handshake messages are in this packet. As discussed earlier, SSL/TLS is a layered protocol in which the record protocol sits at the lowest level. You can see that in this packet, each handshake message was encapsulated in a TLS record. The Content Type field in the TLS record indicated what message type was carried.

- The structure of one of the handshake messages, ServerHello, is shown in the display. As an exercise, you can try to match it with the ServerHello structure shown in the earlier section.

DTLS

The recent success of SSL VPN poses new challenges to the underlying SSL/TLS protocol. As a complete remote access VPN solution, the SSL VPN is required to support various types of applications. UDP applications that are based on real-time protocols, such as voice over IP (VoIP) and streaming media applications, are especially challenging to SSL/TLS.

This challenge to SSL/TLS has emerged because TLS requires a reliable data channel such as TCP, which offers reliable, in-order transmission and flow control. It cannot be used to secure datagram traffic. SSL VPN is able to tunnel the UDP applications and then transport them using the TLS connection that runs over TCP. However, the performance can be very poor, especially when SSL VPN handles real-time applications.

Consider the following scenario of transmitting VoIP traffic over the Internet that could introduce out-of-order packets, packet losses, and congestion. When the VoIP traffic is carried over SSL, the underlying TCP will try to retransmit the lost packets and apply flow control when packet losses are severe. These actions can greatly affect the delay and delay jitter of the VoIP traffic and make the user experience very poor.

Eric Rescorla and Nagendra Modadugu designed datagram TLS (DTLS) to solve the issue previously outlined by allowing TLS to run over UDP. Because TLS was originally designed to run over TCP, it has no internal facilities to handle the unreliability in a datagram environment. DTLS makes the following adjustments to the TLS protocol:

- At the record layer, DTLS introduces two new fields, the epoch and the sequence number, as follows:

```
struct {
      ContentType type;
      ProtocolVersion version;
      uint16 epoch;                  // New field
      uint48 sequence_number;        // New field
      uint16 length;
      opaque fragment[DTLSPlaintext.length];
   } DTLSPlaintext;
struct {
      ContentType type;
      ProtocolVersion version;
      uint16 epoch;                  // New field
      uint48 sequence_number;        // New field
      uint16 length;
      opaque fragment[DTLSPlaintext.length];
   } DTLSPlaintext;
```

The epoch numbers are used by the endpoint to determine which cipher state has been used to protect the record data. The sequence numbers are introduced to deal with lost and out-of-order packets. DTLS uses the same antireplay window mechanism that is used by IPsec Authentication Header (AH) or Encapsulating Security Payload (ESP).

- At the handshake layer, DTLS uses the same handshake messages and flows as TLS, with the following additions:

  — A stateless cookie exchange is added to prevent a denial of service (DoS) attack.

  — The handshake message header is modified to add the sequence number, fragment length, and fragment offset to handle message loss, out-of-order messages, and fragmentation.

  — Retransmission timers are used on both client and server sides to handle message losses.

It is worth noting that RC4, the commonly used cipher in TLS, is not easily applied in lossy datagram traffic; hence it is not allowed to be used in DTLS.

Currently, DTLS is defined in an IETF draft, and it has been implemented as part of an open source toolkit, OpenSSL.

SSL VPN

SSL provides secure communications for applications, and it is transparent to the upper-layer applications. The most successful application running on top of SSL is HTTP because of the huge popularity of the World Wide Web. All commercial web browsers that are by default available on all operating systems now support HTTPS (HTTP over SSL/TLS). This ubiquity, if used in remote access VPNs, provides some appealing properties:

- **Secure communication using cryptographic algorithms:** It offers confidentiality, integrity, and authentication.

- **Ubiquitousness:** The ubiquity of SSL/TLS makes it possible for VPN users to remotely access corporate resources from anywhere using any PC, without having to preinstall a remote access VPN client.

- **Low management cost:** The clientless access makes this type of remote access VPN almost deployment free and maintenance free at the end-user side. This is a huge benefit for the IT management personnel, who would otherwise spend considerable resources to deploy and maintain their remote access VPN solutions.

- **Effective operation with a firewall and NAT:** SSL VPN operates on the same port as HTTPS (TCP/443). Most Internet firewalls, proxy servers, and NAT devices have been set up to handle TCP/443 traffic well. So there is no need for any special consideration to transport SSL VPN traffic over the networks. This has been viewed as a significant advantage over native IPsec VPN that operates over IP type 50 (ESP) or 51 (AH), which in many cases need special configurations on the firewall or NAT devices to let them pass through.

As SSL VPN evolves to fulfill another important requirement of remote access VPN—the requirement of supporting any application—some of these properties are no long true depending on which SSL VPN technology the VPN users choose. But overall, these properties are the main drivers for the popularity of SSL VPN in recent years and are heavily marketed by SSL VPN vendors as the main reasons for IPsec replacement.

Today, no official standard exists for SSL VPN. Today's SSL VPN technology uses SSL/TLS as secure transport and employs a heterogeneous collection of remote access technologies such as reverse proxy, tunneling, and terminal services to provide users with different types of access methods that fit different environments. The sections that follow examine some commonly used SSL VPN technologies:

- Reverse proxy technology
- Port-forwarding technology
- SSL VPN tunnel client
- Integrated terminal services

Reverse Proxy Technology

HTTPS provides secure web communication between a browser and a web server that supports the HTTPS protocol. SSL VPN extends this model to allow VPN users to access corporate internal web applications and other corporate application servers that might or might not support HTTPS, or even HTTP. SSL VPN does this by using several techniques that are collectively called reverse proxy technology.

A reverse proxy is a proxy server that resides in front of the application servers, normally web servers, and functions as an entry point for Internet users who want to access the corporate internal web application resources. To the external clients, a reverse proxy server appears to be the true web server. Upon receiving the user's web request, a reverse proxy relays the user request to the internal web server to fetch the content on behalf of the users and relays the web content to the user with or without additional processing.

Many web server implementations support reverse proxy. One example is the mod_proxy module in Apache. With so many implementations, you might wonder why you need an SSL VPN solution to have this functionality. The answer is that SSL VPN offers much more functionality than traditional reverse proxy technologies:

- SSL VPN can transform complicated web and some nonweb applications that simple reverse proxy servers cannot handle. The content transformation process is sometimes called webification. For example, SSL VPN solutions allow users to access Windows or UNIX file systems. The SSL VPN gateway needs to be able to communicate with internal Windows or UNIX servers and webify the file access in a web browser–presentable format for the VPN users.

- SSL VPN supports a wide range of business applications. For applications that cannot be webified, SSL VPN can use other resource access methods to support them. For users who demand ultimate access, SSL VPN can provide network-layer access to directly connect a remote system to the corporate network, in the same manner as an IPsec VPN.

- SSL VPN provides a true remote access VPN package, including user authentication, resource access privilege management, logging and accounting, endpoint security, and user experience.

The reverse proxy mode in SSL VPN is also known as clientless web access or clientless access because it does not require any client-side agents to be installed on the client machine. Figure 2-11 shows how SSL VPN users access corporate resources using the clientless web access mode.

Figure 2-11 *SSL VPN Reverse Proxy Operation*

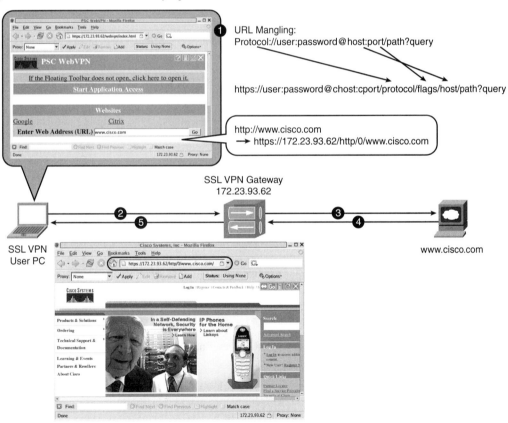

1 The SSL VPN user connects to the SSL VPN device by entering the sign-in URL https://172.23.93.62 into the browser. The client browser and the SSL VPN device first establish an SSL connection. After user authentication at the sign-in page, the user sees the sign-in page with resource bookmarks. To access an internal web server, the user either clicks one of the bookmarks or manually enters the desired URL, in this case, www.cisco.com.

2 Upon receiving the URL request, the client browser changes the requested URL to https://172.23.93.63/0/http//www.cisco.com/. This process is called URL mangling. According to the URL mangling rule shown in Figure 2-11, the mangled URL points to the SSL VPN gateway while preserving the original URL request information. The client browser then sends this request to the SSL VPN gateway instead of sending it directly to www.cisco.com.

3 Upon receiving the request, the SSL VPN gateway restores the mangled URL to its original form. It then sends an HTTP request to the internal web server www.cisco.com.

4 The internal web server returns the content to the SSL VPN gateway.

5 The SSL VPN gateway performs content transformation, also known as content rewriting, on the server content. Then it sends the rewritten content to the client through the established SSL session.

Note the two important techniques in the previous steps: URL mangling and content rewriting. The following sections describe these techniques.

URL Mangling

URL mangling is used to direct user URL requests to the SSL VPN gateway that intermediates the user requests by parsing them to the true destination server address and then forwards the requests to the servers on behalf of the end users. For the web bookmarks on an end user's sign-in page, the bookmarks have been premangled by the SSL VPN gateway. For a URL request that has been input by end users, the URL is mangled by a JavaScript that is downloaded from the SSL VPN gateway at user sign-in time. When the user enters a URL in the SSL VPN sign-in page, the URL mangling routine in the JavaScript is invoked to change the URL properly.

No standards define the format for URL mangling. Mangled URLs can look totally different when handled by different vendors and implementations.

Note that in the previous example, the mangled URL reveals the internal web server address. Because the mangled URL will be displayed in a client browser window and recorded in the browser history file, it might be a security concern for people who don't want to leave the internal web infrastructure information on the client machines, which could be kiosk PCs. One way to resolve this concern is URL obfuscation, also known as URL masking.

Currently, URL obfuscation is a certification requirement by ICSA Labs, yet no standard exists for how URLs should be obfuscated. In general, vendors use a character-encoding table to mask the internal server name and then present the masked mangled URL to the end users.

Content Rewriting

The previous section described URL mangling, which is an important technique in the process by which SSL VPN users access corporate resources using the clientless web access mode. The second important technique is content rewriting.

As a reverse proxy server, the SSL VPN gateway fetches web-based content from an internal web server and performs content rewriting. The main goal of the content rewriting is to change the URL references and Java socket calls so that all users' requests point to the SSL VPN gateway. Also, for Java rewriting, the SSL VPN gateway would need to re-sign with Java bytecode after the rewriting. This is a complicated and resource-intensive process. The content rewriter needs to be able to understand a wide range of complicated web-based objects, such as HTML, JavaScripts, java applets, ActiveX, Flash, and XML and to correctly locate and rewrite the URL references. The loose standard of HTML and web applications makes it more challenging for the content rewriter to properly parse poorly written web contents without breaking the applications.

Server-Side and Client-Side Processing

In the previous example, you saw that the content-rewriting task is carried out at the server side by the SSL VPN gateway. In some occasions, the SSL VPN device merely wraps the web component, and the real content-rewriting task happens at the client-side browser. Client-side processing has the following advantages:

- For web applications that generate dynamic web content at the client side, it is easier to perform the content rewriting at the client side.
- Client-side content rewriting is a form of distributed computing that saves a significant amount of system resources on the SSL VPN device.

The SSL VPN gateway first classifies the web content into different types of web objects, such as JavaScripts, ActiveX, Flash, and images. For the web objects that need client-side processing, the SSL VPN gateway's content rewriter simply tags the web object and sends the content to the client browser along with a JavaScript file that has the proper rewriting routines. The client browser then executes the JavaScript routines to perform the final content rewriting before presenting the content to the end user.

Proxy Bypass

Because of the aforementioned complexity of various web applications and content rewriting, it is almost impossible for vendors to supply a content rewriter that works for all web applications. Sometimes, a complicated content rewriter might not interoperate with new web applications because of its intensive processing of the content. As a possible work-around to this situation, some SSL VPN vendors implement a proxy bypass feature as one of the "fail-safe" options. The proxy bypass feature bypasses the default content-rewriting process and instead follows much simpler content-rewriting steps. It mainly looks for the obvious, static links in the page and rewrites them, but leaves the complicated web component alone. In a many cases, this "simpler is better" design philosophy has proven to work better than applying extremely complicated content-rewriting logic on an unknown application.

To differentiate traffic that needs be proxy bypassed and traffic that needs to go through the normal content-rewriting process, either one of the following two schemes is used:

- **Use of high ports:** For an internal website that needs to be proxy bypassed, a nonstandard high port is assigned on the SSL VPN gateway. To access the internal website, users connect to https://<*SSL_VPN_gateway*>:<*assigned_high_port*>. Upon receiving this request on the predefined high port, the SSL VPN gateway maps the request correspondingly to the internal web server address and applies the bypass-rewriting procedure on the server content.

  The proxy-bypassed internal websites need to be predefined as user bookmarks. This method is not supported by the client-side JavaScript mangling.

  If a firewall is in front of the SSL VPN gateway, the firewall needs to open additional ports other than TCP/443 to accommodate the proxy bypass.

- **Use of alternative host names of SSL VPN gateway:** In this case, the internal web server address is mapped to an alternative host name of the SSL VPN gateway and the user connects to https://<*alternative gateway name*>.

This method has the advantage of not requiring extra ports to be opened on corporate firewalls. However, it requires more configurations, such as DNS configurations, to allocate additional names of the SSL VPN gateway and extra certificates that map to the alternative host names.

Customizable Rewriting

It is desirable for the content rewriter to have customizable rewriting capability to deal with unexpected situations. Today, SSL VPN vendors have the following customized rewriting techniques at different phases of content rewriting:

- **Preprocessing user interface:** This provides administrators with an interface to insert customized content-processing procedures before the content-rewriting engine gets the content. Some examples of the customized processing are cleaning up the HTML content to prepare it for the content rewriter, looking for a specific pattern, and replacing it.

- **Application-specific fine-tuning:** For most common web applications, such as Citrix, Outlook Web Access (OWA), and iNotes, the content rewriter has customized rewriting procedures to make sure that it can handle these applications smoothly.

- **Postprocessing user interface:** Similar to the preprocessing user interface, the postprocessing interface allows administrators to insert additional content-processing steps after the content-rewriting engine performs the content rewriting.

The preprocessing and postprocessing user interfaces are also important troubleshooting tools that can provide temporary remediation in bug situations.

Selective Rewriting

Normally by default, SSL VPN gateways rewrite all the server content. Some vendors offer a selective rewriting, or "split tunneling," feature in their reverse proxy solution. With this feature configured, administrators can specify a list of domain names that do not require content rewriting. The client browser directly accesses the destination site without having to send the request to the SSL VPN gateway first. For example, the VPN administrator can configure the SSL VPN reverse proxy in such a way that only when end users access internal corporate web resources, will the request be sent to the SSL VPN gateway. For other Internet browsing, the request goes to the Internet site directly without going through the SSL VPN gateway. This is similar to the split tunneling in IPsec VPNs, but not exactly the same. The difference is that in SSL VPN, reverse proxy does not have full control of client traffic as the IPsec client does.

Port-Forwarding Technology

Clientless web access supports only a small set of corporate business applications that already have a web interface or can be easily webified. To be a complete remote access VPN solution, SSL VPN–based solutions need to be able to support other types of applications. The port-forwarding client solves part of the problems.

The SSL VPN port-forwarding client is a client-side agent that intercepts specific application traffic and redirects the traffic to the SSL VPN gateway through the established SSL connection. The port-forwarding client is normally a thin client, that is, a small application or applet that is smaller than 100 KB.

SSL VPN vendors use different techniques to implement the port-forwarding function, for example, a Java applet, ActiveX control, Windows Layered Service Provider (LSP), or Windows Transport Data Interface (TDI). The most popular technique is the Java applet–based port-forwarding client. Compared to other Windows-based techniques, Java applet–based port forwarding supports both Windows and non-Windows systems, such as Linux and Mac OS, as long as the client system supports Java.

Figure 2-12 illustrates how a Java applet–based port-forwarding client works.

Figure 2-12 *SSL VPN Port-Forwarding Operation*

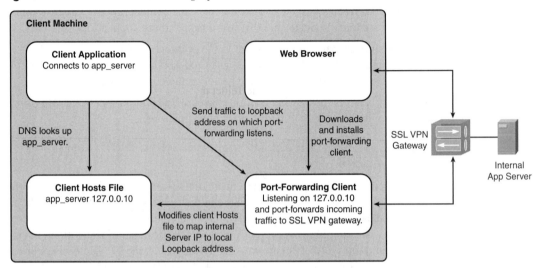

The following list describes the process illustrated in Figure 2-12:

1 The end user launches a web browser to connect to the SSL VPN gateway. After the user signs in, the user clicks to launch the port-forwarding client.

2 The client machine downloads and runs the Java applet–based port-forwarding client. The port forwarding can be configured in the following two ways:

— For each client application that connects to an internal application server, a local loopback IP address and port are predefined. For example, for a Telnet application to internal server 10.1.1.1, the port forwarding client maps it to loop back IP 127.0.0.10 and port 6500. Instead of running Telnet to 10.1.1.1, the end user enters **telnet 127.0.0.10 6500** to telnet to 127.0.0.10 on port 6500. This sends the traffic to the port-forwarding client that is listening on this IP address and port. The port-forwarding client then encapsulates the client Telnet traffic and forwards it to the SSL VPN gateway using an established SSL connection. The SSL VPN gateway then unpacks the traffic and forwards the Telnet request to the internal server at 10.1.1.1.

— With the method described in the previous point, end users have to change the application setting every time to connect to the assigned loopback IP address and port—an operation they find inconvenient.

To solve the problem, a port-forwarding configuration can specify the host name of the internal application server. For example, the Cisco port-forwarding client first backs up the Hosts file on the client machine, and then adds an entry in the Hosts file to map the internal server host name to the assigned loopback IP address. Use the previous example to see how this works. For the internal server 10.1.1.1 with host name router.company.com, the port-forwarding client first backs up the client machine's Hosts file to Hosts.webvpn, and then adds the following entry to the Hosts file: 127.0.0.10 router.company.com. The end user in this case would just enter **telnet router.company.com**. To perform the DNS lookup, the client machine looks up the modified Hosts file and then sends the Telnet traffic to the loopback address on which the port-forwarding client is listening.

With this method, the end users do not have to change the client application setting every time. However, to modify the Hosts file, the end user would need certain user privileges. For example, Linux users would normally require root-level privilege to be able to change the Hosts file.

3 Users launch a client application in the previous steps. The port-forwarding client port-forwards the client application traffic to the SSL VPN gateway under the protection of the established SSL connection.

4 The SSL VPN gateway unwraps the traffic and forwards the client application traffic to the internal application server, and relays the subsequent communication between the client and the server.

5 The end user finishes the application and logs out. The port-forwarding client restores the client machine's Hosts file. The port-forwarding client can either be uninstalled upon user logout or stay on the client machine.

As you can see from previous description, the Java applet–based port-forwarding technique has the following characteristics:

- For each TCP flow, a port-forwarding entry needs to be specifically configured to map to a local loopback address and TCP port.

- The application needs to be initiated from the client side.

Java applet–based port-forwarding clients normally support only simple client-server-based, single-channel TCP applications, such as Telnet, SMTP, POP3, and Windows remote desktop service. For applications that use multiple TCP ports or dynamic TCP ports, such as active FTP and Microsoft Exchange Protocol, Java applet–based port forwarding is not a good choice.

Some Windows-based port-forwarding clients support some multichannel TCP applications and applications that use dynamic ports. They can only track and port-forward traffic from specific Windows processes or to specific destination addresses. Although this allows the port-forwarding clients to support more applications, they are limited to Windows-based client computers and can require end users to have administrative privileges. The Smart Tunnel Access from the Cisco ASA SSL VPN appliance is one example.

Compared to clientless web access, the port-forwarding technology supports more applications but with less granular access control. The level of access control is still much more specific than the traditional IPsec clients, which provide full network-layer access to end users by default. This access and control trade-off makes port-forwarding technology a good choice for business partner access scenarios, where partners can access only specific application resources on the corporate network.

Terminal Services

To use the port-forwarding techniques, users must have client applications installed and configured to point to the local loopback address or the internal server address. You cannot assume that the client computers have these applications available. For some commonly used simple remote control applications, such as Windows terminal service, Citrix terminal service, VNC, Telnet, and SSH, some SSL VPN vendors provide extra convenience by delivering the remote control applications to the client computer.

We use Windows terminal service as an example of how this feature works. End users first log in to the SSL VPN; then they click the bookmark to launch the terminal service application. The client browser then downloads a package, which is often an ActiveX control or a Java applet, from the SSL VPN gateway and installs the package on the client PC. This package contains a customized Windows Remote Desktop Protocol (RDP) client, which enables the user to run a Windows terminal service connection to a corporate internal Windows terminal server. Also, in this case, the end user does not have to configure this RDP client. The traffic is automatically forwarded to the SSL gateway that intermediates the traffic between the RDP client and internal terminal server.

SSL VPN Tunnel Client

Traditional clientless web access and port-forwarding access do not satisfy the needs of power users and telecommuters who run VPNs on corporate-owned machines and like to have full access to the corporate resources. The IPsec VPN is a better fit to provide full network-layer access to the VPN users. Organizations that already have a remote access IPsec VPN can use the existing VPN solution to provide network-layer access and clientless SSL VPN for application-level VPN access. Today, most SSL VPN solutions also provide a tunnel client option for companies that have a greenfield remote access VPN deployment.

Again, unlike IPsec VPNs, SSL VPN tunnel clients have no standards, and different vendors use various tunneling technologies. However they do share some common characteristics:

- The SSL VPN tunnel client can be downloaded on the fly from the SSL VPN gateway and installed on the users' computers. Normally, deliveries are through Java or ActiveX using established SSL connections. This way, there is no need to preinstall the VPN clients, as required by IPsec VPN solutions.

- For installation, in most cases, tunnel clients require users to have administrative privileges.
- The SSL VPN tunnel clients normally function in user space rather than kernel space. Because of this, the VPN users do not need to reboot after the VPN client is installed.
- The tunnel client often installs a logic adapter (for example, a PPP adapter or a virtual adapter) on the user machine and gets an IP address assigned from an internal IP address pool. After the tunnel client captures and encapsulates the client traffic using the logic adapter, it transports the packets to the SSL VPN gateway using the established SSL connections.

Because the SSL VPN tunnel clients can be distributed and installed on the fly during the SSL VPN sessions, they save the IT management cost that would have been required by current IPsec VPN solutions.

Most current SSL VPN tunnel clients transport packets using SSL. The DTLS section covered the performance issue of this approach to support real-time applications. SSL VPN vendors are looking for solutions to resolve these issues. Currently a few methods have been adopted:

- Advanced compression techniques to improve the performance.
- IPsec transport. In this case, the SSL VPN tunnel client is delivered using SSL, but the data transport uses IPsec technology.
- DTLS or alternative UDP mechanisms as data transport mechanisms.

Summary

This chapter covered the SSL and SSL VPN technologies in detail. The chapter started with basic requirements of a secure VPN and discussed how to use various cryptographic algorithms and applications to achieve these requirements. The piecing together of these technologies followed, with a discussion of the workings and implementations of the SSL/TLS protocol, which is the secure transportation base for an SSL VPN solution. The chapter concluded with a discussion of the SSL VPN and various remote access technologies that are deployed to build an SSL VPN solution. In summary, this chapter helps you to understand how SSL VPNs deliver secure communications and application access from a technology standpoint. With this understanding, you are well prepared to move on to the design and deployment of SSL VPN solutions.

References

SSL and TLS, Designing and Building Secure Systems, Eric Rescorla, ISBN 0-201-61589-3.

Applied Cryptography, Bruce Schneier, ISBN 0-471-12845-7.

Network Security, Private Communication in a Public World, Charlie Kaufman, Radia Perlman, Mike Speciner, ISBN 0-13-061466-1.

Network Security Principles and Practices, Saadat Malik, ISBN 1-58705-119-2.

RSA laboratories crypto FAQ, http://www.rsasecurity.com/rsalabs/node.asp?id=2152.

RFC 2246, "The TLS Protocol."

The SSL Protocol, version 3.0, http://wp.netscape.com/eng/ssl3/ssl-toc.html.

RFC 2818, "HTTP over TLS."

PKCS standards, http://www.rsasecurity.com/rsalabs/pkcs.

RFC 3280, "Internet X.509 Public Key Infrastructure Certificate and Certificate Revocation List (CRL) Profile."

RFC 2405, "The ESP DEC-CBC Algorithm with Explicit IV."

RC4 information at wikipedia, http://en.wikipedia.org/wiki/RC4.

The Diffie-Hellman introduction at wikipedia, http://en.wikipedia.org/wiki/Diffie-Hellman.

The RSA introduction at wikipedia, http://en.wikipedia.org/wiki/RSA.

The DSA introduction at wikipedia, http://en.wikipedia.org/wiki/Digital_Signature_Algorithm.

This chapter describes the following topics:

- SSL VPN resource access methods
- User authentication and access privilege management
- Security considerations
- Device placement and platform options
- Virtualization
- High availability
- Performance and scalability

SSL VPN Design Considerations

This chapter discusses design issues you should consider when you build a Secure Socket Layer (SSL) Virtual Private Network (VPN) solution. Readers with experience managing a remote access solution, such as IP security (IPsec)–based remote access VPN, will recognize many common considerations that apply to SSL VPN-based remote access solutions. You will also encounter special considerations that pertain to the characteristics of SSL VPN technology.

No design can fit every network, because everyone's policy and business requirements are different. This chapter provides a list of common design aspects that you need to consider when you design and deploy an SSL VPN solution and possible solutions that you can apply.

Not All Resource Access Methods Are Equal

As mentioned in Chapter 2, "SSL VPN Technology," SSL VPN employs a variety of techniques, each of which has its unique characteristics in terms of user experience, user privilege requirements, and levels of access to the network resources. This is one of the major differences between SSL VPN and traditional remote access solutions, such as IPsec-based remote access VPN.

When you design an SSL VPN network, it is important to understand that not all access methods are equal and different access methods can be deployed to achieve different goals. You should ask yourself several questions when you evaluate SSL VPN technology and before you deploy an SSL VPN access method:

- What level of access does it provide?
- What operating systems does it support, for example, Windows, Linux, Mac, and mobile devices?
- What user privileges does it require?
- What level of access control can you apply?

Table 3-1 provides answers to common questions about SSL VPN access methods.

Table 3-1   *SSL VPN Resource Access Methods*

	Client-Side Agent Required	User Privilege Required	Access Ubiquity	Level of Access	Granular Access Control
Reverse-proxy	No	No	Most ubiquitous	Limited to applications that can be adapted to the web	Very granular application-level control
Port forwarding	Yes; Java applet or ActiveX control	Standard user; administrative privilege sometimes required	Medium	Limited mostly to static server-based TCP applications	Medium; controls client/server application access
Integrated terminal services	Yes	Might require administrative privilege	Medium; mainly Windows systems	Windows Terminal service, Citrix, VNC	Medium; provide only terminal services
Tunnel client	Yes	Typically requires administrative privilege to install the client for the first time	Least ubiquitous; usually limited to corporate-owned/trusted systems	Network-layer access; supports almost all applications	Low

This table compares the special characteristics of an SSL VPN to the traditional remote access VPN solutions. The same network resources can be accessed by using several resource access methods, each of which gives the user different experiences and calls for different system requirements. When you design your SSL VPN solution, it is important to understand this and choose the right access method for the right purpose. Here are some general considerations:

- The reverse-proxy-based method is the most ubiquitous access method and is good for almost all users. It can be applied to support mobile users or business partners who need to access a specific application through web browsers. The applications supported in this case are normally web-based e-mail applications such as Microsoft OWA (Outlook Web Access) and iNotes or a web-based business application, such as salesforce and Oracle iProcurement.

- As mentioned in Chapter 2, the reverse-proxy mode supports only a limited number of applications that can be made suitable for web use.

- The port-forwarding clients can be used to support business partners or contractors who need to access a very limited number of client/server applications that cannot be adapted to the web. As described in Chapter 2, when users use the port-forwarding technology, they often need to reconfigure the application to point to the local loopback address. This can be inconvenient for the users. As tunnel client technology has matured, many companies go directly to using tunnel clients to support various applications.

- Tunnel clients can be used to support power users that need full resource access. Because of their requirement of user privilege and their nature of full network access, tunnel clients are normally deployed on corporate-owned user systems, such as work laptops. Strong security control should be deployed to ensure the proper security posture of the endpoints and the security protection of the corporate networks.

- Some vendors do not use true reverse-proxy to support web browser–based access. A small applet (for example, ActiveX control) is downloaded and installed on the user's computer after the user signs on to the SSL VPN portal. The applet then intercepts the user's web request and sends it off to the established SSL VPN connection. These applet transactions can take place in a manner that is fairly transparent to the end user so that the user does not even realize that he or she is dealing with a client. In this case, you need to understand the operating system, user privilege, and browser setting requirements of the client-side applet (for example, allow ActiveX download and execution) to make sure that they fit into your deployment requirements.

Later sections of this chapter discuss the security and performance considerations of different access methods.

User Authentication and Access Privilege Management

Effectively managing the VPN users and their access privileges is the core consideration in any remote access VPN design. There are mainly two aspects:

- A scalable and secure solution to authenticate users

- Decisions on what access privilege to grant to the users based on various user and security attributes

Many organizations migrate from the existing IPsec-based remote access VPN solutions to SSL VPN, whereas other organizations simply add SSL VPNs to their existing remote access VPN. The good news is that SSL VPNs fit well into the existing authentication infrastructure.

User Authentication

Although this section focuses on user authentication, first step back to have a quick look at the big picture. AAA stands for *authentication* (which defines who you are), *authorization* (which defines what you are allowed to do), and *accounting* (which provides a record of what you did). User authentication is a key step in an SSL VPN solution. Aside from validating users' credentials, user authentication allows an SSL VPN gateway to assign the user to a policy group. The assignment is made by using a user's organization group information, which is derived during the authentication phase, along with other attributes, such as endpoint security posture and time of day. The policy group defines the authorization privileges of the users.

Choice of Authentication Servers

You have a wide variety of identity technologies to choose from for authenticating users. The common choices are passwords, RADIUS, TACACS+, one-time password (OTP) systems, public-key infrastructure (PKI), smart cards, and so on. For remote access VPN authentication, a two-factor OTP system provides the strongest security and manageability combination. It is also common for small- to medium-sized companies to leverage existing user directory infrastructure such as Lightweight Directory Access Protocol (LDAP), Windows NTLM, or Windows XP/2000 Active Directory for VPN user authentication. To use this, you need to apply and enforce strong password policies because the strength of the security relies on those policies.

The design of the AAA system can vary depending on the size of your network and the disparity of access methods. For an SSL VPN device, the choices of authentication servers fall mainly into two categories:

- **A dedicated AAA server running RADIUS:** The AAA server is the interface between the SSL VPN appliance and the identity servers, such as corporate LDAP servers or OTP systems. Cisco Secure ACS is an example of this type of AAA server. The SSL VPN appliance communicates with the AAA server using the RADIUS protocol. Often, the AAA server sends a query to the external identity databases for identity authentication, and returns the authentication result to the SSL VPN appliance. The AAA server can speak different protocol languages with various identity databases such as LDAP, SecureID, and Windows Active Directory. An advanced AAA server, such as Cisco Secure ACS, can also retrieve additional user attributes from the external user identity servers, such as the users' roles in the organization or the users' password expiration information. All these user attributes can be used later in the authorization phase to determine the access privilege.

- **An SSL VPN appliance communicating directly with the identity server:** In this case, the SSL VPN appliance needs to be able to communicate with various types of identity servers, such as LDAP, OTP systems, or Windows domain controllers. This becomes fairly common because most current SSL VPN vendors support multiple types of authentication servers. This mode is most common to small- to medium-sized companies that do not have disparate access methods, and hence have no need to have a central root AAA system.

When you choose to use this method, pay attention to what additional information the SSL VPN appliance can retrieve from the authentication servers, other than the results of the user authentication. For the later authorization phase, it is often useful for the SSL VPN appliance to also be able to get the users' organizational information. Enabling the SSL VPN appliance with this additional capability requires more integration between the SSL VPN appliance and the authentication server.

AAA Server Scalability and High Availability

The scalability and availability of the AAA server directly affect the availability of your VPN network and the user experience.

For a small- to medium-sized VPN network, it is relatively easy to address this design issue. Because the number of the VPN users is relatively small, the scalability of the AAA server is less of an issue. Also, because small to medium deployment normally does not have dispersed Internet VPN access, the AAA servers normally reside on a local network, and network delay and resiliency are not problematic. You should have a backup or secondary AAA server to provide local high availability. Most SSL VPN appliances support checking a secondary AAA server in case the primary server is not available.

For a medium to large enterprise network, the scalability and resiliency of the AAA systems are important and need to be carefully designed. For a remote access VPN deployment, you probably need to integrate your authentication requirements with the AAA infrastructure that is already in place to support other access methods.

Some good design guidelines for deploying a Cisco Secure Access Control Server (ACS) have been documented in the white paper "Guidelines for Placing ACS in the Network," which can be found at http://www.cisco.com/en/US/products/sw/secursw/ps2086/ products_white_paper09186a0080092567.shtml. In this white paper, the general design recommendations documented for scalability, resiliency, and device placement should apply to most AAA server deployments.

The following sections briefly highlight the important factors that need to be considered.

AAA Server Scalability

When you consider AAA server scalability, keep the following points in mind:

- The maximum number of users supported by the AAA server.
- The number of authentication requests per second the AAA server can handle.
- The type of database. For an internal user database on the AAA server itself, check its scalability to find out how many local users can be defined.

AAA Server High Availability and Resiliency

When you consider AAA server high availability (HA) and resiliency, keep the following points in mind:

- Consider a local secondary AAA server.

- For dispersed network access and VPN geographic HA design, consider placing a AAA server at each location that has business-critical impact.

- Incorporate a robust AAA server database synchronization mechanism.

Resource Access Privilege Management

After user authentication, the remote access VPN device should be able to authorize the user with resource access privileges based on the user's attributes. As described earlier, because of the ubiquity of the SSL VPN, its design needs to ensure the integrity of the endpoint. Hence the resource authorization also goes beyond the standard user attributes to include other security attributes. The following is a list of attributes that can be used to determine resource access privilege:

- **Sign-in URL:** For an SSL VPN device that offers different sign-in URLs to different groups of users, the sign-in URL can be used to decide the type of resource this group of users is entitled to.

- **User's digital certificate:** The organization information in the user's certificates can be used to map users to corresponding roles that allow different resource access.

- The result of endpoint security assessment: This point is discussed in more detail within the context of the security considerations. In essence, the posture of the endpoint can be used as a dynamic factor to decide users' access privilege to sensitive corporate resources.

- Time of day.

- Browser types.

- **User attributes:** These are the typical user attributes in the user identity database. For example, the marketing group in the LDAP database can be mapped to an internal marketing group in the SSL VPN.

Some of these attributes, such as endpoint security posture and users' IP addresses, are collected prior to user authentication. Some of the attributes, such as endpoint security posture, should be periodically reevaluated during the user session to dynamically determine the user's access privileges based on the most current situation.

To clarify these concepts, we give an example of how an SSL VPN system can use some of these attributes to perform dynamic access privilege management. In this case study, a salesperson attempts to access corporate resources using an SSL VPN. Depending on the result of the endpoint assessment, the salesperson is granted different levels of resource access.

Scenario 1: Salesperson Accesses the VPN from a Kiosk Computer at a Sales Conference

Step 1 The salesperson initiates the VPN request by entering https://vpn.companyxyz.com into the browser.

Step 2 Upon receiving the access request, the SSL VPN appliance collects some user attributes and performs the endpoint security checking. The results are as follows:

IP address = Outside

Client digital certificate = Not present

Proper antivirus client installed and enabled = No

Step 3 Based on the results in Step 2, the SSL VPN chooses an authentication method for the user and performs user authentication:

Authentication method = Strong, OTP

Step 4 After successful user authentication, the SSL VPN appliance also retrieves the user's organization information through a separate authorization step:

User's organization group = Sales

Step 5 Based on the user attributes so far, the SSL VPN appliance maps the user to a VPN group or role:

VPN role = sales_insecure

Step 6 The sales_insecure role decides the user access privilege:

User privilege = Web access only

Session timeout = 30 minutes

Periodic security checking = Yes

Require secure desktop = Yes

Note: The secure desktop can be launched much earlier at the preauthentication phase based on the IP address attribute. This way, the user password entered into the client browser can be protected from software such as keystroke loggers.

Step 7 The salesperson logs in and starts to access the bookmarked web applications, such as OWA. More granular application-level access control can be applied at this phase.

Scenario 2: The Same Salesperson Accesses the VPN from a Corporate-Owned Laptop at Home

Step 1 The salesperson initiates the VPN request by entering https://vpn.companyxyz.com into the browser.

Step 2 Upon receiving the access request, the SSL VPN appliance collects some user attributes and performs the endpoint security checking. The results are as follows:

IP address = Outside

Client digital certificate = Yes

Proper antivirus client installed and enabled = Yes

Step 3 Based on the results in Step 2, the SSL VPN chooses an authentication method for the user and performs user authentication:

Authentication method = Strong, OTP

Step 4 After successful user authentication, the SSL VPN appliance also retrieves the user's organization information through a separate authorization step:

User's organization group = Sales

Step 5 Based on the user attributes so far, the SSL VPN maps the user to a VPN group or role:

VPN role = sales_secure

Step 6 The sales_secure role decides the user access privilege:

User privilege = Tunnel client

Session timeout = 12 hours

Periodic security checking = Yes

Require secure desktop = No

Step 7 The salesperson logs in and starts to access the corporate network using the tunnel client mode. Additional granular IP-based access control can be applied at this phase.

Security Considerations

A remote access VPN extends the perimeter of your network to the remote endpoints. An SSL VPN has been an entry point for security threats to enter the network. The ubiquity, versatility, and clientless nature of the SSL VPN provide significant business benefits and cost savings, but they also pose additional security challenges compared to traditional remote access VPNs.

The following sections first examine the security threats that need to be addressed in SSL VPN security design. The sections then cover some of the security design measures you can take that help to mitigate those threats.

Security Threats

The following sections look at the common security risks that are associated with SSL VPNs.

Lack of Security on Unmanaged Computers

As mentioned earlier, SSL VPNs can support users coming from any computer on the Internet, such as public domain machines (for example, kiosk PCs) that are not controlled by the corporate IT department. This department ensures that the machines have proper service packs and security software, such as antivirus software. This poses a major threat to security. If, for example, SSL VPN users sign in to the SSL VPN from a compromised or infected PC, they can become a source for spreading viruses, worms, network attacks, and Trojan horses into the corporate network.

Several other security risks mentioned in the sections that follow are also related to these security threats. In general, as you deal with uncontrolled endpoints, you face increased security risks.

Data Theft

Several types of security threats lead to data theft or password theft:

- **Sensitive data left in a browser's cache:** Web browsers cache the various web objects that users downloaded during browsing. This caching helps browsers to improve the browsing experience. The browser cache files are physically stored on the user's computer in predefined directories. For example, the Temporary Internet Files folder is used for Internet Explorer browsers. After users finish browsing and leave the computer, the browser cache is left on the computer and can be accessed by other users who later log on to the same computer. This can be a security risk in a kiosk scenario that uses SSL VPN clientless web access. In this case, a VPN user logs in to the SSL VPN portal from a kiosk machine to access corporate resources, such as e-mail or other business applications. During the session, the user can access sensitive documents through the web browser that caches the document on a local hard drive. After the user signs off and leaves, attackers can easily use the kiosk computer and collect the browser cache to retrieve the sensitive information.

- **Browser histories:** Similar to the browser cache, browser histories are stored by the browser to enhance the user experience. The browser histories reveal the user activities and internal web server structure. Similar to the browser cache, browser histories saved on unmanaged computers are vulnerable to data theft.

- **Browser cookies:** A cookie is a text-only string sent by a web server to a web browser. The cookie can reside in the browser's memory or be stored on a local hard drive. A cookie is often used for purposes such as authentication, tracking, and personalization, such as site preference. Depending on their usage and content, cookies could contain sensitive information about users. Similar to a browser cache, cookies saved on unmanaged computers are vulnerable to data theft.

- **Brower-saved forms and user passwords:** Similarly, browser-saved forms and user passwords are vulnerable to data theft and password theft.

- **Documents on unmanaged computers:** More generally, documents and other types of sensitive data left on the unmanaged computers are vulnerable to data theft. For example, it is common for a VPN user to temporarily download a sensitive document to the local computer for reading or editing and later forget to delete the sensitive document before logging off. Furthermore, even if the user deletes the files before the VPN logoff, it is fairly easy for attackers to recover the deleted files by using common file-recovery utilities that are readily available on the Internet.

- **Data theft and password theft using keystroke loggers or other Trojan horse programs:** In the SSL VPN web-based clientless mode, users can access corporate resources from an already compromised computer that contains malware. For example, loggers that are preinstalled by the attackers can capture user input, such as e-mail IDs and passwords, and take screen shots of the e-mails.

Man-in-the-Middle Attacks

There have been known man-in-the-middle (MITM) attacks to the SSL protocol, and this is how they can work. The attacker first launches an Address Resolution Protocol (ARP) spoofing attack or Domain Name System (DNS) spoofing attack to the SSL VPN user. The success of the attack will redirect the SSL traffic to the attack host that is configured with SSL proxy software. The attack host then acts as the destination web server by establishing an SSL connection with the user on one side and another SSL connection with the true destination web server on the other side, proxying the traffic back and forth. Because the attack host serves as the endpoint of the two SSL tunnels, it has the proper keys to decrypt the SSL traffic. In this attack, the attack host would need to present a spoofed digital certificate to the end users. In most cases, the web browser prompts the end user with a security alert. However, users often simply ignore the warning and proceed.

Web Application Attack

SSL and SSL VPNs do not have built-in mechanisms to detect application attacks such as SQL injections, buffer overflow attacks of web applications, directory traversal attacks, or cross-site scripting.

Spread of Viruses, Worms, and Trojans from Remote Computers to the Internal Network

Corporate networks are vulnerable to the spread of viruses, worms, and Trojans when the SSL VPN users connect using the tunnel client mode. With the tunnel client mode, the endpoints are directly connected to the corporate network with full network-layer access. Endpoints might not be compliant with corporate security policy, which can require, for example, a proper Windows patching level or up-to-date antivirus DAT files. In this case, a high possibility exists that the endpoints will forward their infection to the internal network.

Split Tunneling

In a remote access VPN deployment, split tunneling gives the user direct access to a public network and VPN access to a private network simultaneously. The end user's computer becomes an extended Internet entry point to the corporate network. If no proper security measures are in place on the end user's computer, attackers have opportunities to compromise the computer from the Internet and gain access to the internal network through the VPN tunnel. For this reason, many organizations choose to disable split tunneling in their remote access VPN deployment. Figure 3-1 illustrates the split tunneling topology.

When split tunneling is disabled, one common issue is that users can no longer access the local LAN for tasks such as printing. The solution is to disable split tunneling but enable local LAN access. This way, the local LAN traffic will not be tunneled to the head-end SSL VPN gateway.

Figure 3-1 *Split Tunneling*

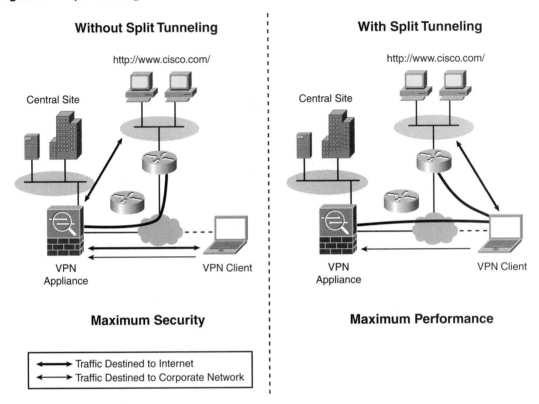

Password Attacks

The password attack is one of the most effective attacks. Common practices such as weak passwords and simple authentication methods such as static passwords are vulnerable to various attacks through password cracking or eavesdropping.

Security Risk Mitigation

The following sections detail the design considerations and security measures that you should consider when implementing an SSL VPN deployment.

Strong User Authentication and Password Policy

Using a strong user authentication mechanism is critical to the security of a remote access VPN. If possible, consider using two-factor authentication techniques, such as hardware tokens and smart cards. If static passwords are used, enforce strong password policy.

Choose Strong Cryptographic Algorithms

The SSL VPN device normally allows you to choose SSL/TLS protocol versions and cipher suites. Consider enforcing SSLv3 or Transport Layer Security (TLS) rather than SSL version 2. Also, choose strong cipher suites for data encryption and integrity. For example, choose Triple DES (3DES) or AES instead of RC4.

Session Timeout and Persistent Sessions

On the SSL VPN device, configure a short session timeout to prevent potential piggybacking unauthorized access to your internal network through a public computer.

Some vendors support persistent sessions that keep the SSL VPN session even after the user closes the browser without signing off. End users might think that closure of the browser is equal to termination of the session. This could lead to unauthorized access to the internal network from a public computer.

Endpoint Security Posture Assessment and Validation

A thorough preconnect security assessment is necessary. As discussed earlier, this helps prevent viruses, worms, and Trojan horses from spreading into the internal network and helps administrators make intelligent decisions on what access privilege to grant to the VPN users based on the endpoint security posture. The preconnect security posture validation can include the following aspects:

- **Location checking:** Using information such as IP address, Windows registries, or even PC screen banners, the SSL VPN device can figure out whether the user is coming from the Internet or from a corporate LAN, using corporate-owned PCs or a kiosk PC.

- **Security posture checking:** This refers to a checklist that can be used to determine whether the endpoint has proper antivirus protection, a personal firewall, or other required security agents that are installed and enabled with up-to-date policies.

- **Malware scans:** A malware scan can detect items such as keystroke loggers, spyware, and other Trojan horse programs on the endpoints.

VPN Session Data Protection

Although SSL VPNs provide secure communication, the session data is not encrypted on the endpoints and can be vulnerable to various malicious programs already on the compromised endpoints, such as a compromised kiosk computer. To protect the VPN session data, consider deploying secure desktop technology. This secure desktop is typically protected from other processes on the computer and has an "on-the-fly" encrypted file system. Malicious codes, even if they are present on the computer, might not be able to access the content stored on the secure desktop. This type of implementation also helps ensure that data will be erased in a secure manner at the end of the session. Later chapters describe the Cisco Secure Desktop in more detail.

Techniques to Prevent Data Theft

To prevent the previously mentioned data theft, consider the following techniques:

- **Cookie management:** Many SSL VPN vendors support cookie management so that user cookies are not passed down to the endpoint.

- **Browser cache control:** HTTP (RFC 2616) offers several cache-control headers that can be used to control the caching behavior of the browser.

- **Cache cleaner:** Many SSL VPN vendors offer a cache cleaner that cleans the browser cache at the end of the session when users log off. The cache cleaner can delete the browser cache and browser histories. When deploying a cache cleaner, consider the following:

  — Which folders does the cache cleaner clean? Some applications leave the cache in a different folder from the standard browser cache folder. Make sure that the cache cleaner can clean those locations. For example, the popular web-based e-mail application iNotes leaves its cache in a different folder than the standard browser cache folder. In this situation, the cache cleaner could miss the cache.

  — Which operating systems does the cache cleaner support?

  — Does the cache cleaner perform secure data sanitization? As mentioned earlier, a simple file delete is not secure. The secure cache cleaner complies to higher data sanitization standards than simple file delete to ensure that the deleted files can not be recovered later.

- **Secure desktop:** Because the secure desktop provides a sandbox that traps all the session data, deletion of the secure desktop at the end of the session provides a thorough data cleanup. This method is more thorough than the cache cleaner, which cleans only specific locations.

- **User education and security awareness:** These are also important aspects of the company security efforts. For SSL VPN security, focus on the following:

  — Educate users on the potential security risks associated with accessing corporate resources from a public system.

  — Encourage users to exercise security precautions when they use an SSL VPN on a public computer. This includes terminating the VPN session before leaving the computers, not leaving sensitive documents on the local hard drive of the public computer, and carefully examining certificate messages to guard against MITM attacks.

Web Application Firewalls, Intrusion Prevention Systems, and Antivirus and Network Admission Control Technologies

As mentioned earlier, the SSL protocol does not have a built-in mechanism to defend against web application attacks, and the SSL VPN tunnel client mode makes it easier for viruses and worms to spread into the Internet network from infected endpoints. Consider integrating threat defense technologies and security compliance technologies with your SSL VPN solution to mitigate these security risks:

- **Web application firewalls:** These are OSI Layer 7 firewalls that can understand and analyze HTTP application traffic to detect protocol conformance violations and attacks. They normally use a combination of protocol conformance enforcement and attack signature pattern-matching techniques to either prevent application anomalies or look for specific attack patterns.

- **Intrusion prevention systems (IPS) and gateway-level antivirus systems:** These systems offer a broader level of threat prevention. They help to prevent network attacks, viruses, worms, Trojan horses, spyware, and other security threats from entering the internal networks.

- **Network Admission Control (NAC):** This is an emerging technology that addresses security compliance enforcement issues. The basic idea is to make sure that the endpoints are compliant with corporate security policies, such as having proper antivirus software and Windows patching level, before the network devices grant users access to network resources. The endpoint security integrity checking that we just discussed is a form of Network Admission Control, and it can be integrated with the overall NAC framework to provide a consistent security validation for all types of network access methods.

Device Placement

SSL VPN appliances are normally placed at the Internet edge of the corporate network. At the Internet edge of the network, other security devices are often deployed to protect the internal network from attacks. This section discusses the device placement issues you should consider when placing the SSL VPN devices among other security services at the edge.

For companies that already have an IPsec-based remote access VPN solution deployed, the device placement considerations should also apply to SSL VPN deployment.

Figure 3-2 shows three common designs for placing the SSL VPN appliances in a medium-sized network.

Figure 3-2 *SSL VPN Device Placement*

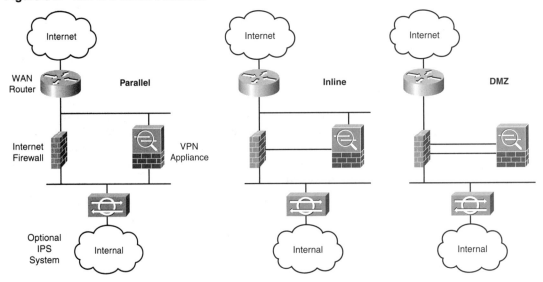

The device placement relationship between the SSL VPN appliance and Internet firewall is mainly based on the following two considerations:

- Do you trust the VPN traffic? In parallel mode, the VPN traffic is trusted and thus sent directly into the internal network after decryption. A high level of security risk is associated with this design. In the other two modes shown in Figure 3-2, VPN traffic is semitrusted and goes through a stateful firewall for access control and access logging.

- Do you need a firewall to protect the SSL VPN appliance? In parallel and inline mode, apply access control lists (ACL) on the WAN router to allow only the SSL VPN traffic to the SSL VPN appliance. In the DMZ mode, you can put that access control on the

Internet firewall and configure more advanced session control to guard against denial of service (DoS) attacks. Because the traffic is encrypted, the firewall will not be able to inspect much SSL traffic. Also, with this design, the firewall sees the VPN traffic twice: once before decryption and once after decryption. Hence, higher performance is required of the firewall.

In all cases, an optional IPS is placed after the VPN decryption to inspect the traffic for attacks. Depending on your security policy and requirements, the IPS can operate in an inline mode or promiscuous mode.

Platform Options

SSL VPNs are evolving in a manner similar to IPsec technology. This technology started as dedicated VPN concentrators and slowly became integrated with other network and security services. Two types of SSL VPN solutions are on the market: the pure-play SSL VPN appliances and the solutions that integrate SSL VPN functionalities with other network devices such as routers and firewalls. The emerging Unified Threat Management (UTM) market provides enterprises with options to deploy a single security device that offers multiple security services such as a firewall, a VPN, an IPS, antivirus and antispam software, and other content security services. Each solution has its merits and deployment benefits. Cisco offers the integrated solution with Cisco routers and Adaptive Security Appliances (ASA). A UTM appliance, the Cisco ASA appliances allows security administrators to deploy additional security services to the SSL VPN traffic.

Virtualization

The concept of virtualization is becoming more and more popular among enterprise customers. For SSL VPNs, the need for virtualization is natural. Enterprises like to provide different remote access VPN presences to different user groups, such as partners and different departments of employees. The following are some basic capabilities you should consider for a "virtualized" SSL VPN deployment:

- Provides a customized SSL VPN presence for individual user groups. For example, each business partner has its own SSL VPN sign-in page with a customized user interface.

- Provides customized authentication methods and VPN group policies for different user groups.

- Provides management roles for running each VPN separately.

- Has total separation of different VPNs in terms of system resources, routing tables, user databases, and policy management interfaces.

Some SSL VPN vendors supply the first three capabilities in the previous list without having to provide a full virtualized implementation. For each VPN user group, the SSL

VPN provides a dedicated sign-in URL. For example, partner A has a sign-in URL of https://www.companyxyz.com/vpn_for_partnerA, and partner B has a different sign-in URL of https://www.companyxzy.com/vpn_for_partnerB. Each sign-in URL has a customized user interface, such as a logo, page layout, and resource bookmarks. Each sign-in URL is associated with a different set of authentication methods and policy flows that are also specifically designed to meet different user group requirements. To the end user, the experience is "virtualized." However, from the SSL VPN system perspective, it is not virtualized.

The fourth capability in the previous list calls for a true virtualization, not only at the user level but also at the system resource level and policy management level. This is normally a requirement for service providers who provide managed remote access VPN services to multiple customers. These customers often demand total traffic and resource and management separation from other VPN customers. This can also be a requirement for large enterprises that have remote access VPNs for different trade partners.

High Availability

The high availability (HA) consideration for a remote access VPN deployment has two parts: local and geographic HA.

Local HA methods include the following:

- **Hot standby failover:** The two SSL VPN appliances are in an active-passive failover session. Common failover protocols include Virtual Router Redundancy Protocol (VRRP) and Hot Standby Routing Protocol (HSRP). A stateful failover synchronizes the SSL VPN session information between the two units to ensure minimum user disruption during the failover.

- **Active-active failover:** Both units are active and handle traffic during the normal state. Some administrators like to oversubscribe the resource and have both units working in full or higher than 50 percent capacity. This could lead to a domino effect. For example, when failure occurs, the failover unit will be overwhelmed by the aggregated user requests.

- **Multiunit clustering:** This is similar to active-active failover but with more than two units. The clustering is mainly used to improve scalability, but it can also provide high availability.

Geographic HA extends the VPN resiliency beyond local network availability. The VPN appliances are placed in multiple locations to serve the local users and also work as backup appliances for other locations.

Performance and Scalability

Performance considerations for an SSL VPN design are a bit different from those of the IPsec-based VPN because of the multiple technologies that the SSL VPN features. When you try to determine the performance of an SSL VPN appliance, you need to be clear about which resource access method you have in mind. The performance of different access methods varies greatly. The following list outlines the performance characteristics of the two most popular access methods:

- **Reverse-proxy-based web access method:** This access method challenges performance and resources more than any other. The SSL VPN appliance needs to perform content rewriting for each web application page and object. This involves resource-consuming pattern searching and matching. The complexity of the web page, which includes the number of URLs and Java scripts, directly affects the performance of the system. Resources permitting, a performance testing using the web pages from your web application can give you a good estimate of real-world performance. Light Reading Lab published a test methodology for clientless performance measurement. It is posted at http://networktest.com/ssl03/ssl03meth.html.

  Consider enabling the server-side caching feature if it is available on your SSL VPN system. With caching enabled, the frequently accessed web content will be cached by the SSL VPN appliance after it is rewritten the first time.

- **Tunnel client mode:** This mode is less complicated than the clientless mode and has higher performance. Instead of having to be inspected and rewritten, the web content goes through the simple encryption process, which can be easily hardware accelerated.

Chapter 2 covers the potential performance challenge that occurs when SSL or TLS supports applications that use real-time protocols. You need to consider this when you need to support applications such as IP telephony.

The scalability of the SSL VPN network is normally addressed by clustering multiple units together. For example, Cisco Adaptive Security Appliances (ASA) support pay-as-you-grow clustering techniques. Enterprises can start with a small cluster, and as the company grows, VPN administrators can easily add more units to the cluster to support more users.

Summary

This chapter discussed some of the important design considerations in an SSL VPN deployment. The areas covered include the characteristics of various SSL VPN resource access methods, user authentication and access privilege management, security, device placement, platform options, virtualization, high availability, performance, and scalability. The remainder of this book discusses in detail how to configure the Cisco SSL VPN product to implement these design considerations.

References

SSL VPN security white paper at http://www.cisco.com, Steven Song, http://www.cisco.com/web/about/security/intelligence/05_08_SSL-VPN-Security.html.

Cisco SAFE VPN IPSec Virtual Private Networks in Depth, Jason Halpern, et al., http://www.cisco.com/en/US/netsol/ns340/ns394/ns171/ns128/networking_solutions_white_paper09186a00801dca2d.shtml#wp48088.

Networkers 2006 presentation SEC-2010, Deploying Remote Access IPSec and SSL VPNs, Pete Davis.

This chapter covers the following topics:

- Overview of Cisco SSL VPN product portfolio
- Cisco ASA 5500 series
- Cisco IOS routers

CHAPTER 4

Cisco SSL VPN Family of Products

Cisco Systems first introduced the Secure Socket Layer (SSL) Virtual Private Network (VPN) functionality in its VPN 3000 concentrator product line. The first phase of SSL VPN functionality included the clientless and thin-client modes of connectivity. In the later software images, Cisco introduced the full-tunnel client mode functionality along with a number of SSL VPN–specific security features to provide a complete SSL VPN solution.

In mid-2005, Cisco introduced the 5500 series Adaptive Security Appliance (ASA) to provide a complete security solution to an enterprise, whether it is a firewall, VPN, intrusion prevention system (IPS), intrusion detection system (IDS), or even content filtration. To provide a state-of-the-art VPN solution, Cisco ported all the VPN-specific features from the VPN 3000 product line into its ASA products. Additionally, a number of significant IPsec and SSL VPN features were also introduced in the ASA product line.

Furthermore, Cisco introduced the SSL VPN functionality in almost all of its IOS router product line to leverage customers' existing investment in routers.

Overview of Cisco SSL VPN Product Portfolio

Cisco currently offers the SSL VPN functionality in a number of its product offerings, including the following:

- **Cisco VPN 3000 series concentrator:** The Cisco VPN 3000 series concentrator was the first Cisco product to offer the SSL VPN functionality. The clientless and thin-client modes were introduced in the 4.1 version of code, whereas the full-tunnel client support was added in the 4.7 version of code. Cisco VPN 3000 series concentrators are now end-of-life units. Cisco recommends that you plan to migrate your VPN infrastructure to the Cisco security appliances for continued support.

- **Cisco ASA 5500 series:** Cisco ASA integrates all the firewall, IDS, and VPN capabilities of its existing products. This provides an all-in-one solution for your network. Incorporating all these solutions into Cisco ASA secures the network without the need for extra overlay equipment or network alterations. Cisco ASA was developed to respond to the many Cisco customers and network professionals who requested the type of integration that ASA supplies in a security product.

- **Cisco VPN routers:** As stated previously, Cisco introduced the SSL VPN functionality in most Cisco IOS routers so that customers can leverage their existing investment in routers. This functionality was offered in the Cisco IOS routers in Release 12.4(6)T of the code. A list of supported Cisco IOS routers is presented in Table 4-3, later in this chapter.

To provide a complete SSL VPN solution for enterprises, Cisco also offers a number of software-based applications and products, including the following:

- **Cisco AnyConnect VPN client:** Cisco AnyConnect is a software application that can be pushed to or installed on a user machine. The AnyConnect client is used to provide full network access to corporate resources after the SSL VPN tunnel has been negotiated. Cisco AnyConnect client is supported by the security appliances running 8.0 or higher versions of code and by Cisco IOS routers running 12.4(15)T or higher versions of code. Before releasing the Cisco AnyConnect client, Cisco used to provide full network access through a different software application called Cisco SSL VPN client (SVC). SVC is supported by the security appliances running version 7.1 or higher of code and by the Cisco IOS routers running Release 12.4(11)T or higher of code. However, you should consider using the Cisco AnyConnect client over the Cisco SVC client because the former is a superset of the original SSL VPN functionality. Furthermore, no further development is planned for the SVC client.

- **Cisco Security Device Manager (SDM):** Cisco Security Device Manager provides an easy-to-navigate GUI to set up and manage features that Cisco IOS routers offer. Although configuring SSL VPN in IOS through SDM is optional, it is highly recommended that you use SDM. Using a command-line interface (CLI) to configure the SSL VPN features is a convoluted process, whereas SDM provides a user-friendly interface for SSL VPN configuration.

- **Cisco Adaptive Security Device Manager (ASDM):** Cisco Adaptive Security Device Manager also provides an easy-to-navigate and simple graphical interface to set up and manage the different features that the security appliances provide. It is bundled with a variety of administration and monitoring tools to check the health of the appliance and the traffic traversing through it. Using ASDM is a requirement if you plan to configure SSL VPN on a security appliance running version 8.0 or higher.

- **Cisco Security Manager (CSM):** Cisco Security Manager provides a centralized management platform to configure and monitor your entire Cisco security infrastructure. CSM can manage devices including Cisco IOS routers, firewalls, VPNs, and IPS/IDS sensors. You can use CSM version 3.1 or higher to manage the SSL VPN functionality on the security appliances and Cisco IOS routers.

This chapter primarily focuses on the SSL VPN functionality on Cisco security appliances and Cisco IOS routers because the Cisco VPN 3000 concentrators are already end-of-life devices.

Cisco ASA 5500 Series

The Cisco ASA 5500 series Adaptive Security Appliance provides an advanced Adaptive Identification and Mitigation (AIM) architecture and is a key component of the Cisco Self-Defending Network. As mentioned earlier in this chapter, the security appliances integrate firewall, IDS/IPS, and VPN capabilities and provide an all-in-one solution for an organization.

Seven Cisco ASA 5500 series models are available in the current Cisco ASA 5500 series product line. They include the following:

- Cisco ASA 5505
- Cisco ASA 5510
- Cisco ASA 5520
- Cisco ASA 5540
- Cisco ASA 5550
- Cisco ASA 5580-20
- Cisco ASA 5580-40

The Cisco 5500 series security appliances are designed to provide a spectrum of security features to an organization of any size. Cisco ASA 5505, for example, is suitable for home or small offices, whereas Cisco ASA 5580-40 is more suitable for the headquarters locations of large enterprises.

SSL VPN History on Cisco ASA

When Cisco introduced its ASA platform, it also introduced the SSL VPN functionality in its first release of version 7.0. The SSL VPN features were in parity with the SSL VPN features of the Cisco VPN 3000 concentrator of version 4.1. The two main features in the ASA 7.0 release were clientless and thin-client modes. Using the clientless mode, users can establish a secure connection to the security appliance using a web browser. Users do not need to install any additional software on the workstation to use this feature. In the thin-client mode, also known as port forwarding, users can access the internal TCP-based applications over the SSL VPN tunnel.

Cisco enhanced the SSL VPN functionality in the next release of the security appliances by offering a number of features. With this release, Cisco brought the security appliance in parity with the SSL VPN features of version 4.7 of the Cisco VPN 3000 concentrator. The two most important features of this release were the SSL VPN client (SVC) and the support for Cisco Secure Desktop (CSD). The SSL VPN client provides full access to the internal resources in a manner that is similar to the Cisco IPsec client. The use of CSD in the SSL VPN environment provides reliable endpoint security to eliminate sensitive data from a workstation when the session is disconnected.

Cisco also introduced a number of SSL VPN features in version 8.0 of the security appliance. Some of the important features in version 8.0 included the AnyConnect VPN client, dynamic access policies (DAP), Smart tunnels, and Host Scans. The Cisco AnyConnect VPN client provides access to the corporate network, just as the SVC does, but supports Microsoft Windows Vista, Windows XP, Windows 2000, Linux, and Macintosh OS X. Cisco recommends that you leverage the AnyConnect VPN client for full network access. You can use DAP, on the other hand, to create a set of access control attributes that you map to a specific user session or connection. This way, the security appliance can allow access to a specific user for a particular session, based on the policies that you create.

Smart tunnels work much like port forwarding, in that you can allow certain TCP applications to be tunneled over the SSL VPN connection. Smart tunnels define which application can be forwarded over the SSL VPN tunnel, whereas port forwarding defines what TCP ports can be forwarded over the tunnel. The Host Scan module is a part of CSD that can scan the remote client machine, either using Cisco AnyConnect or a clientless SSL VPN connection, against a collection of antispyware and antivirus applications, their associated signature definition updates, firewalls, and operating systems. The results from the host scan are used to determine whether the host is allowed to connect, and if allowed, it is used to determine what access should be provided to the host.

NOTE   The security appliances provide SSL VPN acceleration through the use of an on-board hardware acceleration chip.

SSL VPN Specifications on Cisco ASA

As with any network design, you need to determine the size and scope of the SSL VPN implementation, especially the number of concurrent users that will connect to gain network access. If one Cisco ASA is not enough to support the required number of users, the available load-balancing features, such as ASA clustering, must be considered to accommodate all the potential remote users.

Table 4-1 lists the supported security appliances, their VPN throughput, and the number of supported SSL VPN users for each platform. It also specifies whether a security appliance can participate in SSL VPN load balancing.

Table 4-1   *Cisco ASA SSL VPN Specifications*

Platform	Maximum 3DES/AES VPN Throughput	Maximum Concurrent Sessions*	SSL VPN Load Balancing
ASA 5505	100 Mbps	25	Not available
ASA 5510	170 Mbps	250	Available if licensed

Table 4-1   *Cisco ASA SSL VPN Specifications (Continued)*

Platform	Maximum 3DES/AES VPN Throughput	Maximum Concurrent Sessions*	SSL VPN Load Balancing
ASA 5520	225 Mbps	750	Available
ASA 5540	325 Mbps	2500	Available
ASA 5550	425 Mbps	5000	Available
ASA 5580-20	1 Gbps	10,000	Available
ASA 5580-40	1 Gbps	10,000	Available

*Cisco ASAs include a free two-user SSL VPN license.

SSL VPN Licenses on Cisco ASA

Unlike IPsec, the SSL VPN capability in the security appliance is not included free of charge in the base system price. If you want to enable SSL VPN on a security appliance, you must purchase appropriate licenses. The base security appliance includes two SSL VPN users by default for evaluation, lab testing, and remote management purposes. Anything beyond that requires you to buy a separate SSL VPN license. For example, if your environment will have 75 SSL VPN users, you can buy the SSL VPN license that can accommodate up to 100 potential users. Table 4-2 lists the available licenses and their respective part numbers. Note that an SSL VPN license file for ten users will be supported on all platforms, because all security appliances support ten users. However, a 10,000-user license can be installed only on ASA 5580. Similarly, a 750-user license can be installed on ASA 5520, ASA 5540, ASA 5550, and ASA 5580.

Table 4-2 shows the various licensing options available for the various models.

Table 4-2   *Available Licenses for ASAs*

SSL VPN User Requirement	License Part Number
10 Users	ASA5500-SSL-10=
25 Users	ASA5500-SSL-25=
50 Users	ASA5500-SSL-50=
100 Users	ASA5500-SSL-100=
250 Users	ASA5500-SSL-250=
750 Users	ASA5500-SSL-750=
1000 Users	ASA5500-SSL-1000=
2500 Users	ASA5500-SSL-2500=
5000 Users	ASA5500-SSL-5000=
10,000 Users	ASA5500-SSL-10K=

Cisco IOS Routers

Cisco Systems introduced the SSL VPN functionality in Release 12.4(6)T of code of the Cisco IOS routers. Small- to medium-sized enterprises are perfectly positioned to use IOS SSL VPN to extend a remote access VPN solution to their employees and partners. Using a Cisco IOS router as an SSL VPN gateway, customers can deploy a single-box device to meet their routing, voice, wireless, firewall, IPS/IDS, and remote access VPN requirements.

Seven Cisco IOS router product series support SSL VPN. They include the following:

- Cisco 870 series
- Cisco 1800 series
- Cisco 2800 series
- Cisco 3700 series
- Cisco 3800 series
- Cisco 7200 series
- Cisco 7300 series

The support of SSL VPN into the breadth of IOS products can enable any enterprise, whether small or medium, to provide a cost-effective and robust remote access VPN solution in its existing Cisco infrastructure.

SSL VPN History on Cisco IOS Routers

As mentioned in the previous section, the SSL VPN functionality on the Cisco IOS routers was introduced in Release 12.4(6)T. You must run the advanced security or higher Cisco IOS image to enable SSL VPN. Some of the features available in this release include clientless, thin-client, and full tunnel SSL VPN client modes. Cisco, however, recommends that you run at least Cisco IOS Release 12.4(9)T or higher because the earlier version had a number of SSL VPN–specific issues. Additionally, Cisco added numerous SSL VPN– specific features in the later versions of code. For example, support for AnyConnect VPN client and customized web portal were added in IOS Release 12.4(15)T.

SSL VPN Licenses on Cisco IOS Routers

Just as with Cisco ASAs, you need to purchase licenses to enable SSL VPN on a Cisco IOS router. Before you implement SSL VPN on an IOS router, or in a cluster of IOS routers, you need to determine the size of SSL VPN deployment, especially the number of concurrent users of this service. For example, if one IOS router is not enough to support the required number of users, you must consider traditional load balancers or server-clustering schemes to accommodate all potential remote users.

SSL VPN is supported on a number of Cisco IOS routers. Table 4-3 lists the Cisco IOS routers and the supported number of simultaneous SSL VPN users on each platform.

Table 4-3   *Supported IOS Routers and SSL VPN Users*

Supported Routers	Supported Concurrent Users
870	2
1811	10
1841, 2801	25
2811, 2821	50
2851, 3725, 3745	75
3825, 3845	100
7200, 7301	150

Cisco Systems provides two-user complimentary licenses on the supported routers. You do not have to purchase licenses if you want to test SSL VPN features in a lab environment where the user count will not exceed two. The SSL VPN license is available in packs of 10, 25, and 100 users. For example, if you know that the maximum concurrent user count will not exceed 85, you can purchase three 25-user licenses and one 10-user license. Table 4-4 lists the available licenses and their respective part numbers.

Table 4-4   *Available Licenses for Cisco IOS Routers*

SSL VPN User Requirement	License Part Number
10 Users	FL-WEBVPN-10-K9=
25 Users	FL-WEBVPN-25-K9=
100 Users	FL-WEBVPN-100-K9=

Summary

Cisco offers a breadth of products that offer SSL VPN functionality. They include Cisco ASA, Cisco IOS router, and Cisco VPN 3000 concentrators. Cisco stepped into the SSL VPN market by introducing it in its flagship VPN 3000 concentrators and then porting the functionality into other product lines. This chapter discussed the SSL VPN functionality on Cisco ASA and Cisco IOS routers and provided product specifications that were focused on SSL VPN.

This chapter covers the following topics:

- SSL VPN design considerations
- SSL VPN prerequisites
- Pre-SSL VPN configuration guide
- Clientless SSL VPN configuration guide
- AnyConnect VPN Client configuration guide
- Cisco Secure Desktop
- Host Scan
- Dynamic access policies
- Deployment scenarios
- Monitoring and troubleshooting

CHAPTER 5

SSL VPNs on Cisco ASA

Secure Socket Layer (SSL) Virtual Private Network (VPN) is the rapidly evolving VPN technology that complements the existing IPsec remote access VPN deployments. As discussed in the earlier chapters, for the clientless SSL VPN tunnels, the actual data encryption and decryption occur at the application layer usually by a browser. Consequently, you do not need to install additional software or hardware clients to enable SSL VPN in your network infrastructure. Furthermore, if you want to provide full network access to your remote users, you can leverage the full tunnel mode functionality of the SSL VPN tunnels. Most users prefer this option because a VPN client is automatically pushed to a user after a successful authentication.

Cisco Adaptive Security Appliances (ASA) are the all-in-one devices that provide all the major security services to an enterprise. Whether you are looking for a firewall solution to protect a server farm, an intrusion prevention system (IPS) to proactively defend against the spread of new or old attacks, or a flexible VPN solution to provide connectivity to remote offices or remote users to corporate resources, Cisco ASAs can be set up to adapt to your network environment.

The SSL VPN implementation on Cisco ASAs provides the most robust feature set in the industry. In the current software release, Cisco ASA supports all three flavors of SSL VPN. They include clientless, thin client, and full tunnel modes. These modes are discussed in earlier chapters in detail. In many recent Cisco documents, clientless and thin client solutions are grouped under one umbrella and classified as a clientless solution.

SSL VPN Design Considerations

Before you implement the SSL VPN services in Cisco ASA, you have to analyze your current environment and determine which features and modes might be useful in your implementation. Some of the SSL VPN design considerations are as follows:

- **User connectivity:** Before designing and implementing the SSL VPN solution for your corporate network, you need to determine whether your users connect to your corporate network from public shared computers, such as workstations made available to guests in a hotel or computers in an Internet kiosk. In this case, using an SSL VPN is the preferred solution to access the protected resources.

- **ASA feature set:** A Cisco security appliance can run various features such as IPsec VPN tunnels, routing engines, firewalls, and data inspection engines. Enabling the SSL VPN feature can add further load if your existing appliance is already running a number of features. You must check the CPU, memory, and buffer utilization before enabling an SSL VPN.

- **Infrastructure planning:** Because SSL VPN provides network access to remote users, you have to consider the placement of the VPN termination devices. Before implementing the SSL VPN feature, ask the following questions:

  — Should it be placed behind a firewall? If so, what ports should be opened?

  — Should the decrypted traffic be passed through another set of firewalls? If so, what ports should be allowed?

  — Do the inside routers redistribute the pool of IP addresses for SSL VPN clients in a routing protocol so that other routers recognize the subnet?

- **Implementation scope:** Network security administrators need to determine the size of the SSL VPN deployment, especially the number of concurrent users that will connect to gain network access. If one Cisco ASA is not enough to support the required number of users, the use of ASA clustering or load balancing must be considered to accommodate all the potential remote users.

Table 5-1 lists the secure appliances and the number of supported simultaneous SSL VPN users for each platform.

Table 5-1 *ASA Platforms and Supported Concurrent SSL VPN Users*

Security Appliance	Maximum VPN Throughput*	Maximum Supported Concurrent Users
5505	100 Mbps	25
5510	170 Mbps	250
5520	225 Mbps	750
5540	325 Mbps	2500
5550	425 Mbps	5000
5580-20	1 Gbps	10,000
5580-40	1 Gbps	10,000

*The VPN throughput is calculated when 3DES/AES encryption is used for VPN tunnels.

NOTE Cisco uses SSL VPN and WebVPN keywords interchangeably.

SSL VPN Prerequisites

You must meet a number of prerequisites before you can start implementing an SSL VPN in your enterprise. They are discussed in the following sections.

SSL VPN Licenses

The SSL VPN functionality on the ASAs requires that you have appropriate licenses. For example, if your environment is going to have 75 SSL VPN users, you can buy the SSL VPN license that can accommodate up to 100 potential users. Table 5-2 lists the available licenses and their respective part numbers. Note that an SSL VPN license file for ten users will be supported on all platforms because all security appliances can support ten users. However, a 10,000-user license can only be installed on ASA 5580. Similarly, a 750-user license can be installed on ASA 5520, ASA 5540, ASA 5550, and ASA 5580.

Table 5-2   *Available Licenses for ASAs*

SSL VPN User Requirement	License Part Number
10 Users	ASA5500-SSL-10=
25 Users	ASA5500-SSL-25=
50 Users	ASA5500-SSL-50=
100 Users	ASA5500-SSL-100=
250 Users	ASA5500-SSL-250=
750 Users	ASA5500-SSL-750=
1000 Users	ASA5500-SSL-1000=
2500 Users	ASA5500-SSL-2500=
5000 Users	ASA5500-SSL-5000=
10,000 Users	ASA5500-SSL-10K=

Cisco Systems provides a two-user complimentary license on all supported ASA devices. You do not have to purchase licenses if you want to test SSL VPN features in a lab environment where the user count is not going to exceed 2.

NOTE   The minimum version of code to run an SSL VPN is 7.0. In the first release of the ASA, Cisco supported the clientless and thin client modes. The full tunnel SSL VPN client support was added in version 7.1. However, it is highly recommended that you use version 8.0 or higher of software to utilize all the SSL VPN features discussed in this chapter. This chapter strictly focuses on version 8.*x* because of the SSL VPN enhancements that were added in this version of code.

In version 8.*x*, you can purchase an additional license to implement the Advanced Endpoint Assessment feature. This feature enables the ASA to scan a remote workstation for active antivirus, antispyware, and personal firewalls and try to update the noncompliant computers to meet the requirements of an enterprise's security policy. This feature is discussed in the Host Scan section of this chapter in more detail. The part number for this license is ASA-ADV-END-SEC.

NOTE   All license keys are associated per device. That means you cannot share a license among multiple Cisco ASAs, even if they are in high-availability or clustered environments. Customers who want to deploy the security appliances in high-availability areas can purchase the SSL/IPsec VPN Edition bundle with a specific license size.

Client Operating System and Browser and Software Requirements

The SSL VPN functionality on Cisco security appliances is supported on a number of client operating systems and on a number of browsers. The supported platforms are discussed next.

Compatible browser: You must use an SSL-enabled browser such as Microsoft Internet Explorer, Firefox, Opera, Safari, Mozilla, Netscape, or Pocket Internet Explorer (PIE). Table 5-3 provides a list of operating systems and the supported Internet browsers.

Table 5-3   *Supported Operating Systems and Internet Browsers*

Operating System	Supported Browser
Windows XP	Internet Explorer version 6.0 and 7.0
	Firefox version 1.5 and 2.0
Windows Vista (both 32- and 64-bit platforms)	Internet Explorer version 7.0
	Firefox version 2.0
Pocket PC 2003 Windows Mobile 2005	Pocket Internet Explorer
Macintosh OS X 10.4 and 10.5	Safari version 2.0
	Firefox version 2.0 and 2.1*
Linux	Firefox version 1.5 and 2.0

*Cisco AnyConnect VPN Client for Mac OS X does not support the Firefox certificate store.

Sun JRE: SSL VPN, in port forwarding, smart tunnel, and full tunnel modes, uses Sun Microsystems' Java Runtime Environment (JRE) and browsers with ActiveX support.

ActiveX: SSL VPN also uses ActiveX for Internet Explorer on Microsoft-based operating systems. ActiveX is used by smart tunnels, AnyConnect VPN Client, and Cisco Secure Desktop.

Web folder: Microsoft hotfix 892211 must be installed on Windows operating systems to access web folders in the clientless SSL VPN mode.

NOTE   Browser cookies must be enabled if you want to access applications through port forwarding or smart tunnels.

Infrastructure Requirements

The infrastructure requirements for SSL VPNs include, but are not limited to, the following options:

- **ASA placement:** If you are installing a new security appliance, determine the location that best fits your requirements. If you plan to place it after a firewall, make sure that you allow appropriate SSL VPN ports to pass through the firewall.

- **User account:** Before SSL VPN tunnels are established, users must authenticate themselves to either the local database or to an external authentication server. The supported external servers include RADIUS (including Password Expiry using MSCHAPv2 to NT LAN Manager), RADIUS one-time password (OTP), RSA SecurID, Active Directory/Kerberos, and Generic Lightweight Directory Access Protocol (LDAP). Make sure that SSL VPN users have accounts and appropriate access. LDAP password expiration is available for Microsoft and Sun LDAP.

- **Administrative privileges:** Administrative privileges are required for all connections with port forwarding if you want to use host mapping. AnyConnect VPN Client requires administrative rights for the initial installations.

Pre-SSL VPN Configuration Guide

After analyzing the deployment consideration and selecting the SSL VPN as the remote access VPN solution, you must follow the configuration steps discussed in the following sections to properly set up the SSL VPN. These sections discuss the configuration tasks that you must follow before an SSL VPN can be enabled on a Cisco security appliance. These tasks include the following:

- Enrolling digital certificates (recommended)
- Setting up Cisco Adaptive Security Device Manager (ASDM)
- Setting up tunnel and group policies
- Setting up user authentication

Enrolling Digital Certificates (Recommended)

Enrollment is the process of obtaining a certificate from a certificate authority (CA). Before starting the enrollment process, you must generate the RSA key pair with the **crypto key generate rsa** command. To generate the keys, you must first configure a host name and domain name. Example 5-1 demonstrates how to configure a domain name of securemeinc.com and how to generate the RSA key pair of 1024-bit modulus size.

NOTE   If you want to test SSL VPN functionality in a lab environment or in a home setup, you can use a self-signed certificate. A self-signed certificate can be used by ASDM and for the SSL VPN sessions.

Example 5-1   *Generating the RSA Key Pair*

```
Chicago(config)# domain-name securemeinc.com
Chicago(config)# crypto key generate rsa modulus 1024
The name for the keys will be: Chicago.securemeinc.com

% The key modulus size is 1024 bits
% Generating 1024 bit RSA keys, keys will be non-exportable...[OK]
```

NOTE   The same RSA key pair can be used for Secure Shell (SSH) connections to the security appliances.

The enrollment process can be broken into three steps, as described in the following sections.

Step 1: Configuring a Trustpoint

The **crypto ca trustpoint** command declares a CA that your Cisco ASA uses and allows you to configure all the necessary certificate parameters. Invoking this command puts you in ca-trustpoint configuration mode, as shown in Example 5-2. A trustpoint called SecureMeTrustPoint is created in the security appliance.

Example 5-2   *Configuring a Trustpoint*

```
Chicago# configure terminal
Chicago(config)# crypto ca trustpoint SecureMeTrustPoint
Chicago(ca-trustpoint)#
```

You can use the manual or Simple Certificate Enrollment Protocol (SCEP) method to enroll an identity certificate on the security appliance. However, for SSL VPNs, the manual method is used to obtain an SSL VPN certificate from a trusted certificate authority.

In Example 5-3, a security appliance is being configured for manual enrollment. The **enrollment terminal** subcommand in securemetrustpoint configuration is used to declare manual enrollment of the CA server.

Example 5-3 *Configuring Cisco ASA for Manual Enrollment*

```
Chicago# configure terminal
Chicago(config)# crypto ca trustpoint SecureMeTrustPoint
Chicago(ca-trustpoint)# enrollment terminal
Chicago(ca-trustpoint)# end
```

NOTE   If you prefer to use enrollment through SCEP, Cisco ASA provides that functionality. The configuration of a security appliance for SCEP enrollment is similar to its configuration for manual enrollment. However, the **enrollment url** subcommand is used instead of the **enrollment terminal** subcommand.

Step 2: Obtaining a CA Certificate

After defining the trustpoint, the next step is to obtain the CA certificate before requesting an identity certificate from the CA server. The administrator retrieves (copies and pastes) the certificate from the CA server. Use the **crypto ca authenticate** command to import the CA certificate. Example 5-4 demonstrates how to manually import the CA certificate to the Cisco ASA.

Example 5-4 *Importing the CA Certificate Manually*

```
Chicago(config)# crypto ca authenticate SecureMeTrustPoint
Enter the base 64 encoded CA certificate.
End with the word "quit" on a line by itself
-----BEGIN CERTIFICATE-----
MIIC0jCCAnygAwIBAgIQIls45kcfzKZJQnk0zyiQcTANBgkqhkiG9w0BAQUFADCB
hjEeMBwGCSqGSIb3DQEJARYPamF6aWJAY2lzY28uY29tMQswCQYDVGEwJVUzEL
MAkGA1UECBMCTkMxDDAKBgNVBAcTA1JUUDEWMBQGA1UEChMNQ2lzY28gU3lzdGVt
czEMMAoGA1UECxMDVEFDMRYwFAYDVDEw1KYXppYkNBU2VydmVyMB4XDTA0MDYy
-----END CERTIFICATE-----
quit
INFO: Certificate has the following attributes:
Fingerprint:     82a0095e 2584ced6 b66ed6a8 e48a5ad1
Do you accept this certificate? [yes/no]: yes
Trustpoint CA certificate accepted.
% Certificate successfully imported
```

As shown in Example 5-4, the CA certificate is manually imported into the Cisco ASA using the manual (cut-and-paste) method. Enter a blank line or the word **quit** after pasting the Base64-encoded CA certificate to the terminal to exit the CA configuration screen. If the certificate is recognized, the security appliance asks whether you would like to accept the certificate; enter **yes**. The Certificate Successfully Imported message is displayed if the CA certificate import is successful.

Step 3: Obtaining an Identity Certificate

After the CA certificate is obtained from the CA server, use the **crypto ca enroll** command followed by the trustpoint name to generate an identity certificate request to the server. Example 5-5 demonstrates how to generate the certificate request.

Example 5-5   *Generating the ID Certificate Request*

```
Chicago(config)# crypto ca enroll SecureMeTrustPoint
% Start certificate enrollment ..
% The fully-qualified domain name in the certificate will be:
 Chicago.securemeinc.com
% Include the device serial number in the subject name? [yes/no]: no
Display Certificate Request to terminal? [yes/no]: yes
Certificate Request follows:
MIIBpDCCAQ0CAQAwLTErMA4GA1UEBRMHNDZmZjUxODAZBgkqhkiG9w0BCQIWDE5Z
LmNpc2NvLmNvbTCBnzANBgkqhkiG9w0BAQEFAAOBjQAwgYkCgYEA1n+8nczm8ut1
AFAAOBgQDGcYSC8VGy+ekUNkDayW1g+TQL41YldLmT9xXUADAmGhyA8A36d0
VtZlNc2pXHaMPKkqxMEPMcJVdZ+o6JpiIFHPpYNiQGFUQZoHGcZveEbMVor93/KM
IChEgs4x98fCuJoiQ2RQr452bsWNyEmeLcDqczMSUXFucSLMm0XDNg==
---End - This line not part of the certificate request---
Redisplay enrollment request? [yes/no]: no
Chicago(config)#
```

TIP   The request is a PKCS 10 certificate request. Make sure that you do not copy and paste the second highlighted line in Example 5-5. The certificate request will be malformed if this is included.

Example 5-5 shows how the certificate request is generated. The security appliance gives you the option to redisplay the certificate request if needed (as shown in Example 5-5). Copy and paste the certificate request to your CA server. After the request is submitted, make sure that certificate request is approved as a web server certificate by your CA server administrator.

NOTE	Obtain a Base64-encoded certificate from your CA server. You will not be able to copy and paste a Distinguished Encoding Rules (DER) encoded certificate.

After the identity certificate is approved by the CA server administrator, use the **crypto ca import** command to import the Base64-encoded ID certificate. Example 5-6 demonstrates how to import the ID certificate.

Example 5-6 *Manually Importing the ID Certificate*

```
Chicago(config)# crypto ca import SecureMeTrustPoint certificate
% The fully-qualified domain name in the certificate will be:
  Chicago.securemeinc.com
Enter the base 64 encoded certificate.
End with the word "quit" on a line by itself
-----BEGIN CERTIFICATE-----
MIIECDCCA7KgAwIBAgIKHJGvRQAAAAAADTANBgkqhkiG9w0BAQUFADCBhjEeMBwG
CSqGSIb3DQEJARYPamF6aWJAY2lzY28uY29tMQswCQYDVGEwJVUzELMAkGA1UE
CBMCTkMxDDAKBgNVBAcTA1JUUDEWMBQGA1UEChMNQ2lzY28gU3lzdGVtczEMMAoG
A1UECxMDVEFDMRYwFAYDVDEw1KYXppYkNBU2VydmVyMB4XDTA0MDkwMjAyNTgw
NVoXDTA1MDkwMjAzMDgwNVowLzEQMA4GA1UEBRMHNDZmZjUxODEbMBkGCSqGSIb3
SGzFQHtnqURciJBtay9RNnMpZmZYpfOHzmeFmQ==
-----END CERTIFICATE-----
Chicago(config)#
```

The Base64-encoded ID certificate is successfully imported to the security appliance. After the certificate is imported, issue the **ssl trust-point SecureMeTrustPoint outside** command to activate the imported certificate on the outside interface to terminate the SSL sessions, as shown in Example 5-7.

Example 5-7 *Activating the Identity Certificate on the Outside Interface*

```
Chicago(config)# ssl trust-point SecureMeTrustPoint outside
```

Setting Up ASDM

Cisco Adaptive Security Device Manager (ASDM) provides an easy-to-navigate and simple graphical interface to set up and manage the different features that the Cisco Adaptive Security Appliance (ASA) provides. It is bundled with a variety of administration and monitoring tools to check the health of the appliance and the traffic traversing through it. Setting up ASDM is mandatory if you are planning to configure features in versions 8.*x* or higher of code. Many advanced features like Cisco Secure Desktop (CSD) and customized web portals can only be configured through ASDM.

Before you can access the ASDM graphical console, you must install the ASDM software image on the local flash of the security appliance. The ASDM console can manage the local security appliance only. Therefore, if you need to manage multiple security appliances, the

ASDM software must be installed on all the Cisco ASAs. However, a single workstation can launch multiple instances of ASDM clients to manage the different appliances. Optionally, you can leverage Cisco Secure Manager (CSM) to set up the SSL VPN on multiple appliances simultaneously.

NOTE   This chapter focuses on setting up SSL VPN through ASDM. You can use CSM version 3.2 to configure SSL VPN on the ASAs running version 8.0 or higher.

A new security appliance is shipped with ASDM loaded in flash with the following default parameters:

- The Gigabit Ethernet 0/1 interface on Cisco ASA 5520, ASA 5540, ASA 5550, and ASA 5580 is set up as inside with an IP address of 192.168.1.1. On Cisco ASA 5510, the Ethernet 0/1 interface is set up as inside with the same address. However, on ASA 5505, VLAN 1 is setup as the inside interface.

- The DHCP server enabled on the inside interface hands out addresses in the range of 192.168.1.2 through 192.168.1.254.

Uploading ASDM

You can use the **dir** command to determine whether the ASDM software is installed. If the security appliance does not have the ASDM software, your first step is to upload the image from an external file server using the one of the supported protocols. The appliance needs to be set up for basic configuration, such as the interface names, security levels, IP addresses, and proper routes. After setting up basic information, use the **copy** command to transfer the image file, as shown in Example 5-8, where an ASDM file, named asdm-603.bin, is being copied from a TFTP server located at 192.168.1.10. Verify the content of the local flash after the file is successfully uploaded.

Example 5-8   *Uploading the ASDM Image to the Local Flash*

```
Chicago# copy tftp flash
Address or name of remote host []? 192.168.1.10
Source filename []? asdm-603.bin
Destination filename [asdm-602.bin]? asdm-603.bin

Accessing tftp://192.168.1.10/asdm-603.bin...!!!!!!!!!!!!!!!!!!!!!!!!!!!!!!!!!!!!!!
! Output omitted for brevity.
!!!!!!!!!!!!!!!!!!!!!!!!!!!!!!!!!!!!!!!!!!!!
Writing file disk0:/asdm-603.bin...
!!!!!!!!!!!!!!!!!!!!!!!!!!!!!!!!!!!!!!!!!!!!!!!!!!!!!!!!!!!!!!!!!!!!!!!!!!!!!!!!!!!!!!!
! Output omitted for brevity.
```

Example 5-8   *Uploading the ASDM Image to the Local Flash (Continued)*

```
!!!!!!!!!!!!!!!!!!!!!!!!!!!!!!!!!!!!!!!!!!!!!!!!!!!!!!!!!!!!!!!!!!!!!!!!!!!!!!!
5876644 bytes copied in 161.420 secs (36500 bytes/sec)
Chicago# dir
Directory of disk0:/
1260    -rw-  14524416    16:47:34 Nov 07 2007  asa803-k8.bin
2511    -rw-  6889764     17:38:14 Nov 07 2007  asdm-603.bin

62881792 bytes total (46723072 bytes free)
```

Setting Up the Appliance

When the ASDM file is accessed, the Cisco ASA loads the first ASDM image that it finds from the local flash. If multiple ASDM images exist in the flash, use the **asdm image** command and specify the location of the ASDM image you want to load. This ensures that the appliance always loads the specified image when ASDM is launched. In Example 5-9, the appliance is set up to use asdm-603.bin as the ASDM image file.

Example 5-9   *Specifying the ASDM Location*

```
Chicago(config)# asdm image disk0:/asdm-603.bin
```

The security appliance uses the Secure Socket Layer (SSL) protocol to communicate with the client. Consequently, the security appliance acts as a web server to process the requests from the clients. You can enable the web server on the appliance by using the **http server enable** command.

The security appliance discards the incoming requests until the ASDM client's IP address is in the trusted network to access the HTTP engine. In Example 5-10, the administrator is enabling the HTTP engine and is setting up the appliance to trust the 192.168.1.0/24 network connected toward the inside interface.

Example 5-10   *Enabling the HTTP Server*

```
Chicago(config)# http server enable
Chicago(config)# http 192.168.1.0 255.255.255.0 inside
```

NOTE   The SSL VPN implementation on the appliance also requires you to run the HTTP server on the appliance. Starting from version 8.0, you can set up the security appliance to terminate both the SSL VPN as well as the ASDM sessions on the same interface by using the default port of 443. Use https://<ASAipaddress>/admin to access the GUI for admin and management purposes.

CAUTION   If the same port is used for both ASDM and SSL VPN to terminate sessions on an interface, you cannot use client certificates for SSL VPN sessions. When SSL VPN is enabled on an interface, ASDM displays the following warning message to indicate such restriction:

"ASDM and SSL VPN both are configured on the same port 443. If ASDM and SSL VPN are accessed on the same port then you cannot enable certificate requirement for SSL VPN and disable certificate requirement for ASDM on the same interface or vice versa. To achieve this, you need to configure different ports for SSL VPN and ASDM. Do you still want to continue?"

Accessing ASDM

ASDM's interface can be accessed from any workstation whose IP address is in the trusted network list. Before you establish the secure connection to the appliance, verify that IP connectivity exists between the workstation and the Cisco ASA.

To establish an SSL connection, launch a browser and point the URL to the IP address of the appliance. In Figure 5-1, the administrator is accessing ASDM by entering **https:// 192.168.1.1/admin** as the URL. The URL is redirected to https://192.168.1.1/admin/ public/index.html.

Figure 5-1   *Accessing the ASDM URL*

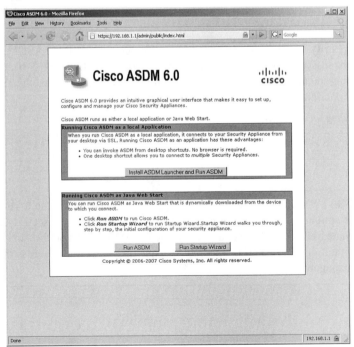

NOTE	ASDM requires Java plug-in 1.4(2), 1.5.0, or 6.0 installed on the web browser. The supported operating systems include Microsoft Windows Vista, 2003 Server, XP, 2000 Service Pack 4, Macintosh OS X, Red Hat Desktop, and Enterprise version 4.

The security appliance presents its certificate to the workstation so that a secure connection can be established. If the certificate is accepted, the security appliance prompts the user to present authentication credentials. If the ASDM authentication is not set up, no default username or password exists. If user authentication is enabled on the security appliance using the **aaa authentication http console** command, provide those login credentials. After a successful user authentication, the appliance presents two ways to launch ASDM:

- **Run ASDM as Java web start:** The security appliance launches ASDM in the client's browser as a Java applet. This option is not feasible if a firewall that filters out Java applets exists between the client and the security appliance.

- **Run ASDM as a local application:** The security appliance offers a setup utility called asdm-launcher.msi, which can be saved to the local hard drive of the workstation.

NOTE	ASDM as a local application feature is currently supported on Windows-based operating systems.

When the ASDM stub application is launched, it prompts for the IP address of the security appliance you are trying to connect to and the user authentication credentials. Figure 5-2 illustrates this, where an SSL connection is being made to an appliance located at 192.168.1.1. If you are using default credentials, leave the username and password blank to log in to ASDM.

Figure 5-2   *Launching ASDM*

NOTE   If you are running version 8.0.3 on the security appliance, make sure that you use version 6.0(3) of ASDM. For more information about ASDM, consult http://www.cisco.com/go/ asdm.

Cisco introduced version 8.1 for its newer ASA 5580-20 and ASA 5580-40 platforms. Use ASDM version 6.1(1) to manage the security appliances running version 8.1.

Setting Up Tunnel and Group Policies

Cisco ASA uses an inheritance model when it pushes network and security policies to the end-user sessions. Using this model, you can configure policies at the following three locations:

- Under default group-policy
- Under user group-policy
- Under user policy

In the inheritance model, a user inherits the attributes and policies from the user policy, which inherits its attributes and policies from the user group-policy, which in turn inherits its attributes and policies from the default group-policy, as illustrated in Figure 5-3. A user, sslvpnuser, receives a traffic access control list (ACL) and an assigned IP address from the user policy, the domain name from the user group-policy, and Windows Internet Naming Server (WINS) information along with the number of simultaneous logins from the default group-policy.

Figure 5-3 *ASA Attributes and Policies Inheritance Model*

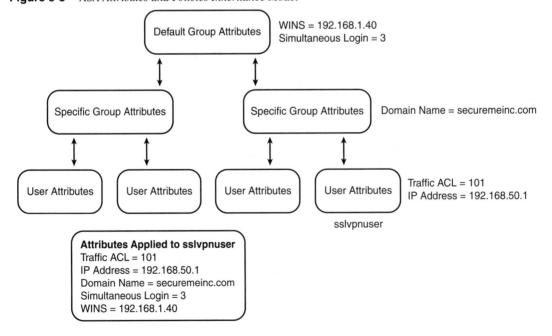

NOTE	DfltGrpPolicy is a special group name, used solely for the default group-policy.

After defining these policies, they must be bound to a tunnel group where users terminate their sessions. This way, a user who establishes his VPN session to a tunnel group will inherit all the policies mapped to that tunnel. The tunnel group defines a VPN connection profile that each user is a member of.

Configuring Group-Policies

The user group and default group policies are configured by choosing **Configuration > Remote Access VPN > Clientless SSL VPN Access** or **Network (Client) Access > Group Policies**. Click **Add** to add a new group policy. As shown in Figure 5-4, a user group-policy, called ClientlessGroupPolicy, has been added. This group-policy only allows clientless SSL VPN tunnels to be established and strictly rejects all the other tunneling protocols. If you would rather assign attributes to default group-policy, you can modify DfltGrpPolicy (System Default). Any attribute that is modified here is propagated to any user group-policy that inherits that attribute. A group-policy name other than DfltGrpPolicy is treated as a user group-policy.

NOTE	The default and user group policies are set up to allow both Cisco IPsec VPN and SSL VPN tunnels. If you want to restrict a policy to solely use SSL VPN, use either clientless SSL VPN or SSL VPN client options under Tunneling Protocols, as illustrated in Figure 5-4.

Figure 5-4 *User Group-Policy Configuration*

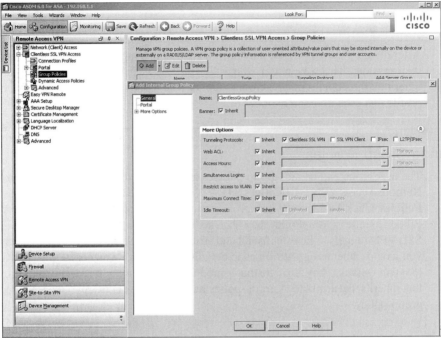

Table 5-4 lists all the SSL VPN attributes that can be mapped to user group, and default group policies.

Table 5-4 *Configurable SSL VPN Attributes*

Attribute	Purpose
Banner	Creates a banner that is displayed to user connections.
Tunneling protocols	Select the remote access protocols that users are allowed to access.
Web ACL	Applies a preconfigured web-type ACL for traffic filtering.
Simultaneous logins	Number of times a user can log in to the security appliance concurrently.
Restrict access to VLAN	Restricts user connection to a specific VLAN on the security appliance.
Maximum connect time	Specifies the maximum time a user is allowed to connect.
Idle timeout	Specifies an idle time a user is allowed to connect.
Bookmark list	Maps a preconfigured bookmark list to the group. If a list is not defined, you can click **Manage** to create a new one.

Table 5-4 *Configurable SSL VPN Attributes (Continued)*

Attribute	Purpose
URL entry	You can allow or deny users to enter URLs directly into the user portal page.
File server entry	Allows or denies users to enter the file server names.
File server browsing	Allows or denies file browsing on the Common Internet File System (CIFS) shares.
Hidden share access	Allows or denies access to hidden shares on a CIFS server.
Port-forwarding list	Applies a port-forwarding list to a group.
Smart tunnel	Applies a smart tunnel list to a group.
ActiveX relay	Allows or denies users to launch Microsoft Office components.
HTTP proxy	Configures an external HTTP proxy server.
HTTP compression	Configures HTTP compression.
Portal customization	Applies a preconfigured user portal list to a group policy.
Homepage URL (optional)	Configures a URL of the web page you want to configure for a user session.
Access deny message	Displays a message to clientless users who log in to the security appliance but do not have SSL VPN privileges.
Post login setting	Prompts the user on whether to download the AnyConnect client.
Default post login selection	Specifies the default login selection if a user does not make a selection in the specified time.
Single sign-on server	Specifies the single sign-on server address.
User storage location	Specifies the location where personalized user information is stored.
Storage key	Specifies the string to provide user access to the storage location.
Storage objects	Specifies object-like cookies, credentials, or both that the server uses in association with the user.
Transaction size	Specifies the time limit. When the time limit is reached, the session times out. The limit is specified in kilobytes.

The user, group, and default group-polices can be applied to clientless, AnyConnect, and IPsec-based remote access VPN tunnels. The SSL VPN–specific attributes are discussed in detail in the next few sections of this chapter.

NOTE   A user policy can be configured by choosing **Configuration > Remote Access VPN > AAA Setup > Local Users**.

Configuring a Tunnel Group

A tunnel group can be configured by choosing **Configuration** > **Remote Access VPN** > **Clientless SSL VPN Access** > **Connection Profiles**. Click **Add** to add a new tunnel group. As shown in Figure 5-5, a tunnel group called SecureMeClientlessTunnel has been added. After defining a tunnel group name, you can bind a user group-policy to a tunnel group. Once a user is connected, the attributes and policies defined under the group-policy will be applied to the user. A user group-policy of ClientlessGroupPolicy is linked to this tunnel group.

Figure 5-5 *Configuration of a Tunnel Group*

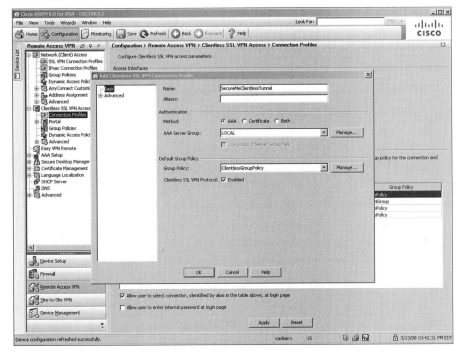

Setting Up User Authentication

Cisco ASA supports a number of authentication servers, such as RADIUS, NT domain, Kerberos, SDI, LDAP, digital certificates, smart cards, and local databases. For small organizations, a local database can be set up for user authentication. For medium to large SSL VPN deployments, it is highly recommended that you use an external authentication server, such as RADIUS or Kerberos, as the user authentication database. If you are deploying the SSL VPN feature for a few users, you can use the local database. The users are defined by choosing **Configuration** > **Remote Access VPN** > **AAA Setup** > **Local Users**. As shown in Figure 5-6, two accounts, sslvpnuser and adminuser, are configured for user authentication. The sslvpnuser account, with a password of user1234, will be used for SSL VPN user authentication, while adminuser, with a password of admin123, will be used to manage the security appliance.

Figure 5-6   *Local Database*

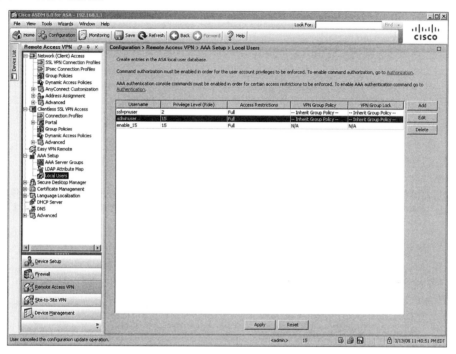

Many enterprises either use a RADIUS server or Kerberos to leverage their existing active directory infrastructure for user authentication. Before configuring an authentication server on Cisco ASA, you must specify authentication, authorization, and accounting (AAA) server groups by choosing **Configuration > Remote Access VPN > AAA Setup > AAA Server Groups > Add**. Specify a server group name that can be referenced by the other AAA processes. Select an authentication protocol for this server group name. For example, if you plan to use a RADIUS server for authentication, select **RADIUS** from the drop-down menu. This option ensures that the security appliance requests the appropriate information from the end users and forwards it to the RADIUS server for authentication and verification.

After enabling RADIUS processing, the next step is to define a list of the RADIUS servers. The Cisco security appliance checks their availability on a round-robin basis. If the first server is not reachable, it tries the second server, and so on. If a server is available, the security appliance keeps using that server until it fails to receive a response. In this case, it checks the availability of the next server. It is highly recommended that you set up more than one RADIUS server, in case the first server is not reachable. A RADIUS server entry can be defined by navigating to **Configuration > Remote Access VPN > AAA Setup > AAA Server Groups** and clicking **Add** under Servers in the Selected Group. You can specify the IP address of the RADIUS server as well as the interface closest to the server. The security appliance authenticates itself to the RADIUS server by using a shared secret key. The security appliance, for security reasons, never sends this shared secret key over the network.

NOTE   User passwords are sent as encrypted messages from the Cisco ASA to the RADIUS server. This protects this critical information from an intruder. The security appliance hashes the password using the shared secret that is defined on the security appliance and the RADIUS server.

Figure 5-7 shows the Cisco ASA configured with two AAA servers under the server group called radius. These servers are located toward the inside interface at 192.168.1.20 and 192.168.1.21. The shared key is cisco123 for both servers.

Figure 5-7   *Defining a RADIUS Server for Authentication*

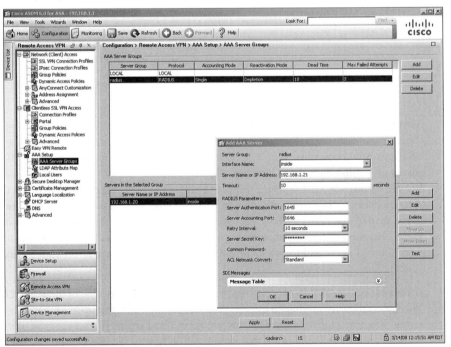

NOTE   You can optionally modify the authentication and accounting port numbers if your RADIUS server does not use the default ports. The security appliance uses UDP ports 1645 and 1646 as defaults for authentication and accounting, respectively. Most of the RADIUS servers use ports 1812 and 1813 as authentication and accounting ports, respectively.

After defining the authentication servers, you have to bind them to the SSL VPN process under a tunnel group. Figure 5-8 illustrates that the newly created radius AAA server group is mapped to the SecureMeClientlessTunnel tunnel group.

Figure 5-8   *Mapping a RADIUS Server to a Tunnel Group*

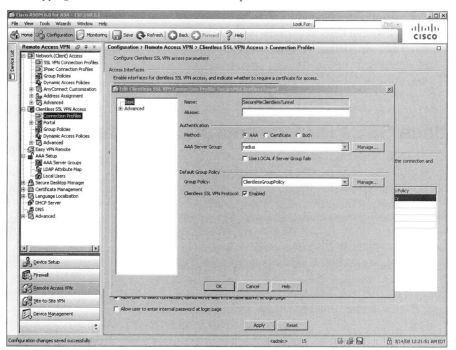

TIP   For large VPN deployments (both IPsec and SSL VPNs), you can even control user access and policy mapping from an external authentication server. You should pass the user group-policy name as a RADIUS or LDAP attribute to the security appliance. By doing so, you guarantee that a user will always get the same policy, regardless of the tunnel group name he connects to. If you are using RADIUS as the authentication and authorization server, you can specify the user group-policy name as attribute 25 (class attribute). Append the keyword OU= as the value of the class attribute. For example, if you define a user group-policy called engineering group, you can enable attribute 25 and specify OU=engineering as its value.

For ease of understanding, this chapter is divided into two configuration sections: clientless SSL VPNs and Cisco AnyConnect VPN Client. The clientless configuration of SSL VPN describes the mandatory steps for enabling SSL VPNs and setting up the user interface for clientless SSL VPN users. The section on AnyConnect VPN Client configuration guides you through the setup of features for full network access.

Clientless SSL VPN Configuration Guide

The SSL VPN functionality on Cisco ASA is the most robust in the industry. The following sections focus on the clientless users who want to access internal corporate resources but do not have an SSL VPN client loaded on their workstations. These users typically access protected resources from shared workstations or even from the hotels or Internet cafés. The clientless configuration on Cisco ASA can be broken down into the following subsections.

- Enable SSL VPN on an interface
- Configure SSL VPN Portal Customization
- Configure Bookmarks
- Configure Web-Type ACLs
- Configure Application Access
- Configure Client-Server Plug-ins

Figure 5-9 is used throughout these sections to demonstrate how to set up Cisco ASA for clientless users. As shown in this figure, the security appliance is set up to accept the SSL VPN connections from the hosts on the Internet. On the private network of the security appliance, we have a number of servers.

Figure 5-9   *SSL VPN Network Topology*

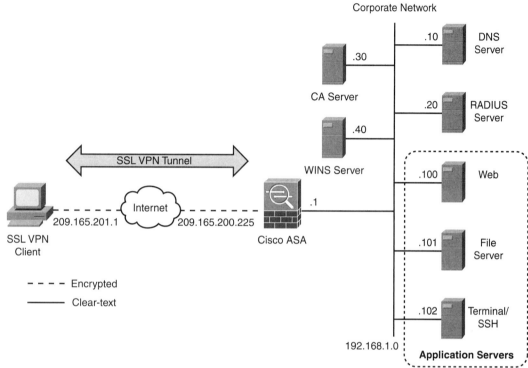

Table 5-5 provides a description of those servers used in this setup.

Table 5-5   *Description and Location of Servers*

Server	Location	Purpose
CA server	192.168.1.30	To issue CA and ID certificates
WINS server	192.168.1.40	To resolve NetBIOS names with IP addresses
DNS server	192.168.1.10	To resolve host names with IP addresses
RADIUS server	192.168.1.20	To authenticate users
Web server	192.168.1.100	To host internal websites
File server	192.168.1.101	To host and present files and folders to SSL VPN users
Terminal server/ SSH server	192.168.1.102	To provide terminal and SSH services to SSL VPN users

NOTE   Cisco has certified HP iPaq H4150 Pocket PC 2003 running Windows CE 4.20.0 build
14053 with Pocket Internet Explorer. The ROM version is 1.10.03ENG with a 07/16/2004
ROM date. You do not need to configure anything special on the security appliance.

Enabling Clientless SSL VPN on an Interface

The first step in setting up a clientless SSL VPN on the security appliances is to enable SSL
VPN on the interface that will terminate the user session. If SSL VPN is not enabled on the
interface, Cisco ASA will not accept any connections, even if SSL VPN is globally enabled.

To enable SSL VPN on an interface through ASDM, choose **Configuration > Remote
Access VPN > Clientless SSL VPN Access > Connection Profiles** and select the **Allow
Access** check box next to the interface on which you want to enable the SSL VPN. As
shown in Figure 5-10, SSL VPN is enabled on the outside interface using the default port
443. Click **Apply** to send the appropriate command from ASDM to the security appliance.

Figure 5-10   *Enable a Clientless SSL VPN on an Interface*

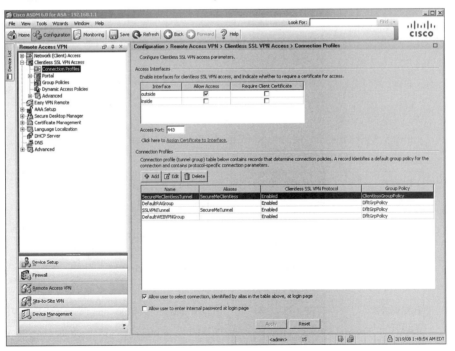

After SSL VPN is enabled on an interface, the security appliance is ready to accept the connections. However, you still need to go through other configuration steps to successfully accept user connections and to allow traffic to pass through.

Configuring SSL VPN Portal Customization

Figure 5-11 shows the default SSL VPN page when a connection is initiated from a web browser. The title of the page is SSL VPN Service and the Cisco Systems logo is displayed in the upper-left corner of the web page. The initial page prompts the user for user authentication credentials.

Figure 5-11 *Default SSL VPN Login Page*

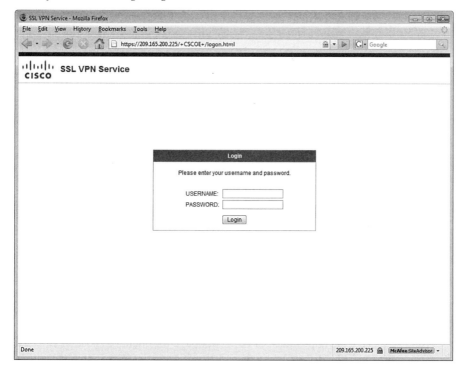

You can customize the initial SSL VPN login page based on security policies of your organization. Cisco ASA also allows you to customize the user web portal by offering a number of options to choose from. The security appliance even allows you to upload images and unique XML data to fully customize the login page. In version 8.0 and higher software, you can even customize the initial login page based on the user group membership.

Using portal customization, you can design and present the SSL VPN page in any way you like. ASA allows you to design the default login page as well as the login page for a group of users. For example, if you want contractors to access a few applications, you can customize a web portal to include those applications and then map that portal to the group policy that contractors use. This way, when a user, who belongs to the contractor group-policy, tries to log in, he will only see applications that are listed in his portal.

NOTE	Portal customization can use dynamic content through the use of a JavaScript include file, <script src="/+CSCOE+/custom.js"></script>. This file is useful if you want to create your own web page using the functions defined for an SSL VPN session.
	If you want to use customization through XML, Cisco ASA contains a customization template. You should export the template to a workstation and modify its content. You can import the customized content into the security appliance as a new customized object.

The user portal customization can be configured by choosing **Configuration > Remote Access VPN > Clientless SSL VPN Access > Portal > Customization**. You can either modify the DfltCustomization object or define a new customized portal. If you want to create a new portal, click **Add** and specify the new object name. After the new object is created, you can select it and click **Edit** to modify its properties. Throughout this book, we use a new object called SecureMePortal. Cisco ASA launches a new browser window to change its properties. You can customize the following three portal pages when a clientless user connects to a Cisco ASA:

- Logon page
- Portal page
- Logout page

Logon Page

You can change the appearance of the logon page for clientless SSL VPN users. You can either customize the default logon page that affects all users or customize a tunnel-specific page that affects users who connect to that tunnel group. For example, if you want contractors to access a different logon page, you can have them access a group-specific logon page. When they access the web page, they will be presented with the logon page specifically designed for them.

At high-level architecture, the login portal customization is broken into four elements. Figure 5-12 illustrates these four elements.

Figure 5-12   *SSL VPN Logon Page Customization*

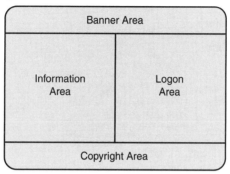

These elements are discussed in the subsequent sections.

Banner Area

The banner area acts as a page title, and thus customers can define their own text for a web page. For example, if you want to present SecureMe SSL VPN Service as the title of the logon page, you can define it under the title panel of the customization editor. This element of a web page can be hidden or displayed by an SSL VPN administrator. You can customize the banner based on your needs. For example, you can change the text and size of the banner text, add or change your company's logo, and position the text and logo on the page. In Figure 5-13, the administrator defines SecureMe SSL VPN Service as the title of the page. An image called securemeinc-sml.png has been set as the logo URL for SecureMe, while the font color is set to #000000 (black) and the background color is set to #ffffff (white). The administrator has enabled a gradient that is used to gradually change the background color.

Figure 5-13 *Logon Page Banner Customization*

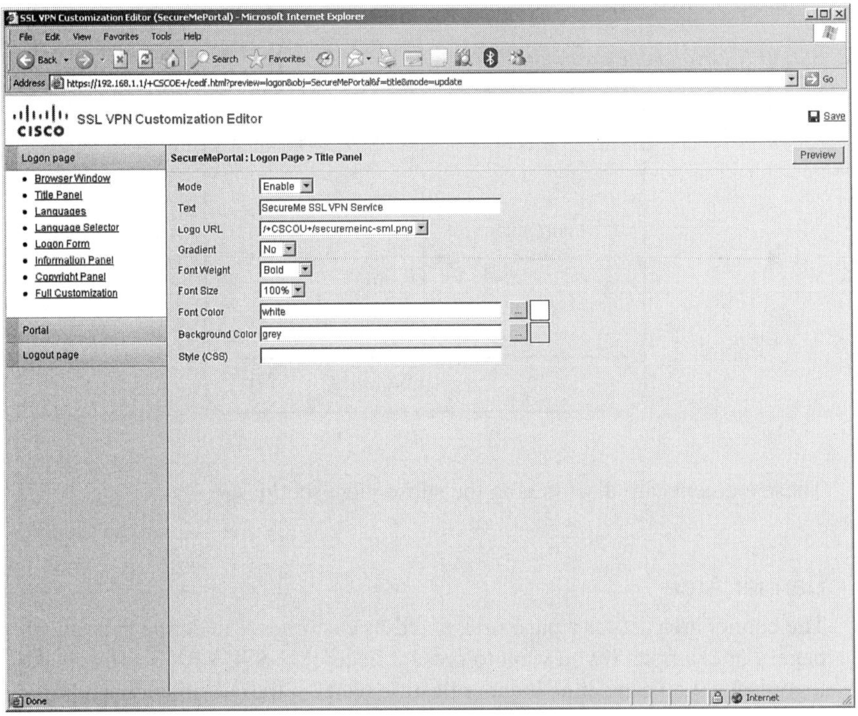

NOTE	The graphical user interface allows you to specify common-sense colors, such as black or white. You do not have to use the font colors in hexadecimal numbers.
	If you want to upload customized images or files, choose **Configuration > Remote Access VPN > Clientless SSL VPN Access > Portal > Web Contents** and upload the files. An example is shown in the section "Full Customization of a Logon Page," later in this chapter.

You can click the **Preview** button to preview the portal that you have designed. This is a great way to test your configuration without actually pushing the configuration or having users establish the clientless SSL VPN tunnel. Click **Save** to save these settings.

NOTE	You cannot preview a portal page if you choose Full Customization or upload an XML file.

Logon Area

The logon area, also known as the logon form, prompts the user to input his or her user credentials. You can customize the title, the logon message, the username and password prompts, and the color and font of the text. You can even choose whether you want users to select a group that they want to use for their authentication. In Figure 5-14, the Cisco ASA administrator has configured the logon form to meet SecureMe's policies. The title of the logon box is changed to SecureMe Logon Box and the message within the logon box is Please Enter Your User Credentials. The text in the username and password prompts is Username: and Password:, respectively. The show internal password prompt is disabled while the text in the group selector prompt is Group:. The text within the login button is Click Here to Log In. The text color of the logon box title is #ffffff (white), while the background color in the title is #666666 (gray). The font color of the text inside the logon box is #000000 (black), while the background color of the logon form is #ffffff (white).

Figure 5-14 *Logon Form Customization*

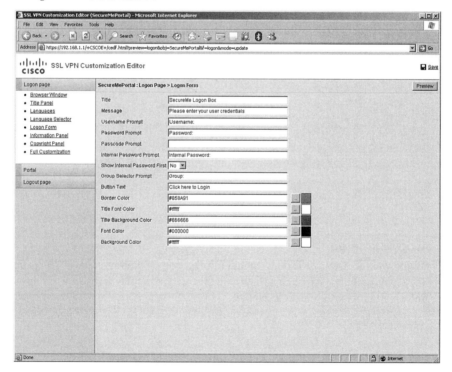

Information Area

The information area shows any text and image that you want to display on the logon page. You can specify whether you want to display the information area to the left or the right side of the logon form. The Cisco ASA administrator can choose to enable or disable this element under the Information Panel option. In Figure 5-15, the information panel is disabled by the administrator.

Figure 5-15 *Logon Page Information Area Customization*

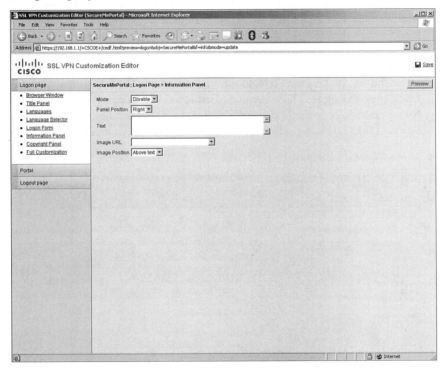

Copyright Area

If you want to display the copyrighted information on the logon page, you can specify it in the Copyright area. Most customers use this area to display a logon warning or important information regarding user logons.

Portal Page

In addition to changing the appearance of the logon page, administrators can change how a portal is displayed to the user after he or she is authenticated. This includes designing their home pages as well as their application access windows when they launch an application.

At high-level architecture, the web portal is broken into four elements: the title panel, toolbar, navigation pane, and content area. Figure 5-16 illustrates these four elements.

Figure 5-16 *SSL VPN User Web Portal Customization*

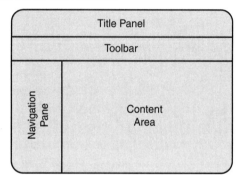

These elements are discussed next.

Title Panel

The title panel designs the title frame on the user portal after the user is logged in. You can specify the title text and logo and customize the font size and colors of the frame. For example, you can present SecureMe SSL VPN Service as the title and load SecureMe's company logo as the title, as shown in Figure 5-17. The font color is #800000 (maroon), and the background color is #ffffff (white). The font size is set to 150 percent of the regular font size. This title panel can be hidden or displayed by an SSL VPN administrator.

Figure 5-17   *SSL VPN Web Portal Title Panel Customization*

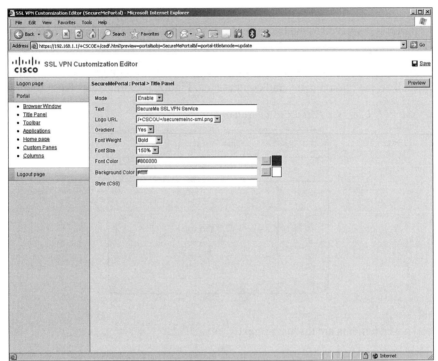

Toolbar

The toolbar is used to define user prompts such as the URL box and logout. You can also define browser button text here. An administrator can hide the toolbar from the user portal for additional security.

Navigation Pane

The navigation pane is a list of all applications that you want SSL VPN users to access. These applications are defined vertically in the left pane. An administrator can choose to enable or hide an application, or move an application up or down the list. As illustrated in Figure 5-18, the administrator has enabled the following applications:

- Home
- Web applications
- Browse networks
- Application access

- AnyConnect
- Telnet/SSH servers

You can move these applications up or down based on your preferences.

Figure 5-18 *SSL VPN Web Portal Application Customization*

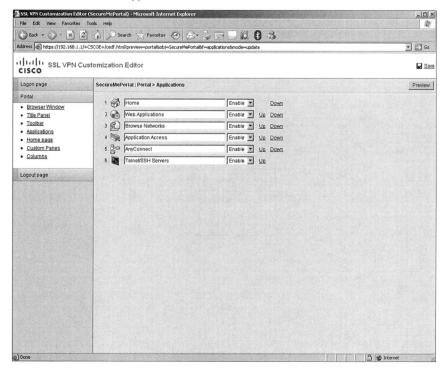

Content Area

The content area shows content for each application. An administrator can choose to split the content area into multiple frames of text, HTML, RSS feeds, or image panes. You can even define an initial web-page URL in case you want SSL VPN users to see important notifications when their connection is established.

Logout Page

Cisco ASA even allows you to customize the logout page. You can define the logout message and provide an option for whether users can be allowed to log back in. You can pick the color of the title font and title background, and the font and background colors of the logout page. In Figure 5-19, the administrator has added the logout message Please

Clear Your Browser's Cache, Delete Any Downloaded Files, and Close All Open Browsers Before You Sign Out. The login button is not allowed, and thus the user needs to specify the SSL VPN server IP address in the browser to start a new session. The text color of the logout box title is #ffffff (white), while the background color of the title is #666666 (gray). The font color of the text inside the logout box is #000000 (black), while the background color of the logout form is #ffffff (white).

Figure 5-19 *SSL VPN Logout Page Customization*

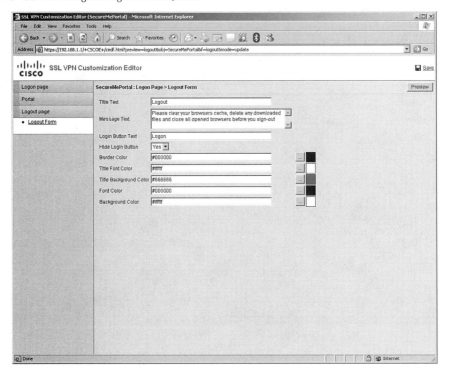

Portal Customization and User Group

When you are done customizing the login, portal, and logout pages, you need to understand how these customized objects can be applied to the appropriate user connection profile. We discuss two scenarios in the following sections.

Customized Login Page and User Connection Profile

After customizing the login page, the next logical step is to display it to the users who are logging in. You have two ways to display the login page to the user:

- **DefaultWEBVPNGroup connection profile:** If you want your customized login page to be displayed to all users who access the security appliance using its FQDN (fully qualified domain name) or the IP address, apply the customized object under the DefaultWEBVPNGroup connection profile by choosing **Configuration > Remote Access VPN > Clientless SSL VPN Access > Connection Profiles**. Select DefaultWEBVPNGroup and click **Edit** to modify its contents. Cisco ASDM will launch a new window. Choose **Advanced > Clientless SSL VPN** and select **SecureMePortal** under Portal Page Customization, as shown in Figure 5-20. Click **OK** when finished. The clientless SSL VPN users can access the customized login portal by navigating to https://*<FQDN>* or https://*<IPAddressOfASA>*.

Figure 5-20 *Mapping of a Customized Portal to a Default Tunnel Group*

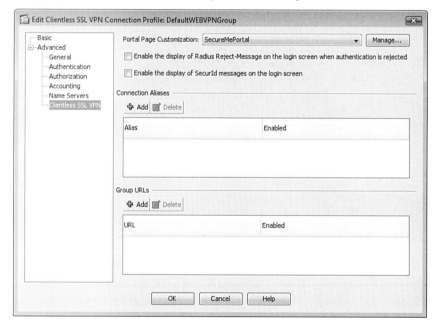

- **User connection profile:** You can also present the customized login page to a user by applying the object under a user connection profile. However, the customized login page will only be displayed if the user accesses a specific login URL that is set up by the administrator. To apply under a user connection profile, choose **Configuration > Remote Access VPN > Clientless SSL VPN Access > Connection Profiles**. Select a user connection profile or create a new one. Throughout this book, we use a use connection profile called SecureMeClientlessTunnel for the clientless SSL VPN session. Select the profile and click **Edit** to modify its settings. Cisco ASDM launches a new window. Under Aliases, specify a name that will be used by the users to connect to the security appliance. In Figure 5-21, SecureMeClientless is configured as the alias. After setting up the alias, the next step is to map the preconfigured customized object to this connection profile. Choose **Advanced > Clientless SSL VPN** and select **SecureMePortal** under Portal Page Customization. Click **OK** when finished. The clientless SSL VPN users can access the customized login portal by navigating to https://*<FQDN>* or https://*<IPAddressOfASA>*/SecureMeClientless.

Figure 5-21 *Connection Profile Alias*

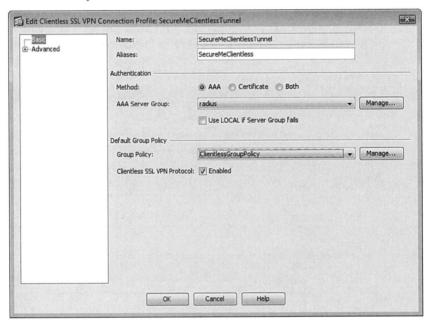

Customized Portal Page and User Connection Profile

When a user first connects to the security appliance, the logon portal is presented based on how the SSL VPN connection is established. For example, if a user selects a logon group, after a successful user authentication, a user portal is shown based on what customization object is mapped to that user connection profile. You have the following three ways to display the customized portal page to a user:

- **Default Login without Group Selection:** When a user accesses the login page and authenticates himself without selecting a group to log in to, he is presented with the user portal page that is mapped to the DefaultWEBVPNGroup.

- **Default Login with Group Selection:** When a user accesses the login page and authenticates himself after selecting a login group, he is presented with the user portal page that is mapped to that specific user connection profile.

- **User Connection Profile Login:** When a user logs in to the system using the group-specific URL, he is presented with the user portal page that is mapped to that specific user connection profile. For example, if a user accesses the security appliance by entering **https://209.165.200.225/SecureMeClientless**, a web portal that is defined in SecureMePortal will be applied for the user sessions.

Full Customization

As mentioned earlier, you can use the full customization feature available in Cisco ASA running version 8.x. You can customize the logon, portal, and logout pages. Customers prefer the full customization functionality so that their SSL VPN portal has the same look and feel as their internal web portal. For ease of understanding, we will show steps how to customize the logon and web portals.

Full Customization of a Logon Page

The default logon page is shown in Figure 5-11. If instead you would rather have a customized logon page as illustrated in Figure 5-22, follow these steps.

Figure 5-22 *Customized Logon Page*

Step 1 Begin with your own logon page. If you already have an HTML code, you can leverage it to define the logon customization. In the following example, a simple code is developed to design the logon page. You can see that we have left space after "Please log in using your user credentials." This is where we will insert the code for the user logon box.

```
<head>
<title>SecureMe SSL VPN Portal</title>
</head>
<body lang=EN-US style='tab-interval:.5in'><div class=Section1>
<span style='mso-fareast-font-family:"Times New Roman"; mso-no-
  proof:yes'><img width=85 height=93 id="_x0000_i1025" src="Doc1_files/
  image003.jpg"></span><b style='mso-bidi-font-weight:normal'><span
  style='font-size:30.0pt;mso-fareast-font-family:"Times New
  Roman"'>Welcome to SecureMe SSL VPN Logon Page<u1:p></u1:p></span></
  b><span style='mso-fareast-font-family:"Times New Roman"'><o:p></
  o:p></span></p>
<br><br><br><br>
<b><span style='font-size:16.0pt'>Please Login using your user
  credentials</b></p>
```

```
<br><br><br>
<!--Insert Logon Dialogue Box code here>
<br><br><br>
<b><style='mso-bidi-font-weight:normal'><i style='mso-bidi-font-
    style:normal'><u>Unauthorized users will be prosecuted according to
    the Federal and State Laws</u></i></b></p>
</div>
</body>
</html>
```

Step 2 Replace any reference to the images with the keyword /+CSCOU+/.
When you upload an image to the security appliance, it is stored in the /
+CSCOU+/ directory, which resides on the local flash. Thus, when you
instruct the security appliance to load an image, it checks the content in
that directory. The snippet of the modified code is highlighted in gray.

```
<span style='mso-fareast-font-family:"Times New Roman"; mso-no-
    proof:yes'><img width=85 height=93 id="_x0000_i1025" src="/+CSCOU+/
    image003.jpg"></span><b style='mso-bidi-font-weight:normal'><span
    style='font-size:30.0pt;mso-fareast-font-family:"Times New
    Roman"'>Welcome to SecureMe SSL VPN Logon Page<u1:p></u1:p></span></
    b><span style='mso-fareast-font-family:"Times New Roman"'><o:p></
    o:p></span></p>
```

Step 3 Before saving the HTML code, you need to insert the logon box. In the
following example, we inserted the logon dialog box by replacing <!--
Insert Logon Dialog Box code here>.

```
<br><br><br>
<body onload="cisco_ShowLoginForm('lform');cisco_ShowLanguageSelector
    ('selector')" bgcolor="white">
<table><tr><td colspan=3 height=20 align=left>
<div id="selector" style="width"300px"></div></td></tr>
<tr><td align=middle valign=middle> <div id=lform> Loading credentials
    </div></td></tr></table>
<br><br><br>
```

Step 4 Save the HTML code as an include file so that the security appliance can
add the appropriate JavaScript to support the login box. In this example,
we named this file logonscript.inc.

Step 5 Import the appropriate images and logon script into the security
appliance. Choose **Configuration > Remote Access VPN > Clientless
SSL VPN Access > Portal > Web Contents** and upload the
logonscript.inc and image003.jpg files from the local workstation to the
flash of the security appliance. Make sure that you select No for the
Destination Require Authentication to Access This Content option.

Step 6   After uploading the web content, choose **Logon Page** > **Full Customization** and change the mode to Enable. Select /+CSCOU+/ logonscript.inc under Custom Page URL.

Step 7   Associate the customized object to a tunnel group that the user can connect to.

NOTE   You can upload images and logos in the JPEG, GIF, and PNG formats.

Full Customization of a User Portal Page

If you want to customize the user web portal, you can use the following steps to provide full customization. These steps are similar to the steps described for the logon page customization. The default user web portal is shown in Figure 5-23.

Figure 5-23 *Default User Web Portal Page*

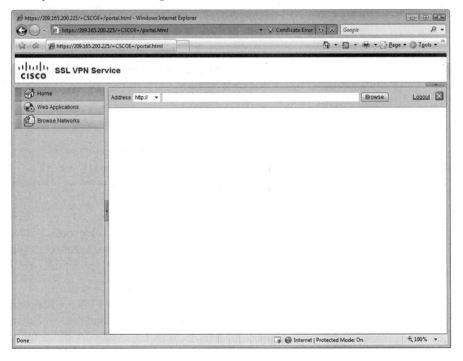

Step 1   Choose **Configuration > Remote Access VPN > Clientless SSL VPN Access > Portal > Customization** and edit the object you care to change under **Portal > Custom Panes**.

Step 2   Under type HTML, make sure that the mode is set to Enable and then
specify a title of the web link. In Figure 5-24, a title of Cisco Systems
Web Page is added. Under URL, add the URL that you want users to see.
In the previous example, the link to the Cisco System web page, http://
www.cisco.com, is shown.

Figure 5-24 *User Web Portal Full Customization*

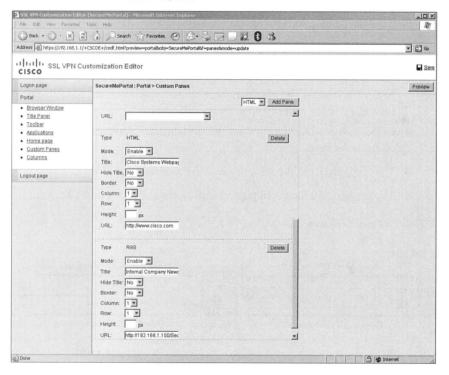

Step 3   Under type RSS, make sure that the mode is set to Enable and then
specify a title of the RSS feed link. In Figure 5-24, a title of Internal
Company News is added. Under URL, specify the link to the RSS feed.
In the previous example, an RSS feed file resides at http://192.168.1.100/
SecureMe.xml. Click **Save** to save these changes.

Step 4   Associate the customized object to a tunnel group that the user can
connect to. If you already have the object mapped to a tunnel group, you
do not need to link it again.

Configuring Bookmarks

Using a clientless SSL VPN, remote users can browse their internal websites, file server shares, and Outlook Web Access (OWA) servers. Cisco ASA achieves this functionality by terminating the SSL tunnels on its outside interface and then rewriting the content before sending it to the internal server. For example, if a user tries to access an internal website, the user's HTTPS connection is terminated to the outside interface. The ASA then forwards the HTTP or HTTPS request to the internal web server. The response from the web server is then encapsulated into HTTPS and forwarded to the client. This mode is illustrated in Figure 5-25. The following sequence of events takes place when UserA tries to connect to a web server located at 192.168.1.100:

1 UserA initiates an HTTP request to the web server, located on the other side of the SSL VPN tunnel. The user request is encapsulated into the SSL tunnel and is then forwarded to the security appliance.

2 Cisco ASA deencapsulates the traffic and initiates a connection to the server on behalf of the web client.

3 The response from the server is sent to the security appliance.

4 The security appliance, in turn, encapsulates and sends it to UserA.

Figure 5-25 *HTTP Requests Through ASA*

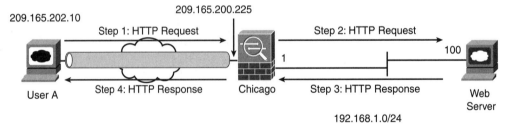

NOTE If you frequently use Java and ActiveX coding in a web page, Cisco ASA might not be able to rewrite web pages that embed that content. You can enable the smart tunnel option within bookmarks to tunnel HTTP traffic directly to the web server.

The security appliance does not allow SSL VPN communication with the websites that present expired certificates during session negotiations.

You can define bookmarks for the internal servers. A user, after logging in, can see those bookmarks and browse the content of the servers by clicking them. Bookmarks are links to commonly used websites that your clientless SSL VPN users connect to. Furthermore, by defining all the websites or servers that you want to allow access to, you can deny users access to any other site or server. This is one way to restrict their access to the internal network after establishing the VPN tunnel.

You can configure bookmarks by choosing **Configuration > Remote Access VPN > Clientless SSL VPN Access > Portal > Bookmarks > Add**. You can specify a bookmark list name that is then mapped to a user or group policy. After specifying a list name, you can click **Add** to specify a URL heading that appears on the main portal page after a successful user authentication. Under Bookmarks, you can add many different types of application servers, including the following:

- Websites (HTTP and HTTPS)
- File servers (CIFS)
- FTP
- SSH/Telnet
- Remote Desktop Protocol (RDP)
- Virtual Network Computing (VNC)

NOTE   You will not see options for VNC, RDP, SSH, and Telnet if you do not import their plug-ins first. Consult the section "Configuring Client-Server Plug-Ins," later in this chapter, for details.

Configuring Websites

After adding a bookmark list, you can add a bookmark entry for the internal web servers that you want to give access to the clientless users. In Figure 5-26, a bookmark list name of InternalServers has been added. Because it is a new list, the administrator has added a bookmark title of InternalWebServer with a URL value of http://intranet.securemeinc.com. Under advanced options, a subtitle of "This is the internal web portal for SecureMe Inc. employees" is added with a thumbnail of the securemeinc-sml.png icon. The administrator has enabled the smart tunnel option to tunnel HTTP traffic directly to the web server.

Figure 5-26 *Website Bookmark Configuration*

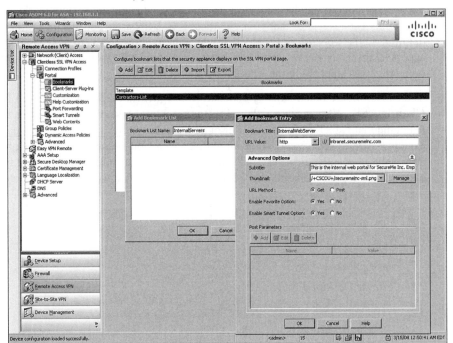

NOTE　If you configure your internal websites using the fully qualified domain name (FQDN), you must configure a Domain Name System (DNS) server on the security appliance to resolve the host names. The DNS server can be configured by choosing **Configuration > Device Management > DNS > DNS Client** and clicking **Add** to add a DNS server under DNS Server Group.

CAUTION　The clientless SSL VPN does not ensure that the communication from the client is secure to all the websites it is accessing. For example, if an external website is accessed by a user, and the traffic is proxied by the security appliance, the connection from the security appliance to the external web server will not be encrypted.

Additionally, web-type ACLs, discussed later in this chapter, do not block a user from accessing the resources outside the SSL VPN tunnel. These ACLs ensure that SSL VPN traffic denied by the ACLs will not pass through the security appliance.

Configuring File Servers

In addition to the web servers, you can also define a bookmark list of the file servers that the clientless users can access. Cisco ASA supports network file sharing using the Common Internet File System (CIFS), a file system that uses the original IBM and Microsoft networking protocols. Through CIFS, users can access their file shares located on the file servers. Users can download, upload, delete, or rename the files under the shared directories, but only if the file system permissions allow them to perform those actions. They can even create subdirectories, assuming that they are allowed to do so.

The configuration of CIFS requires the use of a NetBIOS Name Server (NBNS), also known as Windows Internet Naming Server (WINS). When a clientless user queries to browse the network, the security appliance contacts the WINS and acquires the list of available domains, workgroups, and workstations. Use the following steps to successfully configure Windows file server for clientless SSL VPN users:

Step 1 In ASDM, specify a NetBIOS server by choosing **Configuration > Remote Access VPN > Clientless SSL VPN Access > Connection Profile > SecureMeClientlessTunnel > Edit > Advanced > Name Servers**. Click **Add** under NetBIOS Servers and specify the IP address of the NBNS server for CIFS name resolution. The Master Browser option specifies that the configured NBNS server acts as the master browser in addition to being a WINS server. The Timeout value instructs an appliance to wait for the configured number of seconds (the default is 2 seconds) before sending another query to the next server. The Retry option is used to specify the number of times the security appliance has to go through the list of the configured NBNS servers. The default number of retries is 2, and it can range from 0 to 10. In Figure 5-27, a NetBIOS server located at 192.168.1.40 is added. The Master Browser option is also enabled.

Figure 5-27 *WINS Server Definition*

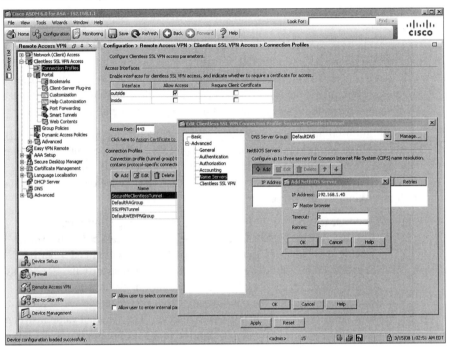

Step 2 Define a bookmark for the file server by choosing **Configuration >
Remote Access VPN > Clientless SSL VPN Access > Portal >
Bookmarks > Edit > InternalServers > Add**. Specify a bookmark title
of InternalFileServer, select **cifs** as the URL value, and add the IP address
of the file server. In Figure 5-28, a CIFS file server that is located at
192.168.1.101 is added. The administrator has added the following
description for this file server: "This is the internal FileServer for
SecureMe Inc. Employees."

Figure 5-28 *File Server Definition*

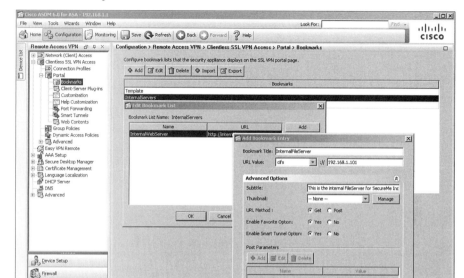

Applying a Bookmark List to a Group Policy

You can apply the bookmark list to a user or group policy. As shown in Figure 5-29, choose **Configuration > Remote Access VPN > Clientless SSL VPN Access > Group Policies > ClientlessGroupPolicy > Edit > Portal** and select **InternalServers** under Bookmark List.

Figure 5-29 *Bookmark to Policy Group Mapping*

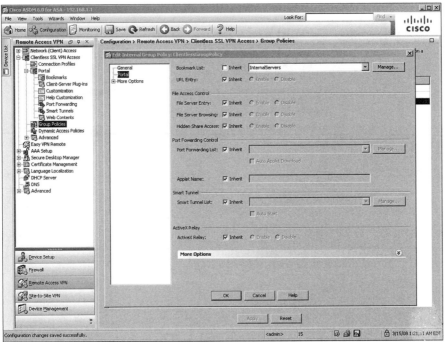

Single Sign-On

Optionally, you can add a single sign-on (SSO) server to ensure that clientless users do not get prompted again to enter their user credentials if they try to access windows-based shares. In SSO, the security appliance acts as a proxy between the clientless SSL VPN user and the authentication server. The security appliance uses users' cached credentials (an authentication cookie) when the user tries to access secure websites or shares within the private network. If you use NT LAN Manager (NTLM) authentication in your environment, you can define SSO attributes under user or group policies. As shown in Figure 5-30, SSO is enabled for all clientless SSL VPN users that send authentication requests to the servers in the 192.168.1.0 subnet using NTLM authentication.

Figure 5-30 *Single Sign-On Server Definition*

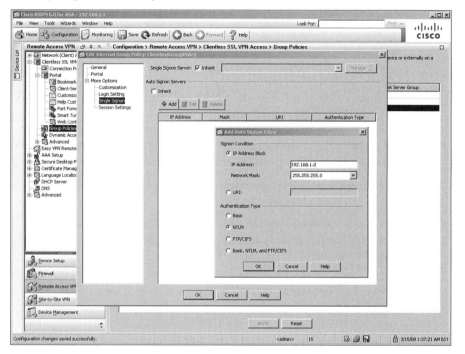

In addition to NTLM, Cisco ASA also supports many other authentication methods, including basic (HTTP), SSO authentication using SiteMinder, SAML browser post profile and the HTTP Form protocol.

Configuring Web-Type ACLs

Cisco ASA enables network administrators to further their clientless SSL VPN security by configuring web-type access control lists (ACL) to manage access to web, Telnet, SSH, citrix, FTP, file, e-mail servers, or all types of traffic. These ACLs affect only the clientless SSL VPN traffic and are processed in sequential order until a match is found. If an ACL is defined but no match exists, the default behavior on the security appliance is to drop the packets. On the other hand, if no web-type ACL is defined, Cisco ASA allows all traffic to pass through it.

Moreover, this robust SSL VPN feature allows these ACLs to be downloaded from a Cisco Secure Access Control Server (CS-ACS) by using vendor-specific attributes (VSA). This allows central control and management of user access into the corporate network by offloading ACL definitions locally on the security appliance.

TIP	Using CS-ACS, a web-type ACL can be configured by specifying the webvpn:inacl# prefix in the downloadable ACLs, where # indicates the sequence number of an access control entry (ACE).

A web-type ACL is configured by choosing **Configuration > Remote Access VPN > Clientless SSL VPN Access > Advanced > Web ACLs**. Click **Add** and select **Add ACL** to define a new web-type ACL. Specify a web ACL name and click **OK**. Select the newly created ACL name, click **Add** again, and select **Add ACE.** You have two options to add a web-type ACL:

- **Filter on URL:** A URL-based web ACL is used to filter out SSL VPN packets if they contain a URL such as http://.

- **Filter on address and service:** An address- and service-based web ACL is used to filter out SSL VPN packets if they use TCP encapsulation based on the IP address and a Layer 4 port number.

If you prefer to add a URL-based entry to filter out SSL VPN traffic, select **Filter on URL** and select the protocol you want to filter. The security appliance allows you to filter based on cifs, citrix, citrixs, ftp, http, https, imap4, nfs, pop3, smart tunnel, smtp, ssh, and telnet for all types of URLs. Next, specify the URL or a wildcard to filter traffic. For example, if you want all clientless users to deny web traffic to internal.securemeinc.com, select **Deny** as the Action, choose **http** as the filter protocol, and select **internal.securemeinc.com** as the URL entry. This is illustrated in Figure 5-31. Click **OK** when finished.

If you want to include all URLs that are not explicitly matched in the ACL, you can include an asterisk (*) as a wildcard. For example, to block POP3 e-mail access and allow all other protocols, perform the following steps:

- Add an ACE and deny POP3 for the protocol and add * as a wildcard URL entry.
- Add another ACE and allow any for the protocol type.

If you would rather permit or block TCP traffic that is destined to particular addresses on specific ports, choose the Filter on Address and Service option. For example, to block all clientless traffic destined to 192.168.0.0/16 on port 23, select **Deny** as the Action, specify **192.168.0.0/16** under Address, and choose **23** under Service. Click **OK** when finished.

Figure 5-31 *Defining Web-Type ACLs*

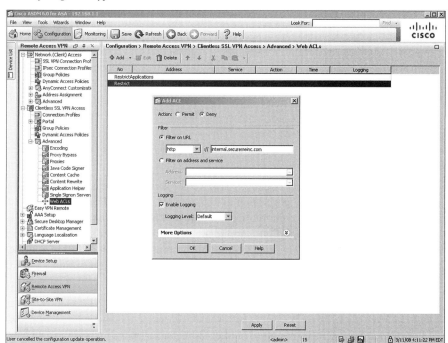

TIP   When you define an ACE that has deny as its first entry, make sure that you configure
            another entry to permit all other clientless SSL VPN traffic.

            After a web ACL is configured, link it to a default user group or user policy. Choose
            **Configuration > Remote Access VPN > Clientless SSL VPN Access > Group Policies >
            ClientlessGroupPolicy > Edit > General** and select the WebACL list on the Web VPN
            drop-down menu.

CAUTION   Web ACLs do not block a user from accessing the resources outside the SSL VPN tunnel.
            These ACLs ensure that SSL VPN traffic denied by the ACLs will not pass through the
            security appliance.

Configuring Application Access

Cisco ASA allows clientless SSL VPN users to access applications that reside on the protected network. Application access only supports applications that use TCP ports such as SSH, Outlook, and Remote Desktop, to name a few. In version 8.0 or higher, Cisco ASA allows the following two methods to configure application access:

- Port forwarding
- Smart tunnels

Configuring Port Forwarding

Using port forwarding, the clientless SSL VPN users can access corporate resources over the known and fixed TCP ports such as Telnet, SSH, Terminal Services, SMTP, and so on. The port-forwarding feature requires you to install Sun Microsystems' Java Runtime Environment (JRE) and configure applications on the end user's PC. If users are establishing the SSL VPN tunnel from public computers, such as Internet kiosks or web cafés, they might not be able to use this feature. The installation of Sun's JRE requires administrative rights on the client computer.

NOTE Port forwarding is only supported on the 32-bit-based operating systems such as Windows Vista, XP, and Windows 2000.

To use port forwarding, the authenticated user selects Application Access from the navigation pane and clicks the **Start Applications** button. The port-forwarding Java applet is downloaded and then executed on the user's computer. This applet starts listening on configured ports, and when traffic is destined to those ports, the applet makes an HTTP POST request to the port-forwarding URL such as https://ASA-IP-Address/tcp/remoteserver/remoteport.

NOTE You can customize the Application Access name in the navigation pane. Choose **Configuration > Remote Access VPN > Clientless SSL VPN Access > Group Policies > ClientlessGroupPolicy > Edit > Portal**, deselect the inherit check box under Applet Name, and specify the customized text that you want to display in the navigation pane.

When port forwarding is in use, the HOSTS file on the client computer is modified to resolve the host name using one of the loopback addresses. Cisco ASA uses an available address in the range from 127.0.0.2 to 127.0.0.254. This requires the logged-in user to have admin rights so that the HOSTS file can be modified. In case the HOSTS file cannot be modified, the host listens on 127.0.0.1 and the configured local port. When the session is terminated, the application port mapping is restored to the default.

NOTE   Certain security applications such as Cisco Security Agent (CSA) detect the modifications of the HOST and other files. You might be asked to acknowledge these modifications.

Configuration of port forwarding on a security appliance is a two-step process:

Step 1   Defining port-forwarding lists

Step 2   Mapping port-forwarding lists to a group policy

Step 1: Defining Port-Forwarding Lists

You must define a list of servers and their respective applications that you want clientless SSL VPN users to access. A port-forwarding list is defined by choosing **Configuration > Remote Access VPN > Clientless SSL VPN Access > Portal > Port Forwarding > Add**. Specify a name for the new port-forwarding list. This list name has local significance and it is eventually used to map the port-forwarding attributes to a group policy, discussed in the next step. To define a specific application to be used for port forwarding, click **Add** and specify the following attributes:

- **Server IP address:** The IP address of the server hosting the application.
- **Server port on which service is listening:** The application port number, such as 22 for SSH service.
- **Port on client PC:** You should use a local port between 1024 and 65535 to avoid conflicts with the existing network services.
- **Description:** A description to identify this list.

As shown in Figure 5-32, a port-forwarding list called SSHServer is defined. A server, located at 192.168.1.102 and listening on port 22, is added in this list. The administrator has configured to use a local port of 1100 for this connection and has added a description of Access to Internal Terminal/SSH Server.

Figure 5-32 *Defining Port-Forwarding List*

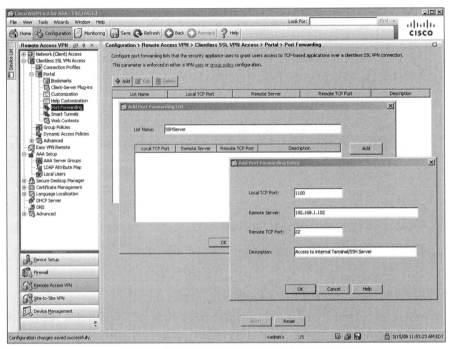

Step 2: Mapping Port Forwarding Lists to a Group Policy

The port-forwarding list, defined in Step 1, is then mapped to a user or group policy. Choose **Configuration > Remote Access VPN > Clientless SSL VPN Access > Group Policies > ClientlessGroupPolicy > Edit > Portal** and select the list on the Port Forwarding List drop-down menu. Additionally, select the **Auto Applet Download** option to automatically install and start the applet as soon as the clientless SSL VPN user establishes a connection to the security appliance. As shown in Figure 5-33, a port-forwarding list of SSHServer is selected.

Figure 5-33 *Mapping of a Port-Forwarding List*

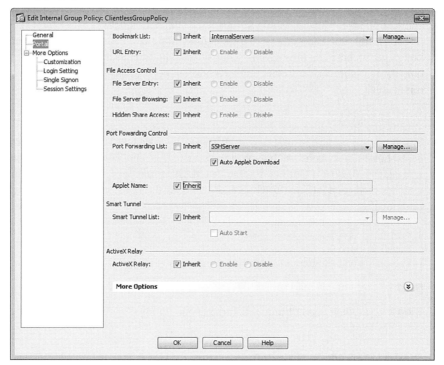

After the applet is loaded on the client, the user launches an SSH client such as Putty.exe to establish a connection to the server by using the loopback IP address of 127.0.0.1 on the local port 1100. This redirects the connection over the SSL VPN tunnel to the server at 192.168.1.102 on port 22.

Configuring Smart Tunnels

As discussed earlier, port forwarding provides access to applications that use static TCP ports. It modifies the HOSTS files on a host so that traffic can be redirected to a forwarder that encapsulates traffic over the SSL VPN tunnel. Additionally, with port forwarding, the Cisco ASA administrator needs to know what addresses and ports the SSL VPN users will connect to, and requires the SSL VPN users to have admin rights to modify the HOSTS file. To overcome some of the challenges related to port forwarding, Cisco ASA presents a new method to tunnel application-specific traffic called smart tunnels. Smart tunnels define which application can be forwarded over the SSL VPN tunnel, whereas port forwarding defines which TCP ports can be forwarded over the tunnel.

Smart tunnels do not require administrators to preconfigure the addresses of the servers running the application or the ports for those applications. In fact, smart tunnels work at the application layer by establishing a Winsock 2 connection between the client and the server. It loads a stub into each process for the application that needs to be tunneled and then intercepts socket calls through the security appliance. Thus, the principal benefit of smart tunnels over port forwarding is that users do not need to have administrative rights to use this feature.

NOTE Smart tunnels require browsers with ActiveX, Java, or JavaScript support. Only 32-bit-based operating systems such as Windows Vista, XP, and Windows 2000 are supported. If you use the Microsoft Outlook Exchange (MAPI) proxy, you must use AnyConnect Client, which is discussed later in this chapter. Port forwarding or smart tunnels do not support this functionality.

Like port forwarding, smart tunnel configuration is also a two-step process:

Step 1 Defining a smart tunnel list

Step 2 Mapping a smart tunnel list to a group policy

Step 1: Defining a Smart Tunnel List

You must define a list of the applications that you want clientless SSL VPN users to access. Smart tunnel list is defined by choosing **Configuration > Remote Access VPN > Clientless SSL VPN Access > Portal > Smart Tunnels > Add**. Specify a name for the new smart tunnel list. This list name has only local significance, and it is eventually used to map the smart tunnel attributes to a group policy, discussed in the next step. To define a specific application to be used for smart tunneling, click **Add** and specify the following attributes:

- **Application ID:** Name or ID of the application to be tunneled. The application ID only has local significance.

- **Process name or full path:** Name of the process to be tunneled. For example, if you want the SSH traffic to be tunneled through Putty, specify putty.exe as the process name.

- **Hash (optional):** The hash is only used to provide additional security so that a user cannot change the filename and gain access to the resources over the tunnel.

As shown in Figure 5-34, a smart tunnel list called SSHServer is defined. The application ID is Putty, while the process name is putty.exe.

Figure 5-34 *Defining a Smart Tunnel List*

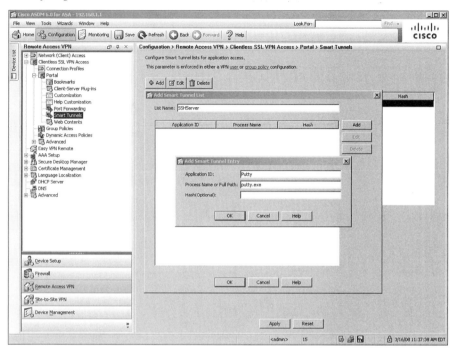

NOTE   The process name should be in the system path. If the application is not in the system path, the smart tunnel will not be able to forward traffic. In such a case, define the application path under Process Name.

Step 2: Mapping a Smart Tunnel List to a Group Policy

The smart tunnel list, defined in Step 1, is then mapped to a user or group policy. Choose **Configuration > Remote Access VPN > Clientless SSL VPN Access > Group Policies > ClientlessGroupPolicy > Edit > Portal** and select the list on the Smart Tunnel List drop-down menu. Additionally, select the **Auto Start** option to automatically install and start the applet as soon as the clientless SSL VPN user connects to the security appliance. As shown in Figure 5-35, a smart tunnel list of SSHServer is selected.

Figure 5-35 *Mapping a Smart Tunnel List*

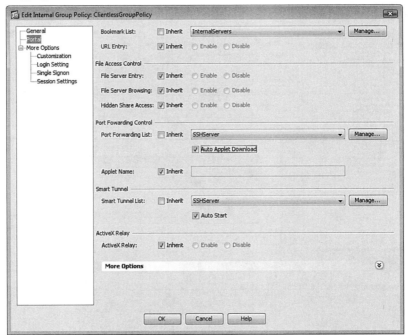

After the applet is loaded on the client, the user launches an SSH client such as Putty.exe to establish a connection to any server that offers SSH service.

NOTE   Smart tunnel and port-forwarding sessions are not failover enabled. Users must start a new SSL VPN session if a failover occurs.

Configuring Client-Server Plug-Ins

For known applications, such as VNC, Remote Desktop, Telnet, and SSH, you can allow the clientless SSL VPN users to connect to the protected network using the supported applications. This way, when a clientless SSL VPN user is authenticated, the user can choose to launch an application plug-in such as VNC and connect to an internal server running the VNC application. Cisco provides the client-server plug-ins for VNCs, Remote Desktop, and SSH/Telnet. These plug-ins can be downloaded from the website and are packaged in the .jar file format. After the plug-ins are uploaded and activated on the security appliance, they can be defined as a URL similar to HTTP:// and cifs:// under a user web portal. For example, for Remote Desktop, a user selects rdp:// and specifies the IP address of the server it connects to. If you want to use a plug-in not provided by Cisco Systems, you can contact third parties to develop the .jar file for their applications.

TIP	Some of the client-server plug-ins can be obtained from the following websites:
	http://javassh.org
	http://properjavardp.sourceforge.net
	http://www.ultravnc.com

You must import the .jar files into the security appliance before you can activate a specific application for this feature. Choose **Configuration > Remote Access VPN > Clientless SSL VPN Access > Portal > Client-Server Plug-ins > Import** and select the plug-in name from the drop-down menu. You can select to import the plug-in from a workstation, from the local flash of the security appliance, or from a remote server using FTP. After you select the file you want to import, click **Import Now**. This should upload the file into the security appliance. In Figure 5-36, the ssh-plugin.jar file is being uploaded from a local workstation to be used for SSH and Telnet sessions.

Figure 5-36 *Importing Client-Server Plug-ins*

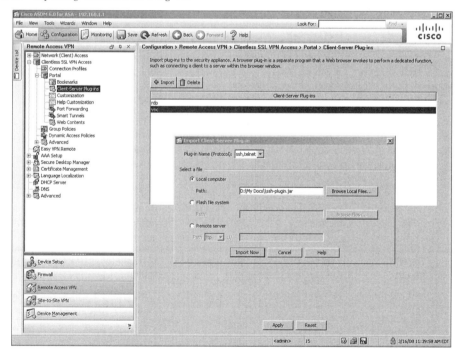

After a plug-in has been uploaded, the authenticated clientless SSL VPN users can select the appropriate protocol from the Address drop-down menu.

AnyConnect VPN Client Configuration Guide

During the early development period of SSL VPNs, network administrators needed a VPN client that had similar benefits of an IPsec remote access VPN client, but required less administrative overhead than installing and maintaining the IPsec VPN client. To accommodate those requirements, the idea of a full tunnel SSL VPN client emerged. In the pre-version 8.0 releases, Cisco provided the SSL VPN Client (SVC). This is a self-downloading, self-installing, self-configuring, and self-uninstalling VPN that offers all benefits that are currently available in the Cisco IPsec client. However, in version 8.0 or later versions of Cisco ASA, Cisco introduced a newer SSL VPN client called Cisco AnyConnect VPN Client. The AnyConnect VPN clients leverage the SSL encryption engine that is already present on the client computer. If you currently use the pre-version 8.0 of code on the security appliances and have SVC clients deployed, test the AnyConnect in a lab environment first before upgrading the code to version 8.0 or higher of the software. Table 5-6 discusses the differences between the SVC and AnyConnect VPN clients. If you decide that the AnyConnect VPN Client will be beneficial in your environment, you can plan to upgrade your security appliance to version 8.*x* of the code by thoroughly testing it in the lab environment first.

Table 5-6 *Contrasting SVC and AnyConnect*

Feature	SVC	AnyConnect
Operating system support	Supported in Windows XP and Windows 2000	Supported in Windows Vista (both 32- and 64-bit), Windows XP, Windows 2000, Mac OS X (version 10.4 or 10.5), and Red Hat Linux (version 9 or higher)
DTLS with SSL connections	Not supported	Fully supported
Package size	Approximately 400 KB	Approximately 1.2 MB
Administrative rights	Required to install and upgrade the package	Required to install the package initially; no administrative privileges are required subsequently
Platform support	Supported on VPN 3000, Cisco IOS routers, and Cisco ASA	Only supported on Cisco ASA and IOS routers
Start before login	Not supported	Supported on Windows 2000 and Windows XP systems
IPv6 support	Not supported	Supported on Windows XP SP2 and Windows Vista
Standalone connection	Requires SVC to be downloaded from Cisco ASA through a web browser	Can be installed as a standalone application or through a web browser

Because versions 8.*x* of code solely support the AnyConnect VPN Client, we only discuss AnyConnect in this chapter.

NOTE   If you use 64-bit (x64) platforms, Cisco provides support only through the Cisco AnyConnect VPN Client. Cisco AnyConnect VPN Client supports both Windows XP as well as Windows Vista x64 platforms. Cisco currently does not have plans to provide support for 64-bit platforms for the Cisco IPsec VPN Client or even the Cisco SSL VPN Client (SVC).

The AnyConnect VPN Client can be installed on a user's computer using one of these two methods:

- **Web-enabled mode:** In this method, the client is downloaded to a user computer through a browser. The user opens a browser and references the IP address or the FQDN of Cisco ASA to establish an SSL VPN tunnel. The user is presented with the standard SSL VPN logon page and is prompted for credentials. If credentials are valid, users are allowed to log in, and if they are using Internet Explorer, they are prompted to download the client using ActiveX. Otherwise, they are prompted to start it manually through the AnyConnect link. If ActiveX fails, the browser tries to download the client through Java. If either ActiveX or Java is successful, the client is downloaded and installed. After it is installed, it tries to connect to the security appliance and establishes an SSL VPN tunnel.

- **Standalone mode:** In this method, the client is downloaded as a standalone application from a file server or directly from the Cisco Systems website. The Microsoft Software Installer (MSI) installed is executed to install the client to the workstation. If the client is not preconfigured, the user needs to specify the IP address or FQDN of the security appliance, the tunnel group to connect to, the username, and the associated password.

NOTE   If you receive the following message, you need to copy MSVCP60.dll and MSVCRT.dll into the system32 directory. Please consult the Microsoft's article KB259403 for more information.

The required system DLL *filename* is not present on the system.

The configuration of AnyConnect VPN Client is a two-step process:

Step 1   Loading the SVC package

Step 2   Defining AnyConnect VPN Client attributes

Loading the SVC Package

Before you define configuration policies for the AnyConnect VPN Client, you have to load the AnyConnect VPN Client package in the local flash of the security appliance. You can verify whether it is installed by choosing **Configuration > Remote Access VPN > Network (Client) Access > Advanced > SSL VPN > Client Setting**. If an AnyConnect VPN Client image is not installed, you can click **Add** to

- Browse through the local flash of the security appliance and select the AnyConnect file you want to use. As shown in Figure 5-37, anyconnect-win-2.1.0148-k9.pkg is being added from the local flash of the security appliance.

- Upload a file from the local computer to the local flash of Cisco ASA. You should check the latest version of the AnyConnect package file at the Cisco website.

Figure 5-37 *Installing the AnyConnect VPN Client Package*

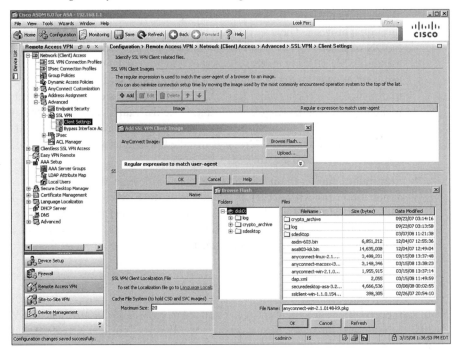

NOTE   You can upload multiple SSL VPN client packages. The order in which the files are listed reflects the order in which they are presented to a user to be downloaded.

If you plan to upload multiple images of the AnyConnect VPN Client (for example, Windows, Linux, or Mac OS X packages), you should increase the maximum size of the cache to hold these images. If you do not have enough cache, the security appliance will take relatively longer to load the image from flash. You can increase the cache file system to 20 MB to be on the safe side if you plan to load multiple images. You can do that by choosing **Configuration > Remote Access VPN > Network (Client) Access > Advanced > SSL VPN > Client Setting** and specifying **20** MB under Cache File System.

CAUTION	Do not rename the package files that you download from the Cisco website. If you change the filename, the hash verification that includes the filename will fail.

Defining AnyConnect VPN Client Attributes

After loading the SVC package in the security appliance's configuration, ASDM allows you to define AnyConnect VPN Client parameters such as the IP address that client should receive. Before an AnyConnect SSL VPN tunnel is functional, you have to configure the following four required attributes:

- Enabling AnyConnect VPN Client functionality
- Defining a pool of addresses
- Configuring traffic filters
- Configuring a tunnel group

Optionally, you can define other attributes to enhance the functionality of the AnyConnect VPN configuration. They include the following:

- Split tunneling
- DNS and WINS assignment
- Keep SSL VPN client installed
- DTLS

All these options are defined in the next sections.

Enabling AnyConnect VPN Client Functionality

After the AnyConnect VPN Client is loaded into flash, the next step is to enable the AnyConnect Client functionality on the interface that is terminating the connection. This is achieved by selecting Enable Cisco AnyConnect VPN Client or Legacy SSL VPN Client Access on the Interfaces Selected in the Table Below in **Configuration > Remote Access VPN > Network (Client) Access > SSL VPN Connection Profiles**. Select the **outside** interface if it is the interface that will terminate the SSL VPN connection. This is shown in

Figure 5-38. Specify the SSL VPN port that the clients should be using to establish the VPN tunnel. By default, it is TCP port 443 and DTLS UDP port 443.

Figure 5-38 *Enabling AnyConnect VPN Client Functionality on an Interface*

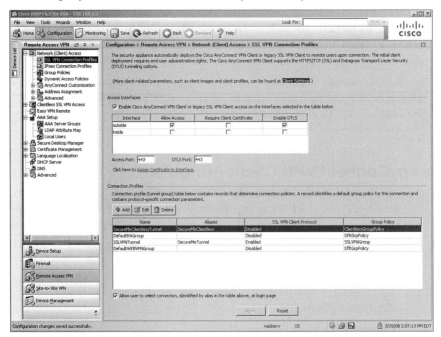

The AnyConnect VPN Client requires administrative privileges on the client computer when it is installed. When AnyConnect Client is launched, no administrative privileges are required subsequently. The AnyConnect Client is pushed through ActiveX as the preferred method. If the ActiveX installation fails, the client is pushed to the workstations through Java. If installation through Java fails, the client is pushed as an executable as the last option.

Defining a Pool of Addresses

During the SSL VPN tunnel negotiations, an IP address is assigned to the VPN adapter of the AnyConnect VPN Client. The client uses this IP address to access resources on the protected side of the tunnel. Cisco ASA supports three different methods to assign an IP address back to the client:

- Local address pool
- DHCP server
- RADIUS server

Many organizations prefer assigning an IP address from the local pool of addresses for flexibility. The IP address is assigned by configuring an address pool and then linking the pool to a policy group. You can either create a new pool of addresses or select a preconfigured address pool. A new pool of addresses can be defined by choosing **Configuration > Remote Access VPN > Network (Client) Access > Address Assignment > Address Pools**. Click **Add** and configure the following attributes, as illustrated in Figure 5-39:

- **Name:** An alphanumeric name to be assigned to this pool. A pool name of SSLVPNPool is assigned.

- **Starting IP address:** The first IP address to be assigned to a client. A starting IP address of 192.168.1.150 is assigned.

- **Ending IP address:** The last IP address to be assigned to a client. A starting IP address of 192.168.1.200 is assigned.

- **Subnet mask:** The associated subnet mask for this pool of addresses. A subnet mask of 255.255.255.0 is configured.

Figure 5-39 *Defining an Address Pool Using ASDM*

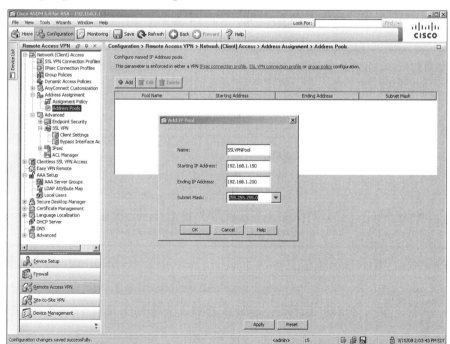

By default, all address assignment methods are allowed. If you want to disable a specific address assignment method, you can do so by navigating to **Configuration** > **Remote Access VPN** > **Network (Client) Access** > **Address Assignment** > **Assignment Policy**.

NOTE	If all three methods are configured for address assignment, Cisco ASA prefers RADIUS over DHCP and address pool. If Cisco ASA is not able to get an address from the RADIUS server, it contacts the DHCP server for address allocation. If that method fails as well, Cisco ASA checks the local address pool as the last resort.

After defining a pool of addresses, the next step is to map the pool to a user group policy. Choose **Configuration** > **Remote Access VPN** > **Network (Client) Access** > **Group Policies** > **Add** and create a new group policy called SSLVPNGroup. Under More Options, select **SSL VPN Client** as the tunneling protocol. Deselect the **Inherit** check box under Address Pools, and then click **Select** to choose a predefined pool of addresses. A new window pops up with all the preconfigured address pools. Select the address pool you want to use and click **Assign** to map the pool to this policy. In Figure 5-40, the SSLVPNPool is assigned to the SSLVPNGroup policy. Click **OK** when finished.

Figure 5-40   *Mapping an Address Pool to a Group Policy*

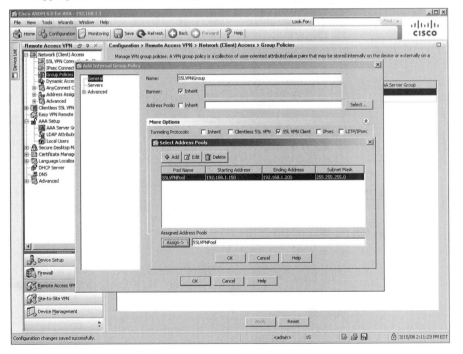

Configuring Traffic Filters

In its default firewall role, the Cisco ASA blocks decrypted traffic and protects the trusted network, unless the ACLs on the ingress interface explicitly permit traffic to pass through it. In case you trust all your remote AnyConnect VPN Clients, Cisco ASA can be configured to permit all decrypted SSL VPN packets to pass through it without inspecting them against the configured ACL. This is done with the **sysopt connection permit-vpn** command, as shown in Example 5-11.

Example 5-11   *Sysopt Configuration to Bypass Traffic Filtering*

```
Chicago(config)# sysopt connection permit-vpn
```

Configuring a Tunnel Group

Set up a new tunnel group by choosing **Configuration > Remote Access VPN > Network (Client) Access > Connection Profiles > Add**. For demonstration purposes, a tunnel group called SSLVPNTunnel has been added for the AnyConnect Clients. After defining a tunnel group name, you can bind the SSLVPNGroup group-policy to this tunnel group. If a user tries to connect to this tunnel group, the user will inherit attributes and policies defined under the user group-policy. Refer to Figure 5-5 for information on how to create a tunnel group.

Advanced Full Tunnel Features

After setting up a basic full tunnel client, you can configure some of the advanced parameters to enhance the SSL VPN implementation in your network. Some of the important full tunnel features are discussed in the next sections.

Split Tunneling

After the tunnel is up, the default behavior of the Cisco AnyConnect VPN Client is to encrypt traffic destined to all the IP addresses. This means that if an SSL VPN user wants to browse to http://www.cisco.com over the Internet, as illustrated in Figure 5-41, the packets will get encrypted and be sent to Cisco ASA. After decrypting them, the security appliance will look at its routing table and forward the packet to the appropriate next-hop IP address in clear text. These steps are reversed when traffic returns from the web server and is destined to the SSL VPN client.

Figure 5-41 *Traffic with No Split Tunneling*

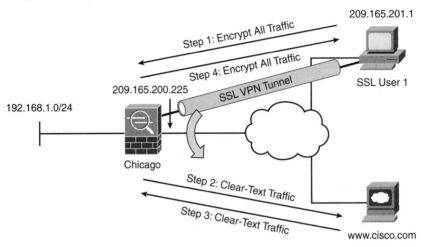

This behavior might not always be desirable for the following two reasons:

- Traffic destined to the nonsecure networks traverses over the Internet twice: once encrypted and once in clear text.

- Cisco ASA handles extra VPN traffic destined to the nonsecure subnet.

With split tunneling, the security appliance can notify the AnyConnect VPN Client about the secured subnets. The VPN client, using the secured routes, encrypts only those packets that are destined for the networks behind the security appliance.

CAUTION With split tunneling, the remote computer is susceptible to hackers, who can potentially take control over the computer and direct traffic over the tunnel. To mitigate this behavior, a personal firewall is highly recommended on the AnyConnect VPN Clients workstations.

Split tunneling can be configured under a user, user group-policy, or default group-policy. Choose **Configuration > Remote Access VPN > Network (Client) Access > Group Policies > SSLVPNGroup > Edit > Advanced > Split Tunneling**. Under Network List, deselect the **Inherit** check box and select a network list from the drop-down menu. If instead you want to define a new network list, click the **Manage** option. Cisco ASDM launches the ACL Manager and prompts you to define a new list. In Figure 5-42, a new list, called SplitTunnelList has been added. Under ACL Manager, click **Add** to add an access control entry (ACE). An ACE entry for 192.168.1.0/24 has been added with a description of List to Allow Access to Inside Network.

Figure 5-42 *Split Tunneling Configuration*

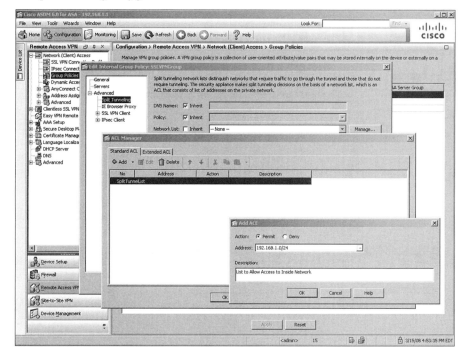

DNS and WINS Assignment

For the AnyConnect VPN Clients, you can assign DNS and WINS server IP addresses so that they can browse and access internal sites after their SSL tunnel is established. You can configure these attributes by choosing **Configuration** > **Remote Access VPN** > **Network (Client) Access** > **Group Policies** > **SSLVPNGroup** > **Edit** > **Servers**. To add multiple DNS or WINS servers, use a comma (,) to separate the entries. In Figure 5-43, the primary DNS server is defined as 192.168.1.10 and the secondary DNS server is 192.168.1.40. The primary WINS server is 192.168.1.40, and the secondary WINS server is 192.168.1.10. The default domain name to be pushed to the AnyConnect VPN Client is securemeinc.com.

Figure 5-43 *Defining DNS and WINS Servers for AnyConnect VPN Clients*

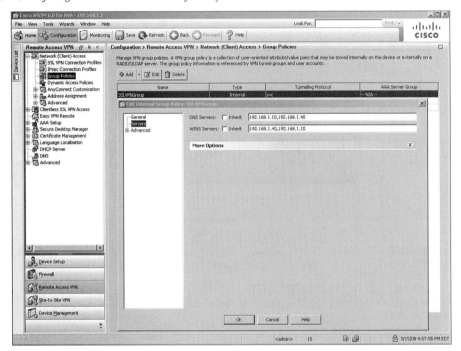

Keeping the SSL VPN Client Installed

After the SSL VPN client is installed successfully, the security appliance allows you to keep the client installed on the computer, even if the tunnel is disconnected. By default, the AnyConnect Client is automatically removed after users log off and is reinstalled when the tunnel is successfully established. You should keep this option enabled so that users do not need to go through the process of installing the client. Additionally, the initial AnyConnect Client installation requires administrative rights. If you do not allow your end users to have administrative privileges, keep the client installed on the workstation. You can configure to keep the client installed by choosing **Configuration > Remote Access VPN > Network (Client) Access > Group Policies > SSLVPNGroup > Edit > Advanced > SSL VPN Client** and selecting the **Keep Installer on Client System** option, as illustrated in Figure 5-44.

Figure 5-44 *Configuration of Keeping the SSL VPN Client Installed*

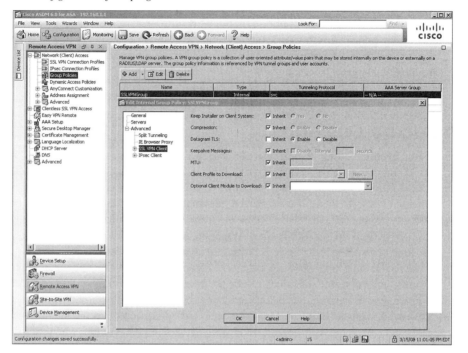

Configuring DTLS

Datagram Transport Layer Security (DTLS), defined in RFC 4347, provides security and privacy for the UDP packets. This allows UDP-based applications to send and receive traffic in a secure fashion without worrying about packet tampering and message forgery. Thus, applications that do not want to be associated with the delays associated with TCP but still want to securely communicate can use DTLS.

Cisco AnyConnect Client supports both SSL as well as DTLS transport protocols. If DTLS is enabled on the security appliance and UDP is blocked or filtered, communication between the client and the security appliance is switched over to the SSL protocol. Enable DTLS settings by choosing **Configuration > Remote Access VPN > Network (Client) Access > Group Policies > SSLVPNGroup > Edit > Advanced > SSL VPN Client**, as shown in Figure 5-44.

NOTE	If you have Cisco Security Agent (CSA) installed on the AnyConnect VPN Clients, you must import the new CSA policies on the workstations. Cisco Systems provides the necessary policies for the workstations running CSA on its software download page. You can import the CSA policies into the CSA management center and use them to attach rules to the CSA agents.

Cisco Secure Desktop

Cisco Secure Desktop (CSD) provides a secure desktop environment to remote users after validating a number of security parameters on the client workstation. The purpose of CSD is to minimize the risk posed by the remote workstations by collecting necessary information from them. If the received information matches the preconfigured criteria, the security appliance can create a secure environment and optionally apply certain policies to and restrictions on the user session. When the user session is disconnected, the secure desktop environment is removed. When this happens, users who want to access corporate resources from a hotel workstation or even from an Internet café can create a secure vault from which corporate resources can be accessed through clientless or even AnyConnect VPN Client. When the user is finished using the public workstation, the vault can be destroyed to ensure that data cannot be accessed by a different user. CSD removes cookies, temporary files, browser history, and even any downloaded content when the secure vault is destroyed.

CSD is designed to help system administrators to enforce security policies for remote users. When a user tries to connect to the SSL VPN gateway, a client component is downloaded and installed on the client workstation. This client component scans the computer and gathers information such as the operating system, installed service pack, antivirus version, and installed personal firewall. This information is sent to the SSL VPN gateway such as the security appliance and then matched against predefined criteria. If the user's computer meets the criteria, the user is given appropriate access to the internal resources. If the criteria are not met, users are granted either limited or no access. For example, an administrator might require that all remote computers must have Windows XP with Service Pack 2 installed. If remote computers meet this condition, they are matched against a profile and then allowed to launch CSD or Cache Cleaner. If dynamic access policy (DAP) is used, appropriate actions such as network restrictions can be applied to the user sessions. Cache Cleaner is discussed in the next section, and DAP is discussed later in the chapter. You can configure a number of parameters and group them together to define a specific location. When a remote host is scanned and the received information matches the criteria, the host is assigned that location. CSD supports five attributes to identify the location of an SSL VPN client. For example, you can define a range of IP addresses and a specific registry key, group them together, and declare them as Work. When clients connect from this address range and have that registry key, they are given access based on the defined policies. The supported attributes include the following:

- Issuer or distinguish name in a certificate
- IP address of the client
- Presence of a file
- Presence of a registry key
- Windows operating system version

CSD uses the proven industry standards such as Triple Data Encryption Standard (3DES) and Rivest Cipher 4 (RC4) to ensure security of the vault. If the logged-in user has administrative privileges, CSD uses the 3DES encryption algorithm, and if the user has lesser privileges, it uses RC4 to encrypt the data.

CSD Components

CSD consists of three components, discussed in the next sections.

Secure Desktop Manager

Secure Desktop Manager is a GUI-based application that allows administrators to define policies and locations for remote users. It currently supports two modules: Secure Desktop and Cache Cleaner. Secure Desktop Manager can be used within ASDM to configure CSD properties.

Secure Desktop

Secure Desktop, also known as system detection process, is a module that creates an encrypted vault in the client computer and allows users to securely access local resources or even allows users to establish SSL VPN sessions. Files created in this vault are encrypted and cannot be accessed by the applications outside this secure desktop. After a user disconnects a session, the vault can be configured so that it is destroyed.

By using Secure Desktop, users are given appropriate access to the corporate network after their system information, such as operating system and service pack, is detected. It can also detect whether the client workstation has any keystroke-logging applications installed before granting access. However, this system detection is transparent to the end user. They do not know what type of information is being collected by CSD, and therefore a different set of features are applied based on the criteria defined by an administrator.

Cache Cleaner

Cache Cleaner securely removes local browser data such as web pages, history information, and cached user credentials when the SSL VPN session is over. Cache Cleaner is supported not only on the Windows operating systems but also on the Linux and MAC OS X systems.

When Cache Cleaner is launched on a client computer, it closes any existing browser windows and initiates the Cache Cleaner process. It monitors the browser data, and when user logs out of the SSL VPN session, it closes the browser and cleans the cache associated with the SSL VPN session.

NOTE   Cache Cleaner and Secure Desktop do not protect your computer from downloaded attachments and therefore do not guarantee full system cleanup.

Cache Cleaner only monitors one browser application per SSL VPN session. If the initial session was established through Internet Explorer, only Internet Explorer–specific browser data will be cleaned after the user session is terminated. If the user launches Firefox after Cache Cleaner has already started, the Firefox browser data will not be wiped out after the user terminates a session.

CSD Requirements

Before you deploy CSD into a production environment, analyze your current system and network architecture first to make sure that they meet the minimum version of supported operating systems and Internet browsers. A list of supported platforms is presented in the next sections.

Supported Operating Systems

When this book was written, Secure Desktop is strictly supported in the Windows environment. The supported Windows platforms include

- Windows Vista 32-bit (x86) in CSD version 3.3
- Windows XP, including options with no service pack, Service Pack 1, and Service Pack 2
- Windows 2000, including options with no service pack, Service Pack 1, Service Pack 2, Service Pack 3, and Service Pack 4

Windows Vista 64-bit, MAC OS X, and Linux-based operating system users can use Cache Cleaner on remote clients. You can also choose to use Cache Cleaner for Windows XP and 2000 operating systems.

NOTE   If you are using Secure Desktop on Windows Vista, you cannot run AnyConnect VPN Client with it.

User Privileges

CSD does not require administrative privileges on the client computer when it is launched. However, the ActiveX installation will fail if you are not logged in as the administrator. Therefore, users cannot run an ActiveX installation when using an Internet café or workstations with no administrative rights. For users without administrative rights, the Java installation should succeed.

NOTE   If you are using Microsoft Java Virtual Machine (JVM), the user must have administrative rights. However, for Sun JVM, you do not have to be a local administrator.

Supported Internet Browsers

You can use the following browsers to manage, use, configure, and administer the currently released version of CSD. When this book was written, the released version of CSD is 3.2.1.126.

- Internet Explorer version 6.0 Service Pack 1 and version 7.0
- Safari 1.0 to 1.3 and 2.0 on Mac OS X
- Mozilla 1.7.*x*
- Mozilla Firefox 1.0, 1.5, and 2.0

Internet Browser Settings

As discussed in the previous section, CSD is installed on the client computer through ActiveX, Java, or an executable file. You must configure the appropriate security settings in your Internet browser to allow those functions. For example, in Internet Explorer, use the guidelines discussed in Table 5-7. These settings are configured by choosing **Tools > Internet Options > Security tab > Internet > Custom Level**.

Table 5-7 *Internet Browser Settings*

Attribute	Setting
ActiveX controls and plug-ins > Download signed ActiveX controls	Enable
ActiveX controls and plug-ins > Run ActiveX controls and plug-ins	Enable
Downloads > File download	Enable
Scripting > Active scripting	Enable
Scripting > Scripting of Java applets	Enable
Microsoft VM > Java permissions	High, medium, or low safety

CSD Architecture

CSD not only checks certain attributes on the client computer to ensure its compliance but also enhances data security by providing an encrypted vault to authorized users. When a user wants to establish an SSL VPN session and CSD is enabled, the client and the gateway go through a number of steps, discussed as follows. These steps are also illustrated in Figure 5-45:

Step 1 A user tries to request the SSL VPN login page by pointing his or her browser to the gateway IP address.

Step 2 The user session is redirected to a different web page (/start.html) because a secure desktop session has not been created. The gateway tries to install the Secure Desktop client component on the user's workstation using ActiveX, Java, or Executable mode.

Step 3 After installing the client component, the system is scanned and necessary information is collected from the client workstation. This information is forwarded to the gateway.

Step 4 The collected information is matched against the policies that are defined in Secure Desktop Manager and are stored in data.xml.

Step 5 A secure desktop cookie is written on the client computer and the secure vault is created on the hard disk. The web session is redirected to the SSL VPN user login page.

Step 6 The user presents authentication credentials, and if authentication is successful, the clientless SSL VPN session or AnyConnect SSL VPN session is created.

Figure 5-45 *CSD System Architecture*

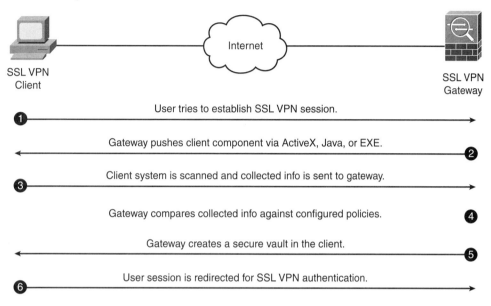

The data.xml file contains CSD-specific configuration information such as

- Location information
- Criteria for SSL VPN features

Configuring CSD

The configuration of CSD is broken into two steps:

Step 1 Loading the CSD package

Step 2 Defining prelogin sequences

Loading the CSD Package

Like Cisco AnyConnect VPN Client, you must load the CSD package in the local flash of the security appliance. If you're not sure whether you have CSD installed in your security appliance, choose **Tools** > **File Management** and look at the contents of the local flash. If you don't see a securedesktop-asa-3.x.xxx-k9.pkg file, upload the file from the local flash of the management host to the flash of the security appliance. After the CSD file is uploaded, choose **Configuration** > **Remote Access VPN** > **Secure Desktop Manager** > **Setup** and click **Browse Flash** to select the CSD file. In Figure 5-46, a securedesktop-asa-3.2.1.126-k9.pkg file is selected from the flash. After the file is selected, the last step is to select the **Enable Secure Desktop** option.

Figure 5-46 *Installing the CSD Package*

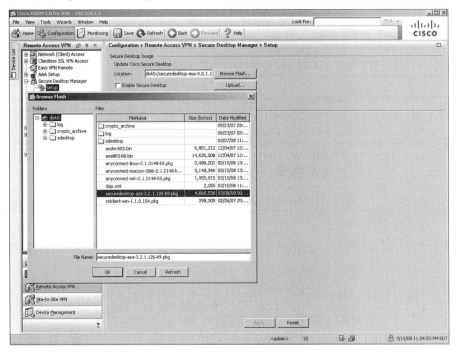

Defining Prelogin Sequences

To configure CSD parameters, choose **Configuration > Remote Access VPN > Secure Desktop Manager > Prelogin Policy**. You can define a prelogin sequence that CSD can use to identify a host and match it to an appropriate profile. If the client's computer matches a certain profile, CSD can either create a Secure Desktop or launch Cache Cleaner. The following sections walk you through the configuration of Secure Desktop Manager in defining the profiles and the respective policies for the SSL VPN users. These sections are as follows:

- Defining prelogin policies
- Assigning CSD policy
- Identifying keystroke loggers
- Defining Secure Desktop general attributes
- Applying Secure Desktop restrictions

- Defining Cache Cleaner policies
- Defining Secure Desktop settings

Defining Prelogin Policies

In the supported Windows, OS X, and Linux-based operating systems, you can define the potential locations where the client computers might be connecting from. For example, if your users connect from the office network, home office network, and even Internet cafés, you can define a location for each setup and give appropriate access to your users. For users connecting from the office network, you classify those hosts fairly securely and allow a less restrictive environment. For users connecting from their home office, you can classify them as somewhat secure and apply more restrictive policies. For users connecting from Internet cafés, you classify them as least secure and apply the most restrictive policies.

Throughout this chapter, we use three prelogin locations to build configurations. They include

- **OfficeCorpOwned:** This location is defined for those workstations that establish an SSL VPN tunnel from the corporate-owned IP addresses. Additionally, the workstation must have a unique registry setting to identify it as a corporate-owned computer. If workstations match this profile, Secure Desktop or Cache Cleaner will not be launched.

- **HomeCorpOwned:** This location is defined for those Windows computers that are corporate-owned but are employed by users who establish an SSL VPN tunnel from their home offices; these addresses do not match the corporate-owned address range. The workstations are classified as corporate owned by identifying a unique registry setting. If workstations match this profile, Secure Desktop will be launched.

- **InternetCafé:** This location is defined for those computers that do not match any of the previous profiles. Cache Cleaner will be launched.

These profiles are defined by choosing **Configuration > Remote Access VPN > Secure Desktop Manager > Prelogin Policy**. You can define prelogin locations by having the workstations meet a number of criteria. CSD supports the following five ways to identify a host:

- **Certificates:** If your client workstations use unique computers, you can use the subject and the issuer names to match a specific profile. The subject and issuer names contain a number of subordinate fields such as common name (CN), organization (O), organizational unit (OU), and country , to name a few. You can use one of the subordinate fields in the subject and issuer names to identify computers that match a specific profile.

NOTE	To identify computers based on certificates, specify the values of the subordinate fields. For example, to identify computers based on organizational unit (OU), simply specify the value of OU but do not list OU in the names.

- **IP address range:** If you know the IP address space of client computers, use this feature to identify computers that match a profile. You can define one or multiple address spaces to identify computers.

NOTE	If the client computer has multiple IP addresses, CSD uses the first identified IP address to match against a profile.

- **File setting:** You can use the location of a file to identify computers. This feature is useful if, for example, you want to identify a specific file to determine whether computers are corporate owned.
- **Registry setting:** You can use a registry key to identify computers. This feature is useful if you want identify a specific registry location to determine whether computers are corporate owned. A registry check is applicable only for Windows-based operating systems.
- **Operating system version:** The host assessment provides the version of operating systems running on the remote workstation. The operating system check is for Windows 9x, 2000, XP, Vista, Mac OS X, and Linux. Secure Desktop is allowed only for Windows Vista (32-bit), XP and 2000 operating systems. For other operating systems, Cache Cleaner is supported.

NOTE	If you specify more than one registry key or file location, CSD applies an OR logical operation. For example, if you define the location of a registry key and define the location of a file, one of the locations must be present to identify a host.

To configure a prelogin location, choose **Configuration** > **Remote Access VPN** > **Secure Desktop Manager** > **Prelogin Policy** and select the appropriate check from the drop-down menu. As illustrated in Figure 5-47, a registry check is being done. If HKEY_LOCAL_MACHINE\SOFTWARE\McAfee\VirusScan exists, CSD continues on and performs other checks. If a workstation does not have this registry key, it is classified as InternetCafe.

Figure 5-47 *Defining a Registry Check*

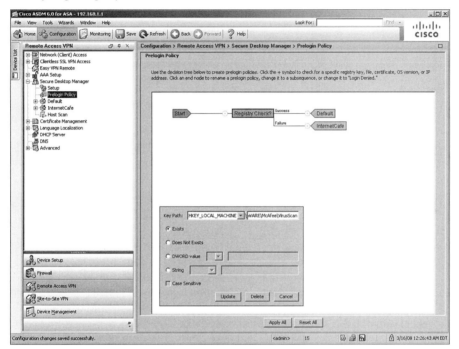

The workstations that have the registry setting are further accessed for additional checks. In Figure 5-48, workstations are checked for their IP addresses. If they are in the 192.168.1.0/24 subnet, they are identified as OfficeCorpOwned workstations. If they are not, they are identified as HomeCorpOwned workstations.

Figure 5-48 *Defining an IP Range Check*

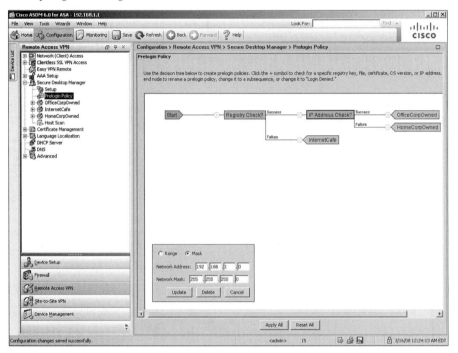

NOTE   If you want to identify a computer by locating a specific file in the system and ensuring the integrity of the file, you can find its checksum. To assist you with calculating the correct checksum of a file, CSD provides the crc32.exe application.

Assigning CSD Policy

When a computer tries to connect to the security appliance, CSD matches it to one of the predefined locations. For each location, you can choose to load either Secure Desktop or Cache Cleaner on the workstation. Choose **Configuration > Remote Access VPN > Secure Desktop Manager > [Prelogin location]** and select the appropriate option. The option should be selected based on your security policies. For example, if a user is identified as a HomeCorpOwned workstation, you can choose to enable Secure Desktop for those computers, as shown in Figure 5-49.

Figure 5-49 *Assigning a CSD Policy*

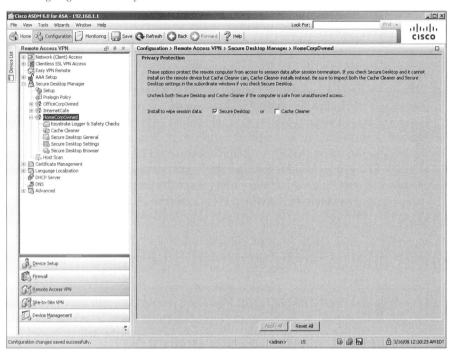

Identifying Keystroke Loggers and Host Emulators

The robust implementation of CSD allows you to detect certain software-based keystroke loggers in a workstation and takes appropriate actions before allowing a user's computer to create a secure environment. Keystroke loggers usually capture keystrokes without informing the legitimate user of the computer. These applications then send the captured information to a server, generally owned by hackers. If, for example, you have a keystroke logger installed on your computer and you are doing online banking, the keystroke logger can potentially capture your user credentials and pass that information to a hacker, who can misuse your personal information for his/her advantage.

You can also detect host emulations to check whether a remote workstation is running virtualization. If the **Always deny access if running within emulation** option is selected, remote workstations will not be allowed to connect through the SSL VPN tunnel. If the **Always deny access if running within emulation** option is not selected but host emulation detection is enabled, CSD prompts users to decide whether they want to continue with the SSL VPN session.

NOTE	Keystroke loggers are detected only when users have administrative rights to their workstations.

To prevent user computers that have a keystroke logger installed from establishing an SSL VPN tunnel, select **Keystroke Logger & Safety Checks** under the name of the location and enable the **Check for keystroke loggers** option. With this option enabled, the system scans and detects a keystroke-logging application on the workstation. If one is detected, the system prompts the user to identify the application as safe. However, if you do not trust user discretion, you can enable Force Admin Control on List of Safe Modules and manually identify which keystroke loggers are safe. Applications, such as Corel PaintShop Pro, usually capture keystrokes to allow users to modify data easily. In that case, an administrator can identify PaintShop Pro as a safe application.

CSD allows you to define a list of safe keystroke-logger application. Click **Add** and then enter the module's path. After an application is added, it appears under List of Safe Modules. You can define as many keystroke-logging applications as you want.

NOTE	If Force Admin Control on List of Safe Modules is enabled, contents under List of Safe Modules are defined, and then you disable Force Admin Control on List of Safe Modules, CSD still keeps the content under List of Safe Modules. It simply deactivates the defined values.

As shown in Figure 5-50, the administrator has enabled the **Check for keystroke loggers** and **Check for host emulation** options.

NOTE	If you receive a message that this tab is not available, that means you either do not have Secure Desktop or that Cache Cleaner is enabled for that specific Windows location.

Defining Secure Desktop General Attributes

In CSD, you can set up general attributes that are applied to all SSL VPN sessions within a predefined location. For example, to allow users to switch between Secure Desktop and the local desktop, you can enable that feature here. The supported Secure Desktop general attributes include

- **Enable switching between Secure Desktop and Local Desktop:** With this option enabled, the user has an option to switch back and forth between Secure Desktop and Local Desktop. In many cases, when an application is launched within Secure Desktop, it sends a notification or user prompt to the Local Desktop. Hence, you should enable this option if you need to switch to Local Desktop to respond to a prompt.

Figure 5-50 *Example of a Keystroke-Logging Application*

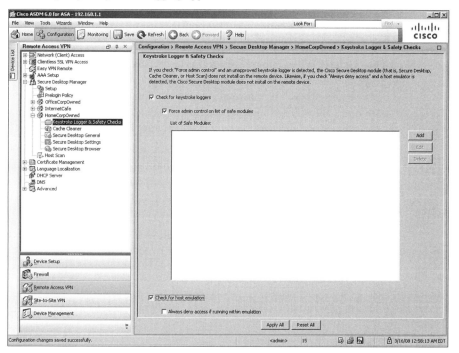

- **Enable Vault Reuse** (User chooses a password)**:** This option is useful if, for example, home users connect to a corporate network from the same desktop computer. Knowing that their computers are fairly secure at home, you can let them use the same vault. This vault is protected by a password that can be up to 127 characters long. In CSD version 3.2, you can enable one of the two options under Enable Vault Reuse. The Suggest Application Uninstall Upon Secure Desktop Closing option prompts and recommends the user to uninstall Secure Session when it closes. On the other hand, the Force Application Uninstall Upon Secure Desktop Closing option uninstalls Secure Desktop on the remote workstation when users close it.

- **Enable Secure Desktop inactivity timeout:** When this option is enabled, the system automatically closes the secure vault after a specified duration of inactivity. This option is useful for sessions that are left behind without properly closing the application. You should enable this option for those locations that are not secure, such as Internet cafés or untrusted host computers. If users are allowed to access critical or sensitive applications over the SSL VPN tunnel, you can configure a lower timeout value such as 5 minutes. If users access insensitive data, you can set a higher timeout such as 30 minutes.

- **Open following web page after Secure Desktop closes:** As the name suggests, this option requires you to input a URL that you want to launch after Secure Desktop disconnects on a user computer. This option is useful if you want to redirect user web sessions to a website that lists a company's policies for SSL VPN usage.

- **Secure Delete:** When Secure Desktop is terminated, CSD converts all data to binary 0s. It then changes all vault space to all 1s and eventually randomized data to 0s and 1s. This entire process is considered one pass. You can change this default setting to run multiple times. After it goes through all the configured passes, it eventually deletes the allocated space that was being used by Secure Desktop.

- **Launch the following application after installation:** You can configure CSD to launch an application after Secure Desktop has been launched. This is useful if you require your users to work on a specific application when they connect through an SSL VPN. The application must reside in the Program Files folder in the Windows-based operating systems.

As shown in Figure 5-51, the administrator has allowed the user to switch desktops. The secure delete is set for five passes for HomeCorpOwned Windows locations.

Figure 5-51 *Defining Secure Desktop General Attributes*

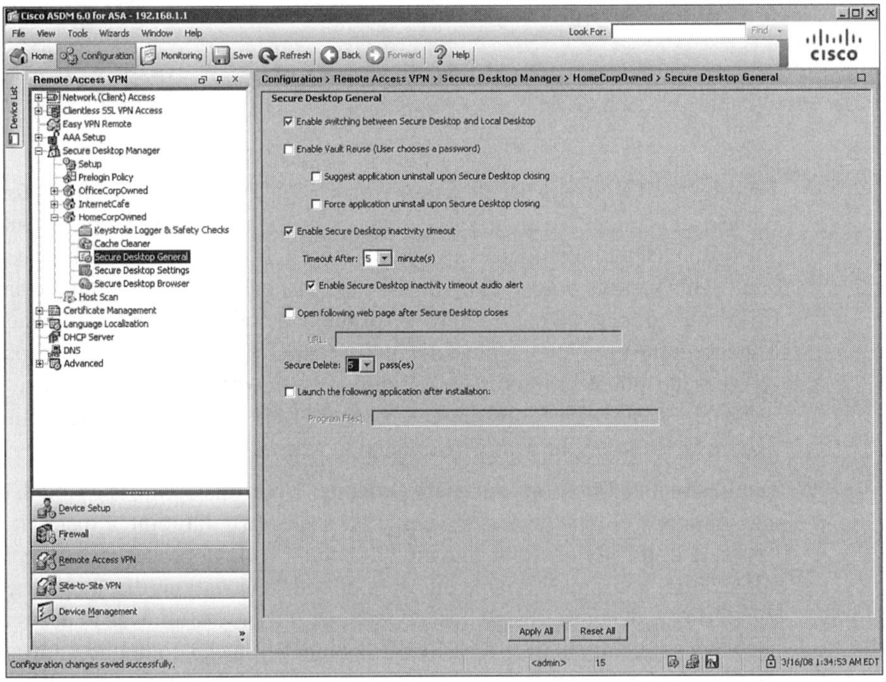

Applying Secure Desktop Restrictions

In addition to the global parameters that can be configured (discussed in the preceding section), you can apply certain restrictions to Secure Desktop to further enhance the level of security for SSL VPN sessions. These restrictions are defined in "Secure Desktop Settings" under a predefined location. These restrictions include the following:

- **Restrict application usage to the web browser only, with the following exceptions:** With this option, you can only allow users to launch multiple windows of the same browser that initiated the Secure Desktop session. For example, if a user launches Secure Desktop using Internet Explorer, he will be denied the ability to launch a different browser, such as Firefox, from within Secure Desktop. This option enhances security on the system because features such as Cache Cleaner do not clean the cache if a different browser is launched. In version 3.2.1 or higher of CSD, the Secure Desktop Manager inserts a text box so that you can select a preconfigured application that can run on Secure Session. If the application you want to allow is not on the preconfigured list, you can type the name of the executable files into the text box.

- **Disable access to network drives and network folders:** With this option, a user is denied access to network folders and drives. This even includes printers and any network shares that use Server Message Block (SMB) protocols. You should enable this restriction for those locations that are the least secure so that unauthorized or illegitimate users do not access protected network shares or resources.

- **Do not encrypt files on network drives:** With this option enabled, users are not able to save encrypted files on network drives. This option is grayed out if Disable Access to Network Drives and Network Folders is enabled.

- **Disable access to removable drives and removable folders:** When this option is enabled, users are denied access to their portable drives such as thumb or external hard drives with the Secure Desktop environment. This restriction is recommended so that users cannot copy sensitive data on a portable drive when accessing data from insecure Windows locations.

- **Do not encrypt files on removable drives:** With this option enabled, users cannot save encrypted files on portable drives. This option is grayed out if Disable Access to Removable Drives and Removable Folders is enabled.

- **Disable registry modification:** To restrict users from modifying the system registry within Secure Desktop, enable this option.

- **Disable command prompt access:** If unauthorized users get access to a system running Secure Desktop, they can launch command-line-based attacks to corporate resources. You should deny users command-prompt access within Secure Desktop to prevent such scenarios.

- **Disable printing:** If an illegitimate user gains access to a Secure Desktop environment, the user can print sensitive data such as software code on a local printer. You should prevent users in the least secure Windows locations from being able to print.

- **Allow e-mail applications to work transparently:** With this option enabled, users can access their e-mails while requiring Secure Desktop to erase the deleted e-mails when the session terminates. This option allows users to save e-mail attachments to the My Documents folder, which can be accessed from Secure Desktop and from the Local Desktop.

In Figure 5-52, the CSD administrator has enabled all restrictions for the HomeCorpOwned predefined location. Additionally, Microsoft Word (winword.exe) is selected as an exception for a Secure Desktop session.

Figure 5-52 *Enabling Secure Desktop Restrictions*

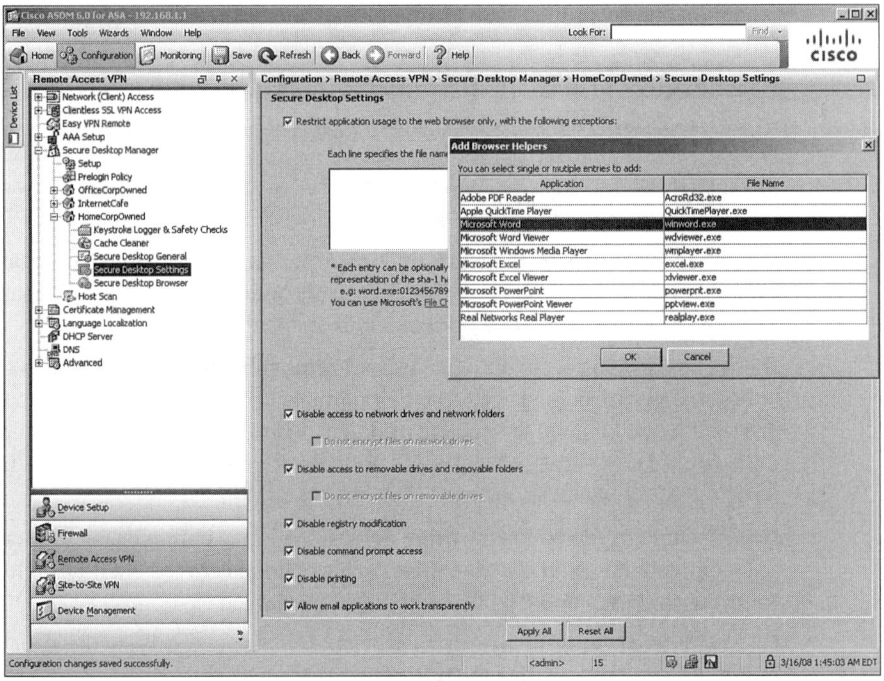

Defining Cache Cleaner Policies

As discussed earlier in this chapter, Cache Cleaner securely removes local browser data such as web pages, history information, and cached user credentials. When Cache Cleaner is launched on a client computer, it closes any existing browser windows and initiates the Cache Cleaner process. It monitors browser data, and when the user logs out of the SSL

VPN session, it closes the browser and cleans the cache associated with the SSL VPN session. Cache Cleaner can be configured under Cache Cleaner of a predefined location.

Cache Cleaner can be launched for any location, if enabled. Table 5-8 lists the options presented to you if Cache Cleaner is enabled for a Windows location.

Table 5-8   *Available Cache Cleaner Options*

Available Option	Description
Launch hidden URL after installation	After Cache Cleaner is installed, you might want the system to access a hidden URL. This way you can track the users and know whether they have successfully installed Cache Cleaner. This is recommended if you want to know how many users use Cache Cleaner.
Show success message at the end of successful installation	Using this option, users are shown a message that Cache Cleaner has been successfully installed. This is recommended so that users know that the cache-cleaning process has started on their computers.
Launch cleanup upon timeout based on inactivity	To start the cache cleanup process after users have been idle for a while, you can enable this option and specify the timeout value in minutes. If this option is enabled, the default timeout value is 5 minutes.
Launch cleanup upon closing of all browser instances or SSL VPN connection	This option is useful if you want to start the Cache Cleaner after users close all their browser windows.
Clean the entire cache in addition to the current session cache (IE only)	If this option is enabled, Cache Cleaner removes the entire Internet Explorer (IE) cache, including the data and files that were generated before CSD was launched.
Secure delete	When Secure Desktop is terminated, CSD converts all cached data to binary 0s. It then changes all cached data to 1 and eventually randomized data to 0s and 1s. This entire process is considered one pass. You can change this default setting to run multiple times. After it goes through all the configured passes, it eventually deletes the allocated space that was being used by Secure Desktop.

In Figure 5-53, the administrator has enabled Launch Hidden URL After Installation and added a hidden URL of http://www.securemeinc.com/cachecleaner.html for the HomeCorpOwned location. All users that match this profile will be shown a message that the Cache Cleaner process has successfully started. If user sessions are inactive for 10 minutes or if users close all browser windows, the Cache Cleaner process will start. Cache Cleaner will also remove the entire IE cache.

Figure 5-53 *Defining Cache Cleaner Policies*

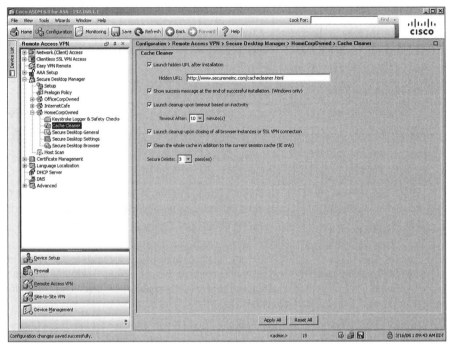

Defining Secure Desktop Browser Settings

Using Secure Desktop, you can present users with a predefined list of browser bookmarks. These bookmarks are generally the most common URLs (or favorite sites) that users connect to after their SSL VPN session is established. These bookmarks are defined under Secure Desktop Browser of a Windows location. You can customize these bookmarks under folders, or if just a few bookmarks exist, define them under the parent folder.

Host Scan

Host Scan is a modular component of CSD. It is installed on the user's computer before the user logs in to the security appliance over an SSL VPN tunnel. If CSD is in use, Host Scan can collect some important endpoint attributes and pass them to other processes such as DAP for appropriate action. Host Scan can scan an end host for information that you want to collect, such as registry entries, filenames, and process names. Host Scan functionality can be greatly enhanced if an advanced Endpoint Assessment license is used, which can collect information regarding antivirus and antispyware applications, firewalls, operating systems, and associated updates.

Host Scan, in CSD version 3.2.1, is currently supported in Microsoft Windows Vista, Windows XP, Windows 2000, MacOS X 10.4 and 10.5, and Linux operating systems.

NOTE   Host Scan functionality occurs after CSD goes through the prelogin assessment and before DAP enforces its policies.

Host Scan Modules

Host Scan currently supports three modules:

- Basic Host Scan
- Endpoint Assessment
- Advanced Endpoint Assessment

Basic Host Scan

Basic Host Scan can be used to identify the following information on a remote computer:

- Operating systems and their respective service packs
- Specific process names in Windows operating systems
- Specific filenames in Windows operating systems
- Registry keys in Windows operating systems

You can use basic Host Scan to determine whether a remote workstation matches a specific user profile by checking information such as its operating system, registry, files, or even an actively running process. When the basic Host Scan is run on a computer, it sends the operating system, service pack information, and any checks that you configure within CSD to the security appliance.

Endpoint Assessment

Endpoint Assessment scans a remote computer for a large collection of firewall, antivirus, and antispyware software, as well as their associated signatures and definition updates. The collected information is then forwarded to the security appliance so that a specific action can be taken and enforced by dynamic access policy (DAP). You do not need to purchase any specific licenses to configure a security appliance to check for the presence of personal firewalls, antivirus software, and antispyware applications.

Advanced Endpoint Assessment

Advanced Endpoint Assessment is a licensed feature that allows you to update noncompliant computers to meet the requirements of an enterprise's security policy. For example, with Advanced Endpoint Assessment, if a remote user logs in to a security appliance that is running an older version of an antivirus definition, this feature can attempt to update the definition on the remote workstation. The Advanced Endpoint Assessment is independent of the basic Host Scan and Endpoint Assessment, which were discussed earlier.

Advance Endpoint Assessment benefits you by forcing the following actions:

- An antivirus or antispyware application turns on the scan functionality if it is disabled.
- An antivirus or antispyware application turns on the scan functionality again if it stops running.
- An antivirus or antispyware application updates the signature definition files if they have not been updated for a configurable number of days.
- A number of configured rules are applied to the supported personal firewalls.

Configuring Host Scan

Host Scan can be configured by choosing **Configuration > Remote Access VPN > Secure Desktop Manager > Host Scan**.

Setting Up Basic Host Scan

To configure CSD to scan a remote computer for basic information, click **Add** under Basic Host Scan and select the type of basic scan you would like to configure. As mentioned in the previous section, a basic Host Scan can identify registry keys, active processes, and files located on the remote workstation. For example, if you want CSD to scan a registry key from the workstation and based on that information you want to apply appropriate action by DAP, add Registry Scan under Basic Host Scan. The system prompts you to configure the following attributes:

- **Endpoint ID:** Specify a meaningful name or unique string that you can later use under DAP to check the endpoint attributes. This endpoint ID is case sensitive. You can, for example, use Corp-Registry as an endpoint ID.
- **Entry Path menu:** Select the initial path of the registry key from the drop-down menu. For example, if the registry key you want to scan resides at HKEY_LOCAL_MACHINE\SYSTEM\CurrentControlSet\Control\Corp, select HKEY_LOCAL_MACHINE from the drop-down menu.

- **Entry Path field:** Specify the complete name of the registry key except the initial directory path that you provided on the Entry Path menu. For example, if the registry key you want to scan resides at HKEY_LOCAL_MACHINE\SYSTEM\CurrentControlSet\Control\Corp, specify SYSTEM\CurrentControlSet\Control\Corp as the Entry Path field, as shown in Figure 5-54.

Figure 5-54 *Defining a Registry Key Scan*

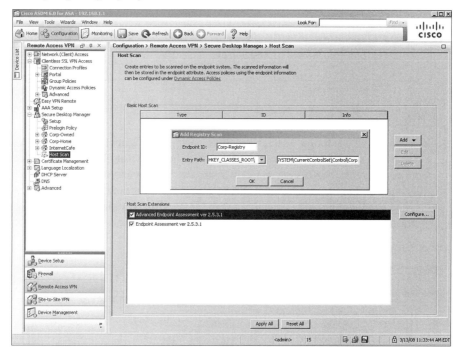

Click **OK** when you are finished defining the attributes.

Similarly, you can add a basic Host Scan for active processes and files residing on the remote workstation. To add a process scan, click **Add** and select **Process Scan**. To add a file scan, click **Add** and select **File Scan**. Refer to Table 5-9 for information on how to configure file and process scans for a basic Host Scan.

Table 5-9 *Basic Host Scan Configuration*

Scan Type	Endpoint ID	Scan Setting	Example
File scan	A unique ID such as Corp-File-Check	Specify the complete path and filename, such as C:\Program Files\ SecureMe\ID.hid, under File Path.	Endpoint-ID: Corp-File-Check File path: C:\Program Files\SecureMe\ID.hid
Process scan	A unique ID such as Corp-Process-Check	Specify the process name that you want to scan, such as mcshield.exe, under Process Name.	Endpoint-ID: Corp-Process-Check Process name: mcshield.exe

Enabling Endpoint Host Scan

You can enable Endpoint Assessment by choosing **Configuration > Remote Access VPN > Secure Desktop Manager > Host Scan** and then selecting **Endpoint Assessment ver w.x.y.z**, where **w.x.y.z** is the version of Endpoint Host Scan you are using. Figure 5-55 illustrates Endpoint Assessment as being enabled and running version 2.5.4.1. After it is enabled, the Endpoint Assessment can scan for antivirus, personal firewall, and antispyware applications and updates.

Figure 5-55 *Enabling Endpoint Assessment*

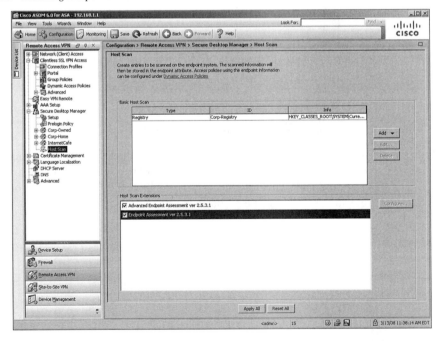

After a user's workstation passes through prelogin assessment, CSD scans the remote computer using the endpoint assessments–defined checks and forwards to the DAP engine for further action. These scan results are used as a condition for the completion of a Cisco AnyConnect or clientless SSL VPN connection.

Setting Up an Advanced Endpoint Host Scan

You can enable Advanced Endpoint Assessment by choosing **Configuration > Remote Access VPN > Secure Desktop Manager > Host Scan** and then selecting **Advanced Endpoint Assessment ver w.x.y.z**, where w.x.y.z is the version of Advanced Endpoint Host Scan you are using. After it is enabled, it allows you to update remote hosts that are noncompliant so that they can meet the configured security requirements.

Configure the Advanced Endpoint Assessment by highlighting **Advanced Endpoint Assessment ver w.x.y.z** and then clicking the **Configure** button. A new window opens that allows you to configure enforcement policies for Windows, Mac OS X, and Linux-based workstations. The enforcement policies can be configured for firewall, antivirus, and antispyware applications.

NOTE   If this option is not available on your Cisco ASA, you must acquire a new activation key that has the advanced assessment feature enabled from Cisco Systems. After you have the new key, you can activate it by choosing **Configuration > Device Management > System Image/Configuration > Activation Key** and entering the new key.

Configuring Antivirus Host Scan

To check remote workstations for antivirus compliance and to update noncompliant computers, click **Add** under AntiVirus. A new window opens with a list of all the supported antivirus vendors and their antivirus products. Select the antivirus vendor and product that you use in your environment from the list and click **OK** when finished. You can enable a couple of options, if your antivirus application supports them. They include the following:

- **Force File System Protection:** To make sure that the remote workstations scan any received files against the antivirus process, enable this option. If the received file contains a virus, the antivirus software should detect the virus and file access will be blocked.

- **Force Virus Definitions Update:** To force the remote workstations to check for a virus definition update, enable this option. This option is beneficial if you do not want workstations running older antivirus definitions to connect to your network. If this option is enabled, you must specify the age in days that triggered the last update.

Configuring Firewall Host Scan

To check remote workstations for personal firewall compliance, click **Add** under Personal Firewall. A new window opens with a list of all the supported firewall vendors and their respective products. Select the firewall vendor and product that you use in your environment from the list and click **OK** when finished. You can also configure a firewall action if your firewall application supports it. This option is useful if you want to make sure that the remote workstation has an active firewall process running. Select Force Enable or Force Disable from the drop-down menu. Certain firewalls also support configuring specific rules. For example, you can configure a Microsoft Windows Firewall Vista firewall to allow or block certain applications from processing traffic on specific ports.

Configuring AntiSpyware Host Scan

To set up the security appliance to scan the remote workstation for antispyware, click **Add** under AntiSpyware. You can check remote workstations for antispyware compliance and update noncompliant computers. A new window opens with a list of all supported antispyware vendors and their respective products. Select the antispyware vendor and product that you use in your environment from the list and click **OK** when finished. Similar to the antivirus scan option, you can also force the remote workstations to check for an antispyware definition update. This way, you can restrict workstations from connecting to your network if they are running older antispyware definitions. To enable this option, select **Force Spyware Definitions Update** and specify the age in days that triggered the last update.

In Figure 5-56, the administrator is setting up the Advanced Endpoint Assessment. He has enabled McAfee VirusScan Enterprise 8.*x* for an antivirus check and Cisco Security Agent 5.*x* for a personal firewall check.

Figure 5-56 *Setting Up Advanced Endpoint Assessment*

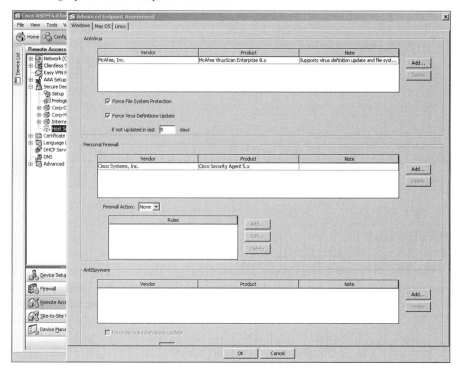

Dynamic Access Policies

In remote access setups, such as SSL VPN, it is becoming extremely difficult to correctly identify users' environments. A remote user can establish an SSL VPN tunnel from his corporate-owned workstation in the morning and then connect to the corporate resources from an Internet café in the evening. Moreover, if you are managing a remote access solution, it is challenging to map appropriate user authorization attributes based on their connection type. To provide a solution to these issues, Cisco introduced the idea of dynamic access policies (DAP).

DAP is defined as the collection of access control attributes that is specific to a user's session. These policies are generated dynamically after evaluating user authorization attributes, such as the tunnel type the user is connecting to and policies associated with that user account, such as access lists or filters. After a DAP policy is generated, it is applied to the user's session to allow or deny access to internal resources.

For example, consider two users who connect to the security appliance through the SSL VPN tunnel. User1 is a member of SSLVPNTunnel, while user2 is a member of SecureMeClientless group. You want to set up policies such that when users connect from workstations running Cisco Security Agent (CSA) as the firewall and have their McAfee antivirus software up to date, they are given full access to the network. However, if either the firewall or antivirus software is disabled, users should not be given access to the network. Therefore, when user1 connects to the security appliance and has both firewall and antivirus software running and up to date, the user is allowed to establish an AnyConnect VPN tunnel. Similarly, when user2 connects to the security appliance, the user is allowed to access smart tunnels and bookmarks if his workstation meets the firewall and antivirus requirements.

NOTE   DAP supports a number of other security appliance features such as IPsec and Cut-through-Proxy.

DAP Architecture

As mentioned earlier, DAP analyzes the posture assessment result of a host and applies dynamically generated access policies when a user session is established. It is designed to complement the AAA services by aggregating the locally defined attributes with the received attributes from the AAA server. In the case of an authorization attribute conflict, the locally defined attribute is selected. Therefore, it is possible to generate DAP authorization attributes by aggregating multiple DAP records from the AAA server and the posture assessment information for a user session.

DAP supports a number of posture assessment methods to collect endpoint security attributes. They include the following:

- **Cisco Secure Desktop:** CSD can collect the file information, registry key values, running processes information, operating system information, and policy information from an end workstation.

- **Cisco NAC:** For NAC deployments, you can use the posture assessment string passed by the CS-ACS server.

- **Host Scan:** Host Scan is a modular component of CSD. It can provide information such as antivirus, antispyware, and personal firewall software information about an end host.

The posture assessment information from end hosts can be complemented by the authorization attributes from the AAA server such as RADIUS or LDAP.

DAP architecture consists of the following components:

- DAP records
- DAP selection configuration file
- DAP selection rules

We briefly discuss these components in the following sections.

DAP Records

The DAP records (DAPR) contain access policy attributes such as user connection type and user's membership, to name a few, and the selection criteria. These records are defined locally on the security appliances. The selection criteria determine what DAP records should be selected during a tunnel negotiation.

DAP Selection Rules

The selection rules are simply the Boolean conditions that identify what DAPRs should be selected when a session gets negotiated. These selection rules reside in the DAP configuration file.

DAP Configuration File

DAP stores its configuration in an XML file (DAP.XML) that is located in the flash of a security appliance. This file contains all the selection criteria for each DAPR.

DAP Sequence of Events

When a user tries to establish an SSL VPN tunnel to the security appliance and DAP is enabled, the following sequence of events occurs:

1 The user negotiates an SSL VPN tunnel and is presented with a login page.

2 The security appliance collects user credentials and passes them to an authentication server.

3 If the user credentials are valid, the user is authenticated and the security appliance receives authorization attributes from the authentication server.

4 The posture assessment process is invoked by the appropriate process, such as Cisco Secure Desktop (CSD).

5 Based on the assessment results, the DAP access policy attributes are requested for the user session. The DAP records are selected using the assessment results collected in the previous step.

NOTE   DAP is supported in a single routed mode security appliance for SSL VPN deployments.

Configuring DAP

When a user tries to establish a connection, DAP can analyze the posture assessment result of a remote host and apply access policies that are dynamically generated. DAP can use the AAA attributes, such as RADIUS, LDAP, and Cisco-specific, and endpoint attributes, such as host scans and prelogin locations, before an action or a series of actions can be applied to a user session. It is designed to complement the authentication, authorization, and accounting (AAA) services by aggregating the locally defined attributes with the received attributes from the AAA server. In the case of an authorization attribute conflict, the locally defined attribute is selected. Therefore, it is possible to generate DAP authorization attributes by aggregating multiple DAP records from the AAA server and the posture assessment information for a user session. This way, the security appliance can use the prelogin sequence, the user login credentials, and the computer scan results before a DAP can be applied to a session.

A user connection might match multiple DAP records. For example, you can have a DAP record that only scans the remote workstations for a registry key. You can have another DAP record that checks the remote computer for an active process. If a remote workstation has the registry key and the process is active as well, that workstation will match against both DAP records. In this case, the security appliance combines both records dynamically and applies an aggregated access policy to a user connection.

The security appliance has a default DAP record called DfltAccessPolicy. This DAP record cannot be deleted and can contain only access policy attributes. It does not allow you to define any AAA or endpoint selection attributes. It is applied to all sessions that do not match any configured DAP records. By default, the DfltAccessPolicy does not restrict a session and allows traffic to pass through without imposing any access policies.

NOTE   The default behavior of DfltAccessPolicy is identical to the pre-DAP-supported security appliance versions, where no policy enforcement existed on user sessions.

You can configure DAP by choosing either of the following commands:

- **Configuration > Remote Access VPN > Network (Client) Access > Dynamic Access Policies**

- **Configuration > Remote Access VPN > Clientless SSL VPN Access > Dynamic Access Policies**

Create a new DAP record by clicking **Add**. ASDM opens a new window, where you can specify a name for this policy. The security appliance also allows you to specify a priority for this record. The priority is used to logically order the DAP records in case a user session matches multiple DAP records. The higher the number of a DAP record, the higher the priority.

For each DAP record, you specify selection criteria and configure appropriate action. For ease of understanding, DAP configuration is divided into the following three subconfiguration sections:

- Selecting a AAA attribute
- Selecting endpoint attributes
- Defining access policies

Selecting a AAA Attribute

Because DAP complements the AAA process, the security appliance can select DAP records based on AAA authorization attributes that it receives from the following storages:

- Cisco
- LDAP
- RADIUS

Table 5-10 defines the attributes that you can select within ASDM.

Table 5-10   *Supported AAA Attributes*

Attribute Type	Supported Attribute	Maximum Length	Attribute Description
Cisco	username	128	Authenticated username
Cisco	memberof	64	Group names that the authenticated user is a member of
Cisco	class	64	Group name value that is passed through the class attribute
Cisco	ipaddress	Not Applicable	Assigned framed IP address
Cisco	tunnelgroup	64	Tunnel group name that the user connects to
LDAP	LDAP attribute ID	128	LDAP attribute value
RADIUS	RADIUS attribute ID	128	RADIUS attribute value

NOTE   You can leverage the advanced option under DAP policy construction by using Lua, which is a lightweight, fast, and powerful scripting language. For more information about Lua, refer to http://www.lua.org. To define AAA attributes under the advanced section, add the aaa and then the attribute type followed by the attribute name. For example, if you want to define a Cisco username using Lua, you would specify it as aaa.cisco.username.

You can create one or multiple AAA attribute pairs to define a condition so that a specific DAP can be selected. In case you have more than one attribute pair defined, you can specify a logical operation (any, all, or none). For example, if you want users who connect to a tunnel group of *employees* or users who are members of a group *fullaccess* to be a part of the same DAP policy, select **user has ANY of the following AAA attribute values**. If you want users to match all conditions before a DAP policy can be selected, choose **user has ALL of the following AAA attribute values.** Additionally, you can select **user has NONE of the following AAA attribute values** if you want to select a DAP action and the authenticated user does not match any defined conditions.

Using the LDAP attribute type, you can leverage the native LDAP response attributes. The memberOf attribute of Active Directory specifies the distinguished name (DN) string of a group record. Specifically, the common name (CN) in the DN string is considered for group mapping. For example, if you are using LDAP authorization and you want to select users who are members of a CN called Employees, follow these directions under AAA attribute:

> AAA Attribute Type: LDAP
> Attribute ID: memberOf
> Value: "=" from the drop-down menu, and Employees as value

NOTE   Using Lua, you can configure the LDAP memberOf as follows:
aaa.ldap.memberOf=Employee.

Like LDAP, the RADIUS attribute type can also leverage the native RADIUS response attributes. These attributes are configured as attribute numbers and value pairs in the DAP record. For example, if you are using RADIUS authorization and you want to select users who belong to the class attribute of Employees, follow these directions under AAA attribute:

> AAA Attribute Type: RADIUS
> Attribute ID: 25
> Value: "=" from the drop-down menu, and Employees as value

NOTE   The attribute ID is always the attribute number; you cannot use the attribute name. Using Lua, you can configure the RADIUS class attribute as follows: aaa.radius.25=Employee.

In Figure 5-57, the SecureMe Inc. administrator is creating a new DAP entry called Clientless-DAP. A description of This Policy Is Applied to Employees Logging In Through Clientless SSLVPN Hosts is being added. SecureMe prefers to apply this policy for users who connect to the security appliance tunnel group of SecureMeClientlessTunnel and are members of the LDAP directory group attribute of Employees.

Figure 5-57 *Defining a AAA Attribute*

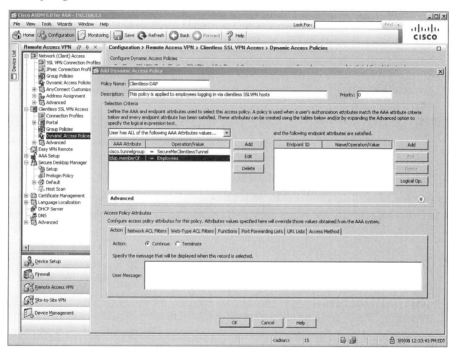

Selecting Endpoint Attributes

After defining the AAA attributes, you can optionally select the endpoint attributes. These attributes are collected by a number of sources, including Host Scans (basic, Endpoint, or Advanced Endpoint), Secure Desktop, and NAC. The AAA attributes are validated during user authentication, whereas the endpoint attributes are collected by the security appliance prior to user authentication. Table 5-11 presents all the available attributes that you can select and configure under endpoint attributes.

Table 5-11 *Available Endpoint Attributes*

Endpoint Attribute Type	Attribute Description
Antispyware	Select this attribute if you want to scan the host computer for antispyware. This option requires the use of CSD. Review the sections on Advanced Endpoint Host Scan for more details.
Antivirus	Select this attribute if you want to scan the host computer for antivirus. This option requires the use of CSD. Review the sections on Advanced Endpoint Host Scan for more details.
Application	Select this attribute if you want to take action if the users connect from clientless, AnyConnect, IPsec, L2TP, or Cut-through-Proxy connections. You can even take action if users connect from methods other than the ones defined.
File	Select this attribute if you want to take action if the users' computers contain the file specified here. This uses endpoint IDs specified in CSD's Host Scan option. This option requires the use of CSD.
NAC	Select this attribute if you want to take action if the posture state matches the defined user status string.
Operating system	Select this attribute if you want to take action if the operating system and the service pack of the end host match the configured operating system and service pack. This option requires the use of CSD.
Personal firewall	Select this attribute if you want to scan the host computer for a personal firewall. This option requires the use of CSD. Review the sections on Advanced Endpoint Host Scan for more details.
Policy	Select this attribute if you want to take action if the prelogin location of a user session matches the configured policy. This option requires the use of CSD.
Process	Select this attribute if you want to take action if the user's computer is running the process specified here. This uses endpoint IDs specified in CSD's Host Scan option. This option requires the use of CSD.
Registry	Select this attribute if you want to take action if the users' computers contain the registry entry specified here. This uses endpoint IDs specified in CSD's Host Scan option. This option requires the use of CSD.

NOTE When defining AAA Attributes as well as endpoint attributes, DAP will use a logical AND operation between the two fields to determine a match. DAP will also use a Logical AND operation between multiple endpoint attribute categories (such as antispyware, antivirus, and file). You can customize the operation performed within categories by clicking the **Logical Op.** button.

In Figure 5-58, SecureMe Inc. is checking the prelogin location and operating system of the remote workstations. For this DAP record, the users' computers must meet the prelogin location of Corp-Owned, and the operating system must match Windows XP Service Pack 2.

Figure 5-58 *Defining an Endpoint Attribute*

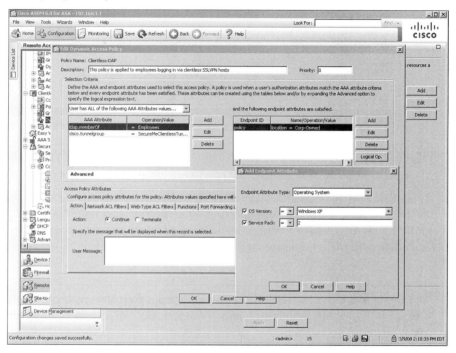

Defining Access Policies

After selecting the AAA and the endpoint attributes, the next step is to configure the policies that you want to apply to user sessions that match the attributes. You can configure VPN access attributes for a specific DAP record by using procedures outlined later in this chapter. For example, if a user's AAA and endpoint attributes match a DAP record, you can choose to allow that connection and apply certain ACLs configured into DAP to restrict user traffic. The DAP enforcements take precedence over other enforcement policies, whether those be AAA filters, user or group polices, or tunnel group attributes.

As an administrator, you can configure a limited set of attribute values for a DAP record. ASDM provides seven configuration tabs to configure such attribute values:

- Action tab
- Network ACL Filters tab

- Web-Type ACL Filters tab
- Functions tab
- Port Forwarding Lists tab
- URL Lists tab
- Access Method tab

The configuration of these tabs is discussed in the following sections.

Action Tab

The Action tab allows you to select which action will be enforced for a single DAP record. If the configured AAA and endpoint attributes match the received information from a user session, you can choose to either allow or terminate the session for that DAP record. Additionally, you can show a message of up to 128 characters to a user. The message blinks three times to get the user's attention.

If multiple DAP records are selected for a user session, the most restrictive action is taken as the aggregated policy. For example, if a user session matches three DAP records and two of them have an action of Continue while the third record has an action of Terminate, the collective policy will terminate the user connection.

TIP   The messages are shown in HTML format. That means you can even display a URL or links to users if they do not comply with policies so that they can take appropriate actions to remediate their workstations.

Network ACL Tab

The Network ACL tab allows you to apply traffic filters for the user session that match the DAP record. You can define traffic filters in the form of network ACLs. Each ACL can have either a permit or deny statement, but you cannot have both. If an ACL has both permit and deny rules, DAP rejects it as a configuration error.

If a user session matches multiple DAP records, an aggregated ACL is applied on the user. The aggregated list considers a number of parameters, such as the priority of each DAP record as well as duplications of access control entries (ACE).

To configure a network ACL, click the Network ACL tab and select a preconfigured ACL from the drop-down menu. Click the **Add** button to move the selected ACLs to the right under Network ACLs. The Network ACL tab even allows you to define a new ACL or modify an existing ACL. Click the **Manage** button to manage ACLs. In Figure 5-59, RestrictACL is selected and applied to this DAP record.

Refer to the section "Split Tunneling," earlier in this chapter, for information on how to manage ACLs.

Figure 5-59 *Defining Network ACLs for DAP*

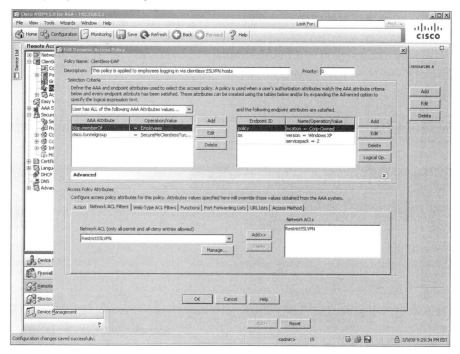

Web-Type ACL Tab

The Web-Type ACL tab, also known as the application ACL tab, allows you to apply application-specific filters for a user session that matches a particular DAP record. You can define traffic filters in the form of network ACLs. Each ACL can have either a permit or deny statement, but you cannot have both. If a web-type ACL has both permit and deny rules, DAP rejects it as a configuration error.

NOTE   If you happen to have an ACL entry that contains both permits and denies as access control entries, the command is rejected and the following message is displayed:

> "Unable to assign an access list with mixed deny and permit rules to a dynamic access policy."

If a user session matches multiple DAP records, an aggregated ACL is applied on the user. The aggregated list considers a number of parameters, such as the priority of each DAP record as well as duplications of ACEs.

To configure a web-type ACL, click the Web-Type ACL tab and select a preconfigured ACL from the drop-down menu. Click the **Add** button to move the selected ACLs to the right under Web-Type ACLs. The Web-Type ACL tab even allows you to define a new ACL or modify an existing ACL. Click the **Manage** button to manage ACLs. In Figure 5-60, RestrictApplication is selected and applied to this DAP record.

Figure 5-60 *Defining Web-Type ACLs for DAP*

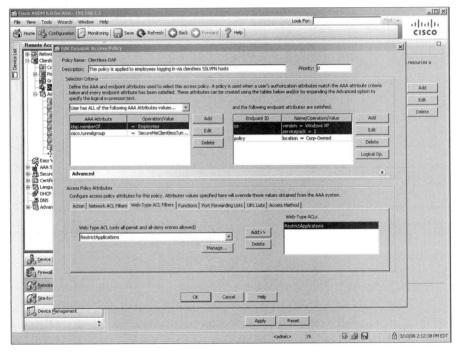

Refer to the section "Configuring Web-Type ACLs," earlier in this chapter, for information on how to manage web-type ACLs.

Functions Tab

The Functions tab allows you to configure file server browsing and entry, HTTP proxy, and URL entry. You can choose to allow or deny users from using these features for a specific DAP record. You can even choose to use the values from the group-policy that the user is connecting to. For HTTP proxy, you have the option to launch an applet by DAP when a user connects. Refer to Table 5-12 for an explanation of file server browsing and entry, HTTP proxy, and URL entry features.

Table 5-12   *Description of Functions Tab Features*

Feature	Unchanged	Enable/Disable	Auto-Start
File server browsing	Applies values from a group policy to which the user is assigned	Allows or denies users from CIFS browsing for file servers	Not applicable
File server entry	Applies values from a group policy to which the user is assigned	Allows or denies user from entering file server paths and names	Not applicable
HTTP proxy	Applies values from a group policy to which the user is assigned	Allows or denies user from using HTTP proxy	Allows DAP to automatically start the applets; also enables HTTP proxy for a user session
URL entry	Applies values from a group policy to which the user is assigned	Allows or denies user from entering HTTP or HTTPS URLs on the portal page	Not applicable

NOTE   You must enable WINS if you want to enable file browsing. Refer to the section "Configuring File Servers," earlier in this chapter, for more details. If WINS is not defined, the security appliance uses a DNS server to resolve names.

If multiple DAP records are selected for a user session, the least restrictive action is taken as the aggregated policy. For example, if a user session matches three DAP records and two of them have an action of disable, while the third record has an action of auto-start, the collective policy will auto-start the user connection for that specific feature.

To configure functions, click the Functions tab and select an option for each feature. In Figure 5-61, file server browsing and entry as well as URL entry are enabled, while HTTP proxy is set to auto-start.

Figure 5-61 *Selection of User Functions*

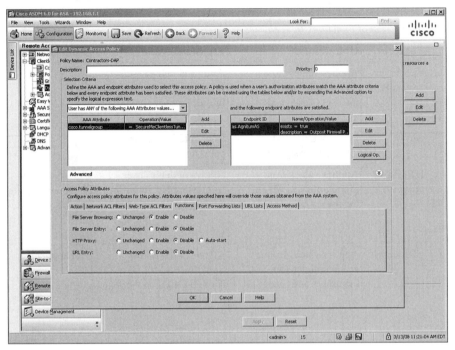

Port Forwarding Lists Tab

The Port Forwarding Lists tab allows you to apply a preconfigured port-forwarding list to a DAP record. If you do not have a preconfigured port-forwarding list, you can define one under this tab. Because DAP enforces action and policies, you can deny users the use of a port-forwarding list even if the group policy that the user is assigned to allows it. Similarly, if a group policy does not have a port-forwarding list mapped to the group policy, you can choose to auto-start the selected list.

To choose a preconfigured port-forwarding list, click the Port Forwarding Lists tab and select a preconfigured list from the drop-down menu. Click the **Add** button to move the selected ACLs to the right. If a new list needs to be defined, click the **New** button. As illustrated in Figure 5-62, a port-forwarding list called SSHServer is selected and applied to this DAP record.

Figure 5-62 *Selecting a Port-Forwarding List*

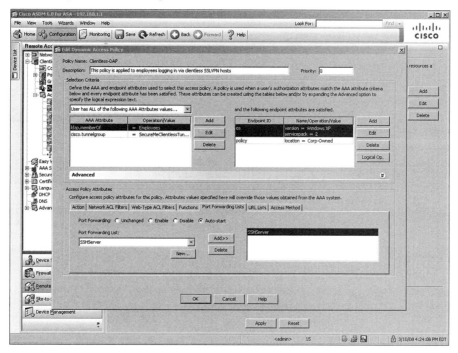

If a user session matches multiple DAP records, an aggregated policy is applied on the user. The aggregated policy concatenates the attribute values from the selected DAP records and removes any duplicates values.

NOTE   Refer to the section "Configuring Port Forwarding," earlier in this chapter, to learn more.

URL Lists Tab

The URL Lists tab allows you to apply a preconfigured URL list to a DAP record. If you do not have a preconfigured URL list, you can define one under this tab as well. To choose a preconfigured URL list, click the URL Lists tab and select a preconfigured list from the drop-down menu. Click the **Add** button to move the selected ACLs to the right. If a new list needs to be defined, click the **New** button. As illustrated in Figure 5-63, a URL list called InternalServers is selected and applied to this DAP record.

Figure 5-63 *Selecting a URL List*

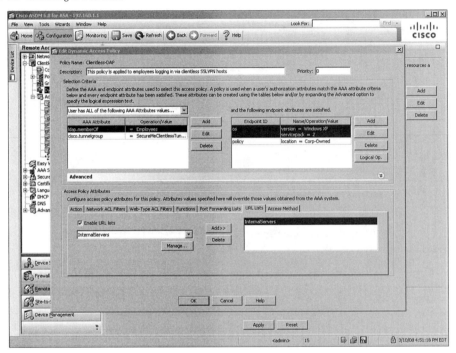

If a user session matches multiple DAP records, an aggregated policy is applied on the user. The aggregated policy concatenates the attribute values from the selected DAP records and removes any duplicates values.

NOTE   Refer to the section "Configuring Websites," earlier in this chapter, to learn more.

Access Method Tab

On the Access Method tab, you can specify an access method for a DAP record. The supported access methods include AnyConnect Client, Web-Portal, Both-Default-Web-Portal, Both-Default-AnyConnect Client, and Unchanged. For example, if users match a DAP record but you do not want to give them AnyConnect Client functionality, select the Web-Portal option for that particular DAP record. If you select either the Both-Default-Web-Portal or Both-Default-AnyConnect Client, users who match the DAP record will have access to both features and the default method will be tried first. If you select Unchanged as the option, the user will be allowed an access method based on the group policies that he acquires for his session. As shown in Figure 5-64, an access method of Web-Portal is selected and applied to a DAP record.

Figure 5-64 *Selecting an Access Method*

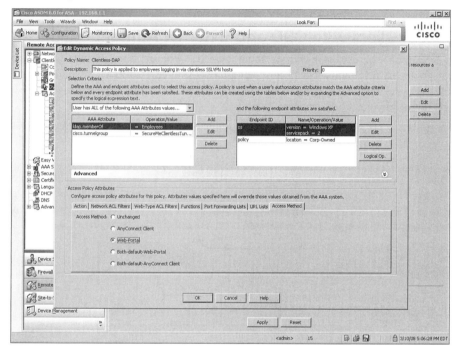

A user session can match multiple DAP records. In this case, the applied aggregated policy selects the least restrictive access method. For example, if a DAP record has Web-Portal as its access method, whereas another DAP record has Both-Default-AnyConnect Client, the user's access method will be Both-Default-AnyConnect Client. However, if Both-Default-AnyConnect Client and Both-Default-Web-Portal are selected for a user session, the aggregates policy applies Both-Default-Web-Portal as the access method.

Deployment Scenarios

The Cisco SSL VPN solution is useful in deployments where remote and home users need access to corporate networks and administrators want to control their access based on a number of attributes. The SSL VPN solution can be deployed in many ways; however, the sections that follow cover two design scenarios for ease of understanding:

- AnyConnect Client with CSD and external authentication
- Clientless connections with DAP

NOTE   The design scenarios discussed in the following sections should be used solely to reinforce learning. They are for reference purposes only.

AnyConnect Client with CSD and External Authentication

SecureMe has recently learned about the SSL VPN functionality in Cisco ASA and wants to deploy it for a number of remote employees in New York. These employees need full access to the internal network without restriction to complete their tasks if they meet criteria defined by the administrator.

Figure 5-65 shows SecureMe's network topology for AnyConnect Client.

Figure 5-65 *SecureMe's SSL VPN for AnyConnect Clients*

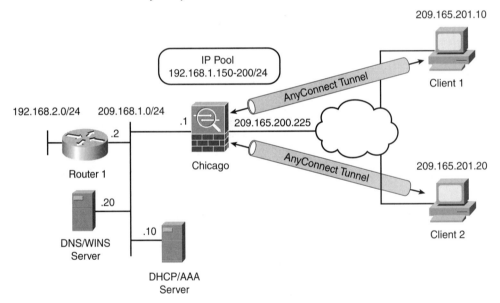

The security requirements of SecureMe are as follows:

- Allow full access to the internal network when a user fulfills certain requirements.
- Use a RADIUS server as the external database for user lookup.
- Use split tunneling and encrypt traffic going over to the 192.168.0.0/16 network.
- Scan remote workstations for corporate registry keys. If the registry key exists, create a secure environment and allow users to connect to the internal network.

To achieve SecureMe's requirements, the administrator has proposed that the security appliance use CSD and collect information from the remote workstation. If workstations have a registry key of HKLM\SYSTEM\CurrentControlSet\Control\Corp and their IP addresses do not fall within the corporate network range, they are declared as CorpOwnedHomeMachine. The security appliance will create a Secure Desktop on the workstation and prompt the user for credentials. The credentials will be checked against the RADIUS database, and if users are successfully authenticated, they will be allowed to establish an SSL VPN tunnel through the AnyConnect Client. After an AnyConnect Client is loaded on the workstation, it should remain installed.

The steps to implement the proposed solution are listed next.

Step 1: Set Up CSD

The first step in achieving the listed goals is to create a secure environment for remote users. This is achieved by following these steps:

1 Choose **Configuration** > **Remote Access VPN** > **Secure Desktop Manager** > **Setup**, click **Browse Flash** to select the CSD file you want to use, and select **Enable Secure Desktop**.

2 Choose **Configuration** > **Remote Access VPN** > **Secure Desktop Manager** > **Windows Location Setting** and define a prelogin sequence based on registry key and IP address range. Create a new Windows location called CorpOwnedHomeMachines that has a registry key check of HKLM\SYSTEM\CurrentControlSet\Control\Corp and an address check where the address should not fall in the 209.165.200.224/27 subnet.

3 Choose **Configuration** > **Remote Access VPN** > **Secure Desktop Manager** > **CorpOwnedHomeMachines** and select the **Secure Desktop** option.

Step 2: Set Up RADIUS for Authentication

The second step is to set up a RADIUS server for user authentication. This is achieved by following these guidelines:

1 Choose **Configuration** > **Remote Access VPN** > **AAA Setup** > **AAA Server Groups** > **Add**. Specify the server group called **RADIUS** and select **RADIUS** from the drop-down menu. Click **OK** when finished.

2 Click the newly created server group, and under Servers in the Selected Groups, click **Add**. Under Interface Name, select **inside** from the drop-down menu and specify 192.168.1.10 as the IP address of the RADIUS server. Configure a shared key of SecureMe123, and click **OK** when finished.

Step 3: Configure AnyConnect SSL VPN

The last step needed to meet the listed requirements is to configure AnyConnect VPN Client on the security appliance for remote users. Follow these guidelines to achieve the goals:

1 Choose **Configuration > Remote Access VPN > Network (Client) Access > Advanced > SSL VPN > Client Settings > Add.** Click **Browse Files** and select **AnyConnect VPN client**.

2 After loading the AnyConnect Client, enable full tunnel client functionality on the outside interface. This is achieved by selecting the **Enable Cisco AnyConnect VPN Client or legacy SSL VPN Client access on the interfaces selected in the table below** option under **Configuration > Remote Access VPN > Network (Client) Access > SSL VPN Connection Profiles** on the outside interface. Make sure that the **Allow Access** check box is selected for the outside interface.

3 Choose **Configuration > Remote Access VPN > Network (Client) Access > Address Assignment > Address Pools > Add.** Under Name, specify **SSLVPNPool** and configure 192.168.1.100 through 192.168.1.150 as the pool of addresses and a mask of 255.255.255.0.

4 Choose **Configuration > Remote Access VPN > Network (Client) Access > Group Policies > Add.** Specify **SSLVPNGroup** as the group policy name. Under Address Pools, deselect the **Inherit** check box and select **SSLVPNPool**.

5 Click the option for **Advanced > Split Tunneling** in the left pane. Under Policy, deselect the **Inherit** check box and select **Tunnel Network List Below.** Under Network List, deselect the **Inherit** check box and click **Manage.** On the Standard ACL tab, click **Add** and add an ACL called **SSLVPNST.** Then click **OK.** Click **Add** and then **Add ACE** to add an access control entry (ACE). Specify **192.168.0.0/16** under Address. Click **OK** when finished. Verify that the SSLVPNST ACL is selected in the drop-down list.

6 Click the **Servers** option in the left pane and configure **192.168.1.20** as the WINS and DNS server addresses.

7 Click the **Advanced > SSL VPN Client** option in the left pane, and select **Keep Installer on Client System**.

8 Create a new tunnel group by choosing **Configuration > Remote Access VPN > Network (Client) Access > SSL VPN Connection Profiles > Add.** Under Connection Profiles, click **Add** and specify **SSLVPNTunnel** as the tunnel group name. Select **RADIUS** under AAA Server Group and select **SSLVPNGroup** under Default Group Policy. Make sure the **SSL VPN Client Protocol** check box is selected.

9 Click the **Advanced > SSL VPN** option in the left pane. Under Group URL, click **Add** and specify **https://sslvpn.securemeinc.com/sslvpnclient**. Verify that the **Enable** check box is selected. Click **OK** to exit.

You can now connect to the ASA using the following URL in your browser: https://sslvpn.securemeinc.com/sslvpnclient.

Clientless Connections with DAP

After successfully implementing the AnyConnect functionality on the security appliance, SecureMe has now decided to provide clientless functionality to a group of mobile contractors. These contractors use a web server for browsing, a terminal server, and a Windows file server to save and retrieve their documents.

Figure 5-66 shows SecureMe's proposed network topology for clientless connections.

Figure 5-66 *SecureMe's Clientless Connection Topology with DAP*

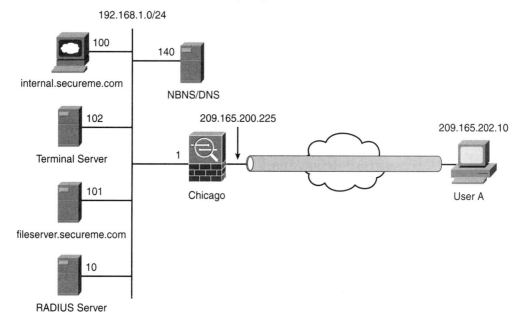

The security requirements for SecureMe are as follows:

* Deny access to the internal web server located at intranet.securemeinc.com.
* Allow web access to all other web servers.
* Allow access to a file server with an IP address of fileserver.securemeinc.com.
* Allow access to a terminal server with an IP address of 192.168.1.102.
* SecureMe uses RADIUS for user authentication and uses attribute 25 for role mapping within the enterprise.

- Contractors must have an active McAfee firewall (McAfee Personal Firewall version 8.*x*) running before access to SecureMe's network can be granted.

- Contractors should not be able to browse or specify any other web server in the SecureMe network.

To achieve SecureMe's requirements, the administrator has proposed that the security appliance be configured for clientless access. Bookmarks and smart tunnels will be configured to provide access to the internal web servers, CIFS servers, and terminal servers. The preconfigured RADIUS will be leveraged for user authentication. Attribute 25 will be used by DAP to assign specific policies based on user roles. Additionally, an endpoint assessment will be done to ensure that contractors have an active firewall running. If the security appliance receives attribute 25 with a value of contractor and endpoint assessment determines that the McAfee firewall is running, contractors will be allowed to connect through the web portal.

The steps to implement the proposed solution are listed next.

Step 1: Define Clientless Connections

The first step in achieving the listed goals is to set up clientless connections for remote contractors as follows:

1 Define bookmarks for the internal servers (web and CIFS) by choosing **Configuration > Remote Access VPN > Clientless SSL VPN Access > Portal > Bookmarks > Add**. Specify a bookmark list name called **Contractors-List** and then click **Add** to specify a bookmark title of **Internal-Web**. Select **http** under the URL Value drop-down menu, and configure a URL value of **http:// intranet.securemeinc.com**. Under advanced options, enable the Smart Tunnel option to tunnel HTTP traffic directly to the web server. Click **OK** when finished. Click **Add** to add another entry for the CIFS server. Under Bookmark Title, specify **Internal-FileServer** and select **cifs** from the URL Value drop-down menu. Configure a URL value of **fileserver.securemeinc.com**.

2 Configure a web-type ACL by choosing **Configuration > Remote Access VPN > Clientless SSL VPN Access > Advanced > Web ACLs**. Click **Add**, select **Add ACL**, and define a list called **RestrictWebServer.** Select the newly created ACL name, click **Add** again, select **Add ACE**, and select **Deny** as the Action. Choose **http** as the filter protocol and specify **internal.securemeinc.com** as the URL entry. Create another ACE, select **Allow** as the Action, and choose **any** as the filter protocol. Click **OK** when finished.

3 Choose **Configuration > Remote Access VPN > Clientless SSL VPN Access > Portal > Smart Tunnels > Add** to define an entry for the terminal server. Specify a list name of **TerminalServer**, an Application ID of **Terminal**, and a Process Name of **mstsc.exe**.

4 Define a group policy to link the bookmark and smart tunnel lists. Choose **Configuration > Remote Access VPN > Clientless SSL VPN Access > Group Policies > Add** and specify **ClientlessGroupPolicy** as the policy name for the clientless users. Under More Options, deselect the **Inherit** check box for Tunneling Protocols and select **Clientless SSL VPN**. Click the **Portal** option in the left pane and deselect the **Inherit** check box for Bookmark List. Select **Contractor-List** from the drop-down list. Now, deselect the **Inherit** check box for Smart Tunnel List and select **TerminalServer** from the drop-down list. Also enable **Auto Start** so that the smart tunnel is automatically initiated when the tunnel is established for a user. Click **OK** when finished.

5 Choose **Configuration > Remote Access VPN > Clientless SSL VPN Access > SSL VPN Connection Profiles**, and under Access Interfaces, select the **Allow Access** check box for the outside interface. Create a new tunnel group by clicking **Add** under Connection Profiles. Specify **SecureMeClientlessTunnel** as the tunnel group name. Select **RADIUS** under AAA Server Group and select **ClientlessGroupPolicy** under Default Group Policy.

6 Because you are using bookmarks for the web and CIFS servers, you need to define a WINS and a DNS server. Choose the **Advanced > Name Servers** option in the left pane. Under NETBIOS Servers, click **Add**, specify **192.168.1.140** as the IP address of the NBNS server, and enable the Master Browser option. Under DNS Server Group, click **Manage** and then **Add**. Specify **SecureMeDNSGroup** as the DNS server group name. Configure **192.168.1.140** under Server IP Address to Add and click **Add** to add the server to the DNS server list. Specify **securemeinc.com** under Domain Name. Click **OK** when finished.

7 Click the **Advanced > SSL VPN** option in the left pane. Under Group URL, click **Add** and specify **https://sslvpn.securemeinc.com/clientless**. Verify that the **Enable** check box is selected. Click **OK** to exit.

Step 2: Configuring DAP

SecureMe wants to apply policy enforcements through DAP. The next step is to configure DAP by choosing **Configuration > Remote Access VPN > Clientless SSL VPN Access > Dynamic Access Policies**.

1 Create a new DAP record by clicking **Add** and specifying the record name of **Contractors-DAP**. Under AAA attribute selection criteria, click **Add** and select **RADIUS** as the AAA Attribute Type. Under Attribute ID, specify **25** and select Value equal to **Contractors**. Insert another AAA attribute type of **Cisco** and select the **Tunnel Group** check box. Specify **SecureMeClientlessTunnel** as the Tunnel Group value. Select **User has ALL of the following AAA Attribute Types** as the Selection Criteria.

2 Configure the endpoint attribute selection. Click **Add**, select **Personal Firewall** as the Endpoint Attribute Type, and select the **Exists** radio button. Under Vendor, select **McAfee, Inc**. and choose **McAfee Personal Firewall version 8.x** as the Product Description. Click **OK** when finished.

3 Configure the Access Policy Attributes. On the Action tab, choose **Continue**. Click the Web-Type ACL tab and select **RestrictWebServer** from the drop-down menu. Click the **Add** button to move the selected ACLs to the right under Web-Type ACLs. Now, select the Functions tab and choose **Enable** for File Server Browsing. Also choose **Disable** for File Server Entry, HTTP Proxy, and URL Entry.

4 On the URL Lists tab, click **Enable URL Lists** and select **Contractors-List** from the drop-down menu. Click the **Add** button to move the selected list to the right. Finally, select **Web-Portal** as the Access Method on the Access Method tab. Click **OK** when finished.

You can now connect to the ASA using the following URL in your browser: https://sslvpn.securemeinc.com/clientless.

Monitoring and Troubleshooting SSL VPN

The following sections discuss the monitoring and troubleshooting steps that are available to help you in running the SSL VPN solution smoothly on a security appliance.

Monitoring SSL VPN

To monitor the WebVPN sessions, first check how many active SSL VPN tunnels are established on the security appliance. You can do this by choosing **Monitoring** > **VPN** > **VPN Statistics** > **Sessions**. The security appliance shows you all the active VPN sessions, including the clientless and full tunnel client connections. As shown in Figure 5-67, an active clientless connection is created by a user called sslvpnuser. The user computer's IP address is 209.165.200.230, and the negotiated encryption type is RC4. The security appliance has received 75,283 bytes of traffic, whereas it has transmitted 153,387 bytes of data to the client. The user is connected for just over a minute. Should you prefer to get detailed information about a user's connection, select that specific user session and then click the **Details** button.

Figure 5-67 *Monitoring SSL VPN Sessions Through ASDM*

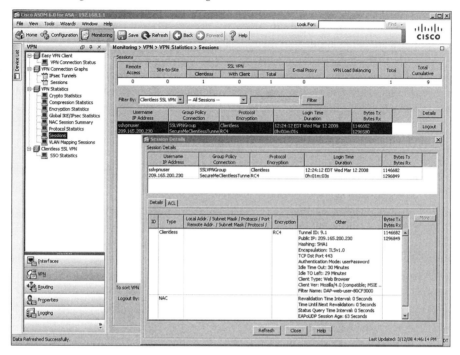

To view the DAP policies that are configured on the security appliance in Lua, issue the **debug menu dap 2** command, as shown in Example 5-12. Two DAP records are configured: Clientless-DAP and Contractors-DAP.

Example 5-12 **debug menu dap** *Command*

```
Chicago# debug menu dap 2
DAP record [    Clientless-DAP  ]:
(EVAL(aaa.ldap.memberOf,"EQ","Employees","string") or
 EVAL(aaa.cisco.tunnelgroup,"EQ","SecureMeClientlessTunnel","string")) and
 ((EVAL(endpoint.os.version,"EQ","Windows XP","string") and
 EVAL(endpoint.os.servicepack,"EQ","2","integer"))) and
 ((EVAL(endpoint.policy.location,"EQ","Corp-Owned","string")))

DAP record [    Contractors-DAP ]:
(EVAL(aaa.radius["25"],"EQ","Contractors","string") and
 EVAL(aaa.cisco.tunnelgroup,"EQ","SecureMeClientlessTunnel","string")) and
 ((EVAL(endpoint.fw.McAfeeFW.exists,"EQ","true","string") and
 EVAL(endpoint.fw.McAfeeFW.description,"EQ","McAfee Desktop Firewall","string")))
Chicago#
```

Additionally, if you want to monitor user sessions through syslogs, you can enable the webvpn, svc, csd, and dap classes. These classes are useful for understanding how users are getting authenticated, what information is being collected, and what type of attributes and policies are being applied on their sessions. As shown in Example 5-13, the administrator is collecting debug-level information for the webvpn, svc, csd, and dap classes. The syslog messages are being collected in the local buffer of the security appliance. Based on the syslog messages, an sslvpn user tries to connect to the SecureMeClientlessTunnel tunnel group. CSD determines that the host connects from the Internet cafe location, and the security appliance applies a DAP called Contractors-DAP. The user session is successfully authenticated, and the user is allowed to connect through a clientless SSL VPN (WebVPN) tunnel.

Example 5-13   **class** *Syslog Commands*

```
Chicago# show log
Chicago# logging enable
Chicago# logging buffer-size 1048576
Chicago# logging class webvpn buffered debugging
Chicago# logging class svc buffered debugging
Chicago# logging class csd buffered debugging
Chicago# logging class dap buffered debugging
Syslog logging: enabled
     Facility: 20
     Timestamp logging: disabled
     Standby logging: disabled
     Deny Conn when Queue Full: disabled
     Console logging: disabled
     Monitor logging: disabled
     Buffer logging:  class webvpn svc csd dap, 133 messages logged
     Trap logging: disabled
     History logging: disabled
     Device ID: disabled
     Mail logging: disabled
     ASDM logging: disabled
%ASA-7-734003: DAP: User sslvpnuser, Addr 209.165.200.230: Session Attribute
  aaa.cisco.username = sslvpnuser
%ASA-7-734003: DAP: User sslvpnuser, Addr 209.165.200.230: Session Attribute
  aaa.cisco.tunnelgroup = SecureMeClientlessTunnel
%ASA-7-734003: DAP: User sslvpnuser, Addr 209.165.200.230: Session Attribute
  endpoint.os.version = "Windows XP"
%ASA-7-734003: DAP: User sslvpnuser, Addr 209.165.200.230: Session Attribute
  endpoint.os.servicepack = "2"
%ASA-7-734003: DAP: User sslvpnuser, Addr 209.165.200.230: Session Attribute
  endpoint.policy.location = "InternetCafe"
%ASA-7-734003: DAP: User sslvpnuser, Addr 209.165.200.230: Session Attribute
  endpoint.protection = "secure desktop"
<snip>
%ASA-7-734003: DAP: User sslvpnuser, Addr 209.165.200.230: Session Attribute
  endpoint.enforce = "success"
%ASA-6-734001: DAP: User sslvpnuser, Addr 209.165.200.230, Connection Clientless:
  The following DAP records were selected for this connection: Contractors-DAP
  %ASA-6-716001: Group <ClientlessGroupPolicy> User <sslvpnuser> IP
  <209.165.200.230> WebVPN session started.
%ASA-6-716038: Group <ClientlessGroupPolicy> User <sslvpnuser> IP <209.165.200.230>
  Authentication: successful, Session Type: WebVPN.
```

NOTE   The debug-level syslogs should be used if you are monitoring sessions in a lab environment. They should be used only for troubleshooting in the production environment and should be disabled when you have collected the necessary information.

Troubleshooting SSL VPN

Cisco ASA provides a number of troubleshooting and diagnostic commands for SSL VPNs. The following sections focus on three troubleshooting scenarios related to SSL VPN.

Troubleshooting SSL Negotiations

If you have a user who is not able to connect to the security appliance using SSL, you can follow these steps to isolate the SSL negotiation issues:

- Verify that the user's computer can ping the security appliance's outside IP address.

- If the user's workstation can ping the address, issue the **show running | include ssl** command and verify that SSL encryption is configured.

- If SSL encryption is properly configured, use an external sniffer to verify whether the TCP three-way handshake is successful.

Troubleshooting AnyConnect Client Issues

The following sections provide guidelines on troubleshooting the commonly seen AnyConnect VPN Client issues and cover troubleshooting two issues.

Initial Connectivity Issues

If you are using AnyConnect VPN Client in your environment and a user is having initial connectivity issues, enable **debug webvpn svc** on the security appliance and analyze the debug messages. Most of the configuration-specific issues can be easily fixed by looking at the error messages. For example, if your security appliance is not configured to assign an IP address, you will receive a No Assigned Address error message in the debugs. This is highlighted in Example 5-14.

Example 5-14 **debug webvpn svc** *Command*

```
Chicago# debug webvpn svc
CSTP state = HEADER_PROCESSING
http_parse_cstp_method()
...input: 'CONNECT /CSCOSSLC/tunnel HTTP/1.1'
webvpn_cstp_parse_request_field()
...input: 'Host: 209.165.200.225'
<snip>
Processing CSTP header line: 'X-DTLS-CipherSuite: AES256-SHA:AES128-SHA:DES-CBC3-
  SHA:DES-CBC-SHA'
Validating address: 0.0.0.0
CSTP state = WAIT_FOR_ADDRESS
webvpn_cstp_accept_address: 0.0.0.0/0.0.0.0
webvpn_cstp_accept_address: no address?!?
CSTP state = HAVE_ADDRESS
No assigned address
webvpn_cstp_send_error: 503 Service Unavailable
CSTP state = ERROR
```

Optionally, you can enable an SVC-specific syslog on the security appliance and look at the messages. For example, if the security appliance does not assign an IP address to an AnyConnect client, you should see the No Address Available for SVC Connection message, as shown in Example 5-15.

Example 5-15 *SVC Logging*

```
Chicago(config)# logging on
Chicago(config)# logging class svc buffered debugging
Chicago(config)# exit
Chicago# show logging
%ASA-3-722020: TunnelGroup <SSLVPNTunnel> GroupPolicy <SSLVPNGroup> User
  <sslvpnuser> IP <209.165.200.230> No address available for SVC connection
```

Additionally, you can look at the AnyConnect VPN Client logs in Windows Event Viewer. Choose **Start > Administrative Tools > Event Viewer > Cisco AnyConnect VPN Client** and review the logs. If an address is not being assigned, you should see an error message.

Traffic-Specific Issues

If you are able to connect but fail to successfully send traffic over the SSL VPN tunnel, look at the traffic statistics on the client to verify that traffic is being received and transmitted by the client. As illustrated in Figure 5-67, the client has encrypted 1146682 bytes and decrypted 1296849 bytes. Therefore, as far as the client is concerned, it is transmitting and receiving traffic.

Next, check the security appliance for received and transmitted traffic, as shown in Figure 5-68. If the security appliance applies a filter, the filter name is shown and you can look at the ACL entries to check whether your traffic is being dropped.

Figure 5-68 *Monitoring SSL VPN Traffic Statistics on AnyConnect VPN Client*

Troubleshooting Clientless Issues

The following sections provide guidelines on troubleshooting the commonly seen clientless issues and cover troubleshooting of three issues.

Issues with Websites

If you use clientless SSL VPN to provide connectivity to remote users and a user is having issues connecting to the websites through bookmarks, follow these steps to isolate the problem:

- Check whether the user is having connectivity issues with all configured websites. If so, check whether other applications, such as CIFS, port forwarding, or smart tunnels, are working well.

- If connectivity issues are limited to one web server, check whether one user or all users are having issues connecting to that website.

- Verify whether using smart tunnels for the configured website bookmark fixes the issue.

- If the issue is still not fixed, disable additional features such as CSD and DAP to see whether that fixes the issue.

- You can also try a different browser to isolate a browser-specific issue.

- As a last option, test connectivity to the server by using AnyConnect VPN Client to rule out other issues.

Issues with CIFS

You can provide CIFS services to the clientless users so that they can access their shared resources on the Windows file servers. If the clientless SSL VPN users have issues with multiple logons when they try to access the servers, you can configure a single sign-on and see whether that resolves the issue.

If users have issues connecting to the servers or have issues access their shared folders or files, you can try to access them by entering the server name and share through the bar inside the web portal page. This helps in isolating issues with CIFS bookmarks.

In some cases, clientless SSL VPN users can receive a Failed to Retrieve Domains error message when they select Browse Entire Networks with the web portal page. You can resolve this issue by adding the WINS (NBNS) server under the correct tunnel group.

At the time of this writing, an issue exists when users periodically get an Error Contacting Host error message when they try to access servers through CIFS bookmarks or click the Browse Entire Network option. The only work-around at this time is to reboot the security appliance. This issue is identified as CSCsl94183.

| NOTE | You can enable **debug ntdomain 255** and **debug webvpn cifs 255** to collect the appropriate information. A packet capture between the ASA and the CIFS server is also helpful. You can submit the debug output and capture to a Cisco TAC engineer for further analysis. |

Troubleshooting CSD

If you have deployed CSD in your environment, users can sometimes experience slow processing when CSD is being loaded. This could be the result of the following issues:

- **Number of registry keys and values reads:** The more registry reads you have, the more time CSD needs to read and process entries.

- **Version of Java running:** Some versions of Java can process many more registry reads than some older versions.

You can help by clearing the SSL state on the Internet browser and by turning off the certificate revocation check. You can also use the latest version of CSD.

Troubleshooting DAP

The best way to troubleshoot DAP-related issues is to enable **debug dap trace**. For example, you can identify who is connecting to the security appliance, what tunnel group is being selected, what CSD prelogin location is chosen, what hotfixes the host is running, and what DAP record is being applied for that connection. As shown in Example 5-16, the username is sslvpnuser and the session is using the SecureMeClientlessTunnel tunnel group. The CSD prelogin location is determined as InternetCafe, and the security appliance assigns the Contractors-DAP policy for this user session.

Example 5-16   **debug dap trace** *Command*

```
Chicago# debug dap trace
DAP_TRACE: DAP_open: D44B80A8
DAP_TRACE: DAP_add_CSD: csd_token = [3463312075D26823695DDD52]
DAP_TRACE: Username: sslvpnuser, aaa.cisco.username = sslvpnuser
DAP_TRACE: Username: sslvpnuser, aaa.cisco.tunnelgroup = SecureMeClientlessTunnel
DAP_TRACE: dap_add_to_lua_tree:aaa["cisco"]["username"] = "sslvpnuser";
DAP_TRACE: dap_add_to_lua_tree:aaa["cisco"]["tunnelgroup"] =
  "SecureMeClientlessTunnel";
DAP_TRACE: dap_add_to_lua_tree:endpoint["application"]["clienttype"] =
  "Clientless";
DAP_TRACE: Username: sslvpnuser, dap_add_csd_data_to_lua:
endpoint.os.version = "Windows XP";
endpoint.os.servicepack = "2";
endpoint.policy.location = "InternetCafe";
endpoint.protection = "secure desktop";
endpoint.device.hostname = "home-pc";
endpoint.os.windows.hotfix["KB873339"] = "true";
endpoint.os.windows.hotfix["KB884016"] = "true";
<snip>
endpoint.fw["MSWindowsFW"].description = "Microsoft Windows Firewall";
endpoint.fw["MSWindowsFW"].version = "XP SP2+";
endpoint.fw["MSWindowsFW"].enabled = "failed";
endpoint.enforce = "success";
DAP_TRACE: Username: sslvpnuser, Selected DAPs: ,Contractors-DAP
DAP_TRACE: dap_request: memory usage = 40%
```

continues

Example 5-16 **debug dap trace** *Command (Continued)*

```
DAP_TRACE: dap_process_selected_daps: selected 1 records
DAP_TRACE: Username: sslvpnuser, dap_aggregate_attr: rec_count = 1
DAP_TRACE: Username: sslvpnuser, dap_comma_str_fcn: [Contractors-List] 16 128
DAP_TRACE: Username: sslvpnuser, DAP_close: D44B80A8
```

Summary

This chapter provided details about the SSL VPN functionality in Cisco ASA. Using the robust features available in Cisco ASA SSL VPN remote access, security administrators can deploy Cisco ASA in almost any network topology. This chapter discussed clientless and full tunnel SSL VPN client implementations. The chapter also focused on Cisco Secure Desktop (CSD) and offered guidance in setting up CSD features. The chapter discussed the Host Scan feature that is used to collect posture information about end workstations. The DAP feature, its usage, and detailed configuration examples were also provided. To reinforce learning, many different deployment scenarios were presented, along with their configurations. This chapter covered extensive **show** and **debug** commands to assist in troubleshooting complicated SSL VPN deployments.

This chapter covers the following topics:

- SSL VPN design considerations
- IOS SSL VPN prerequisites
- IOS SSL VPN configuration guide
- Advanced SSL VPN features
- Cisco Secure Desktop
- Deployment scenarios
- Monitoring SSL VPNs on Cisco IOS

CHAPTER 6

SSL VPNs on Cisco IOS Routers

As mentioned in Chapter 1, "Introduction to Remote Access VPN Technologies," SSL VPNs complement the existing IPsec remote access VPN deployments. In SSL VPNs, the encryption and decryption of packets are performed at the application layer, usually by a browser. Therefore, there is no need to install a software application on the remote access client computers. Because most of the corporate traffic is either e-mail or web processing, the SSL VPN implementation in the Cisco IOS routers fully supports tunneling these services. Using the clientless mode to secure network services, security engineers can take advantage of the inherent capabilities of web browsers. If remote users need full corporate network connectivity, an SSL VPN client application can be installed on the workstations. Most users prefer this option because the VPN client is automatically pushed and installed to the remote workstation after a successful user authentication.

In the current software release, Cisco IOS routers support all three flavors of SSL VPN, which include clientless, thin client, and full tunnel modes.

NOTE   Cisco Systems has been marketing these three modes since it started offering SSL VPN services in its products. However, Cisco is currently marketing two distinct types: clientless connections that include clientless and thin client modes, and SSL VPN connections that include full tunnel mode.

SSL VPN Design Considerations

Before you implement the SSL VPN services in Cisco IOS routers, you have to analyze your current environment and determine which features and modes might be useful in your implementation. SSL VPN design considerations include the following:

- **User connectivity:** Before designing and implementing the SSL VPN solution for your corporate network, you need to determine whether your users connect to your corporate network from public shared computers, such as a computer in a library or a computer in an Internet kiosk. In this case, you have to use clientless SSL VPN mode because usually you are not allowed to install any other applications on public workstations.

- **Router feature:** A Cisco IOS router can run various features, such as IPsec VPN tunnels, routing engines, and firewall processes, to name a few. Enabling the SSL VPN feature can add considerable load if your existing IOS router is already running a number of features.

- **Router hardware:** The SSL VPN process is fairly CPU and memory intensive. Before implementing an SSL VPN on the I OS router, make sure that you leverage the hardware-accelerated SSL VPN engines such as AIM-VPN/SSL-1, AIM-VPN/SSL-2, and AIM-VPN/SSL-3.

  For more information about the SSL VPN hardware modules, refer to http://www.cisco.com/en/US/products/ps5853/products_data_ sheet0900aecd 804ff58a.html.

- **Infrastructure planning:** Because an SSL VPN provides network access to remote users, you have to consider the placement of the VPN termination devices. Before implementing the SSL VPN feature in IOS, ask the following questions:

  — Should the SSL VPN be placed behind a firewall? If so, what ports should be opened?

  — Should the decrypted traffic be passed through another set of firewalls? If so, what ports should be allowed?

  — Do you use the firewall and other security features in the IOS SSL VPN gateways? If so, what traffic needs to be allowed through the routers?

  — Do the inside routers need to redistribute the pool of IP addresses for SSL VPN clients in a routing protocol so that other routers know about the subnet?

- **Implementation scope:** The network security administrators need to determine the size of the SSL VPN deployment, especially the number of simultaneous users that will connect to gain network access. If one IOS router is not enough to support the required number of users, traditional load balancers or server-clustering schemes must be considered to accommodate all potential remote users.

The SSL VPN is supported on a number of Cisco IOS routers. Table 6-1 lists the Cisco IOS routers and the supported number of simultaneous SSL VPN users on each platform.

Table 6-1 *Supported IOS Routers and Concurrent SSL VPN Users*

Supported Routers	Number of Concurrent Users
870	2
1811	10
1841, 2801	25
2811, 2821	50
2851, 3725, 3745	75
3825, 3845	100
7200, 7301	150

As mentioned in Chapter 4, "Cisco SSL VPN Family of Products," the SSL VPN capability in the Cisco IOS routers is not bundled free of charge in the base system price. If you want to enable SSL VPN on a router, you must purchase appropriate licenses. Before implementing SSL VPN in an IOS router, or in a cluster of IOS routers, determine the size of the SSL VPN deployment, especially the number of concurrent users of this service. Cisco Systems provides a two-user complimentary license on the supported routers. You do not have to purchase licenses if you want to test SSL VPN features in a lab environment, where the user count is not going to exceed two. If you plan to deploy SSL VPN in IOS routers, consult Table 6-2 for the available licenses and their respective part numbers.

Table 6-2   *Available Licenses for Cisco IOS Routers*

SSL VPN User Requirement	License Part Number
10 Users	FL-WEBVPN-10-K9=
25 Users	FL-WEBVPN-25-K9=
100 Users	FL-WEBVPN-100-K9=

NOTE   The required minimum code version to run an SSL VPN is Cisco IOS Release 12.4(6)T. You should use Release 12.4(15)T or later to benefit from the SSL VPN features discussed in this chapter. Some features that are discussed in this chapter might not be available in the earlier versions of code.

At the time of this writing, the latest version of IOS code is 12.4(15)T3.

IOS SSL VPN Prerequisites

You must meet the following prerequisites before you can start implementing SSL VPN in your enterprise:

- **Compatible browser:** You have to use an SSL-enabled browser such as Internet Explorer, Firefox, Mozilla, or Safari.

- **User account:** Before SSL VPN tunnels are established, users must authenticate themselves to either the local database or to an external authentication server, such as RADIUS. If you are deploying an SSL VPN, make sure that you already have a user database and that you grant appropriate access to users.

- **Sun JRE:** Port-forwarding and full tunnel modes use Sun Microsystems' Java Runtime Environment (JRE).

- **ActiveX:** An SSL VPN uses ActiveX for Internet Explorer on Microsoft-based operating systems. ActiveX is used by AnyConnect VPN Client and Cisco Secure Desktop.

- **Web folder:** Microsoft hotfix 892211 must be installed on Windows operating systems to access web folders in the clientless SSL VPN mode.
- **Administrative privileges:** If you plan to use port forwarding, administrative privileges are required. However, administrative rights are needed only for AnyConnect VPN Client during the initial installation.

IOS SSL VPN Configuration Guide

After analyzing the deployment considerations and selecting SSL VPN as the remote access VPN solution, you must follow the configuration steps described in the subsequent sections. The configuration guide is divided into the following six configuration sections to match your deployment scenarios:

- Configuring pre-SSL VPN setup
- Initial SSL VPN configuration
- Configuring clientless SSL VPNs
- Configuring thin client SSL VPNs
- Configuring AnyConnect Client SSL VPNs
- Configuring advanced SSL VPN features

Configuring Pre-SSL VPN Setup

Before you set up the SSL VPN features, you need to complete the following configuration tasks on the IOS router:

- Setting up user authentication
- Enrolling digital certificates (recommended)
- Loading SDM (recommended)

Setting Up User Authentication

Cisco IOS routers support a variety of authentication servers, such as RADIUS, TACACS, and the local database. For small organizations, a local database can be set up for user authentication. For medium to large SSL VPN deployments, you should use an external RADIUS server as the user authentication database. If you are deploying the SSL VPN feature for a few users, you can use the local database, as shown in Example 6-1. Two accounts, sslvpnuser and adminuser, are configured for user authentication. The sslvpnuser account, with a password of user1234, is used for SSL VPN user authentication, while adminuser, with a password of admin123, is used to manage the router for administrative purposes.

Example 6-1 *Local User Accounts*

```
Chicago# configure terminal
Chicago(config)# username sslvpnuser secret password user1234
Chicago(config)# username adminuser secret password admin123
```

NOTE   You should encrypt user passwords in the configuration. You can use either the **secret** keyword, as shown in Example 6-1, or you can use the **service password-encryption** command to globally encrypt all passwords in the router's configuration.

After setting up the local user database, the next step is to configure the authentication, authorization, and accounting (AAA) commands. A Cisco IOS router can be set up for AAA by using the **aaa new-model** command, if it is not already configured to do so. This command enables the AAA process globally on a Cisco IOS device, as shown in Example 6-2. To enable local authentication for the SSL VPN process, use the **aaa authentication login sslvpn local** command. The **sslvpn** option is a list name that is mapped when you define the SSL VPN context, discussed later in this chapter.

Example 6-2 *AAA Configuration for Local User Database*

```
Chicago# configure terminal
Chicago(config)# aaa new-model
Chicago(config)# aaa authentication login sslvpn local
```

NOTE   If the **aaa new-model** command is not configured, you will not see any AAA commands in the Cisco IOS command syntax.

For medium to large SSL VPN deployments, the use of a RADIUS server is recommended. Use the **aaa authentication login sslvpn group radius** command to enable RADIUS processing by the AAA process. This command ensures that the Cisco IOS SSL VPN gateway requests the appropriate information from the end users and forwards them to the RADIUS server for authentication and verification. In Example 6-3, a Cisco IOS router is set up for the AAA process to use RADIUS for user authentication. The **group radius** option instructs the Cisco IOS router to send user authentication requests to a group of RADIUS servers, as defined in Example 6-4.

You can optionally enable an **aaa accounting network** if you want the Cisco IOS router to send an accounting record for each authentication request. In Example 6-3, the router is set up to send an accounting record to the RADIUS server after it authenticates a user session and to send another accounting record when it tears down that session.

Example 6-3   *AAA Configuration for RADIUS User Authentication*

```
Chicago# configure terminal
Chicago(config)# aaa new-model
Chicago(config)# aaa authentication login sslvpn group radius
Chicago(config)# aaa accounting network default start-stop group radius
```

After the IOS router is set up for the AAA process, the next step is to define a list of the RADIUS servers. The Cisco IOS SSL VPN gateway checks their availability on a round-robin basis. If the first server is not reachable, the gateway tries the second server, and so on. You should set up more than one RADIUS server, in case the first server is not reachable. A RADIUS server entry can be defined by using the **radius-server host** command followed by the IP address of the RADIUS server and a shared secret. The Cisco IOS router authenticates itself to the RADIUS server by using this shared secret. For security reasons, this shared secret is never sent over the network.

NOTE   The Cisco IOS router sends user passwords as encrypted messages to the RADIUS server. This is useful in protecting this critical information from an intruder. The router hashes the password using the shared secret that is defined on the IOS gateway and the RADIUS server.

You can optionally modify the AAA port numbers if your RADIUS server does not use the default ports. The Cisco IOS routers use User Datagram Protocol (UDP) ports 1645 and 1646 for authentication and accounting, respectively.

TIP   If all your RADIUS servers are configured to use the same shared secret, you can define a global key by using the **radius-server key** command followed by the actual shared secret.

As shown in Example 6-4, two RADIUS servers located at 192.168.1.20 and 192.168.1.21 are configured. Because both servers use the same shared secret, the administrator has defined a global key of cisco123. It is a best practice to encrypt the specified shared secret by using the **service password-encryption** command. If the Cisco IOS router can reach the RADIUS server through multiple interfaces, you should use the **ip radius source-interface** command to send and receive the RADIUS traffic from a particular interface. In this example, the loopback0 interface is configured as the source interface for the RADIUS packets.

Example 6-4   *Configuration of RADIUS Servers*

```
Chicago# configure terminal
Chicago(config)# service password-encryption
Chicago(config)# radius-server host 192.168.1.20
Chicago(config)# radius-server host 192.168.1.21
Chicago(config)# radius-server key cisco123
Chicago(config)# ip radius source-interface loopback0
```

TIP   It is a best practice to use a loopback interface to source packets to the RADIUS server. This is because a loopback interface is always up, and the source IP address in the RADIUS packets will be the same, regardless of the egress interface from the router.

Enrolling Digital Certificates (Recommended)

Enrollment is the process of obtaining a certificate from a certificate authority (CA). Before starting the enrollment process, you must generate the RSA key pair with the **crypto key generate rsa** command. To generate the keys, you must first configure a host name and domain name on a Cisco IOS router. Example 6-5 demonstrates how to configure a domain name of securemeinc.com and how to generate the RSA key pair of 1024 bits modulus size.

Example 6-5   *Generating the RSA Key Pair*

```
Chicago(config)# ip domain-name securemeinc.com
Chicago(config)# crypto key generate rsa modulus 1024

The name for the keys will be: Chicago.securemeinc.com

% The key modulus size is 1024 bits
% Generating 1024 bit RSA keys, keys will be non-exportable...[OK]
```

NOTE   The same RSA key pair can be used for Secure Shell (SSH) connections to the IOS router.

The enrollment process can be broken into the following three steps:

Step 1   Configuring a trustpoint

Step 2   Obtaining a CA certificate

Step 3   Obtaining an identity certificate

Step 1: Configuring a Trustpoint

The **crypto ca trustpoint** command enables you to configure all the necessary certificate parameters. Invoking this command puts you in ca-trustpoint configuration mode, as shown in Example 6-6.

Example 6-6   *Configuring a Trustpoint*

```
Chicago# configure terminal
Chicago(config)# crypto ca trustpoint SecureMeTrustpoint
Chicago(ca-trustpoint)#
```

You can use the manual or Simple Certificate Enrollment Protocol (SCEP) method to enroll an identify certificate on the router. If a CA server does not support SCEP, you can use the manual enrollment method, as shown in Example 6-7. The **enrollment terminal** subcommand is used to show the output of the certificate request on the terminal under **SecureMeTrustpoint** configuration.

Example 6-7   *Configuring the IOS Router for Manual Enrollment*

```
Chicago# configure terminal
Chicago(config)# crypto ca trustpoint SecureMeTrustpoint
Chicago(ca-trustpoint)# enrollment terminal
Chicago(ca-trustpoint)# end
```

NOTE   A Cisco IOS router also supports enrollment through SCEP. If you prefer to perform enrollment through SCEP, the **enrollment url** subcommand is used instead of the **enrollment terminal** subcommand.

Step 2: Obtaining a CA Certificate

After specifying the trustpoint, the next step is to obtain the CA certificate before requesting an identity certificate from the CA server. The administrator retrieves (copies and pastes) the certificate from the CA server. Use the **crypto ca authenticate** command to import the CA certificate. Example 6-8 demonstrates how to import the CA certificate into the Cisco IOS router manually.

Example 6-8   *Importing the CA Certificate Manually*

```
Chicago(config)# crypto ca authenticate SecureMeTrustpoint
Enter the base 64 encoded CA certificate.
End with a blank line or the word "quit" on a line by itself
-----BEGIN CERTIFICATE-----
MIIC0jCCAnygAwIBAgIQIls45kcfzKZJQnk0zyiQcTANBgkqhkiG9w0BAQUFADCB
hjEeMBwGCSqGSIb3DQEJARYPamF6aWJAY2lzY28uY29tMQswCQYDVQQGEwJVUzEL
MAkGA1UECBMCTkMxDDAKBgNVBAcTA1JUUDEWMBQGA1UEChMNQ2lzY28gU3lzdGVt
czEMMAoGA1UECxMDVEFDMRYwFAYDVQQDEw1KYXppYkNBBU2VydmVyMB4XDTA0MDYy
-----END CERTIFICATE-----
```

Example 6-8 *Importing the CA Certificate Manually (Continued)*

```
quit
INFO: Certificate has the following attributes:
Fingerprint:    82a0095e 2584ced6 b66ed6a8 e48a5ad1
Do you accept this certificate? [yes/no]: yes
Trustpoint CA certificate accepted.
% Certificate successfully imported
```

As shown in Example 6-8, the CA certificate is manually imported to the Cisco router through the cut-and-paste method. Enter a blank line or the word **quit** after pasting the Base64-encoded CA certificate to the Cisco router to exit the CA configuration screen. If the certificate is recognized, the Cisco router asks you whether you would like to accept the certificate; enter **yes**. The Certificate Successfully Imported message is displayed if the CA certificate import is successful.

Step 3: Obtaining an Identity Certificate

After the CA certificate is obtained from the CA server, use the **crypto ca enroll** command followed by the trustpoint name to generate an identity certificate request that is sent to the server. Example 6-9 demonstrates how to generate the certificate request.

Example 6-9 *Generating the ID Certificate Request*

```
Chicago(config)# crypto ca enroll SecureMeTrustpoint
% Start certificate enrollment ..
% The fully-qualified domain name in the certificate will be:
  Chicago.secureinc.com
% Include the router serial number in the subject name? [yes/no]: no
Display Certificate Request to terminal? [yes/no]: yes
Certificate Request follows:
MIIBpDCCAQ0CAQAwLTErMA4GA1UEBRMHNDZmZjUxODAZBgkqhkiG9w0BCQIWDE5Z
LmNpc2NvLmNvbTCBnzANBgkqhkiG9w0BAQEFAAOBjQAwgYkCgYEA1n+8nczm8ut1
AQQFAAOBgQDGcYSC8VGy+ekUNkDayW1g+TQL4lYldLmT9xXUADAQqmGhyA8A36d0
VtZlNc2pXHaMPKkqxMEPMcJVdZ+o6JpiIFHPpYNiQGFUQZoHGcZveEbMVor93/KM
IChEgs4x98fCuJoiQ2RQr452bsWNyEmeLcDqczMSUXFucSLMm0XDNg==
---End - This line not part of the certificate request---
Redisplay enrollment request? [yes/no]: no
Chicago(config)#
```

NOTE   This request is for a PKCS 10 certificate request.

After a request is generated, copy and paste it to your CA server. If you manage the CA server, you can approve and issue the request as a web server certificate.

TIP	Make sure not to copy and paste the second highlighted line in Example 6-9. The certificate request will be malformed if that line is included.

NOTE	Obtain a Base64-encoded certificate from your CA server. You will not be able to copy and paste a Distinguished Encoding Rules (DER) encoded certificate.

The Cisco IOS router gives you the option to redisplay the certificate request if needed (as shown in Example 6-9).

After the CA server administrator approves the identity certificate, use the **crypto ca import** command to import the Base64-encoded ID certificate. Example 6-10 demonstrates how to import the ID certificate.

Example 6-10 *Manually Importing the ID Certificate*

```
Chicago(config)# crypto ca import SecureMeTrustpoint certificate
% The fully-qualified domain name in the certificate will be:
  Chicago.securemeinc.com
Enter the base 64 encoded certificate.
End with a blank line or the word "quit" on a line by itself
-----BEGIN CERTIFICATE-----
MIIECDCCA7KgAwIBAgIKHJGvRQAAAAAADTANBgkqhkiG9w0BAQUFADCBhjEeMBwG
CSqGSIb3DQEJARYPamF6aWJAY2lzY28uY29tMQswCQYDVQQGEwJVUzELMAkGA1UE
CBMCTkMxDDAKBgNVBAcTA1JUUDEWMBQGA1UEChMNQ2lzY28gU3lzdGVtczEMMAoG
A1UECxMDVEFDMRYwFAYDVQQDEw1KYXppYkNBU2VydmVyMB4XDTA0MDkwMjAyNTgw
NVoXDTA1MDkwMjAzMDgwNVowLzEQMA4GA1UEBRMHNDZmZjUxODEbMBkGCSqGSIb3
SGzFQHtnqURciJBtay9RNnMpZmZYpfOHzmeFmQ==
-----END CERTIFICATE-----
quit
INFO: Router Certificate successfully imported
Chicago(config)#
```

The Base64-encoded ID certificate is successfully imported to the Cisco IOS router.

Loading SDM (Recommended)

Cisco Security Device Manager (SDM) provides an easy-to-navigate and simple graphical user interface (GUI) to set up and manage different features that a Cisco IOS router provides. It is bundled with a variety of administration, configuration, and monitoring tools to check the health of the device and the traffic traversing through it. Although setting up SDM is optional, you should use SDM in configuring the SSL VPN functionality in Cisco IOS routers.

NOTE   SSL VPN is a relatively new feature in Cisco IOS routers. Older versions of SDM might not be able to manage this functionality. Make sure that you are running at least version 2.4 of SDM. For more information about SDM, consult http://www.cisco.com/go/sdm.

At the time of this writing, the latest SDM version is 2.5.

If you are not sure whether SDM is loaded in your router, simply issue the **show flash** command and look for sdm.tar. Additional .tar files are used by SDM, as shown in Example 6-11.

Example 6-11 *Output of the* **show flash** *Command*

```
Chicago# show flash
28672K bytes of processor board System flash (Intel Strataflash)
Directory of flash:/
    2  -rwx    16391232  Mar 16 2008 13:54:28 -05:00  c870-advsecurityk9-mz.124-
       15.T4.bin
    3  -rwx        1038  Mar 16 2008 14:09:52 -05:00  home.shtml
    4  -rwx        3179  Mar 16 2008 14:09:55 -05:00  sdmconfig-8xx.cfg
    5  -rwx      112640  Mar 16 2008 14:10:00 -05:00  home.tar
    6  -rwx     1505280  Mar 16 2008 14:11:31 -05:00  common.tar
    7  -rwx     6389760  Mar 16 2008 14:33:37 -05:00  sdm.tar
    9  -rwx        4114  Mar 16 2008 22:10:02 -05:00  SDM_Backup
   18  -rwx        8881  Mar 16 2008 23:19:04 -05:00  test.xml
   10  -rwx         660  Jun 19 2006 14:05:34 -05:00  vlan.dat
   12  drwx         256  Mar 17 2008 00:38:57 -05:00  webvpn
   16  -rwx        2516  Mar 16 2008 23:33:15 -05:00  secureme.PNG
```

NOTE   The new Cisco Integrated Services Routers (ISR) are preloaded with SDM. You might have to update the SDM version if you are running an older version.

You can launch SDM by establishing either an HTTP or HTTPS connection to the router. The router acts as a web server to process the requests from the clients. You can enable the web server on the router by using the **ip http server** and **ip http secure-server** commands. The **ip http server** command is necessary if you prefer to access SDM using HTTP. However, it is best practice to access SDM with secure HTTP by enabling **ip http secure-server**.

By default, a Cisco IOS router allows incoming requests from any IP address. It is best security practice to allow only those IP addresses or networks that manage the router in the access control list (ACL). You can then map the ACL to the HTTP server process by using the **ip http access-class** command followed by the ACL number. In Example 6-12, the

administrator is enabling the HTTP engine and is setting up the router to trust the
192.168.1.0/24 network.

Example 6-12 *Enabling the HTTP Server*

```
Chicago(config)# access-list 10 permit 192.168.1.0 0.0.0.255
Chicago(config)# ip http server
Chicago(config)# ip http access-class 10
Chicago(config)# ip http secure-server
```

NOTE   You can use SDM and SSL VPN on the same interface. However, in that scenario, SDM
uses a default port of 4443 for management. For example, if you want to manage your IOS
router through SDM, use https://<*router-ip-address*>:4443. The SDM GUI can be
accessed from any workstation whose IP address is in the trusted network. Before you
establish a secure connection to the router, verify that IP connectivity exists between the
workstation and the Cisco IOS router on port 80 and/or port 4443.

To establish an SSL connection from SDM, launch a browser and point the URL to the IP
address of the router. The router presents a certificate to the workstation. If the issuer is not
in the trusted root database, the browser might prompt the user to accept the certificate. If
the certificate is accepted, the router prompts the user to present authentication credentials.
If it is a new setup for the router, the default username is cisco and the default password is
also cisco.

NOTE   SDM requires Java plug-in 1.4(2), 1.5.0, and 1.6.*x* installed on the web browser.

Figure 6-1 illustrates an SSL connection to a router located at 192.168.1.1. Specify the
username and password to log in to SDM.

Figure 6-1 *Launching SDM*

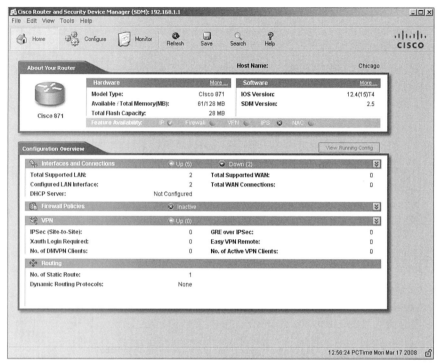

Initial SSL VPN Configuration

The configuration of SSL VPN can be accomplished in five steps. Figure 6-2 is used throughout this section to demonstrate how to set up Cisco IOS router. As shown in this figure, the IOS router is set up to accept the SSL VPN connections from the hosts on the Internet. There are several servers on the private network of the router. Table 6-3 describes the servers used in this setup.

Figure 6-2 *SSL VPN Network Topology*

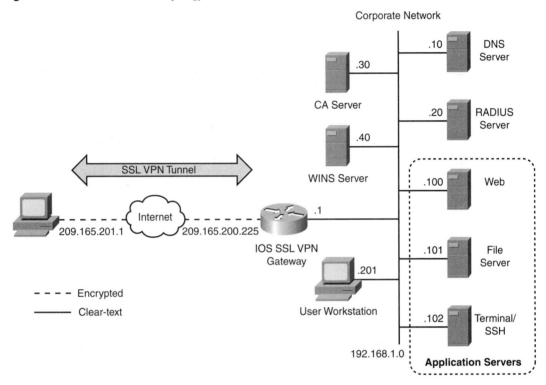

Table 6-3 *Description and Location of Servers*

Server	Location	Purpose
CA server	192.168.1.30	Issues CA and ID certificates
WINS server	192.168.1.40	Resolves NetBIOS names with IP addresses
DNS server	192.168.1.10	Resolves host names with IP addresses
RADIUS server	192.168.1.20	Authenticates users
Web server	192.168.1.100	Hosts internal websites
File server	192.168.1.101	Hosts Windows shares and files for SSL VPN users
Terminal/ SSH server	192.168.1.102	Provides terminal and SSH services to SSL VPN users
Management station	192.168.1.201	Hosts the SDM client to provide management connectivity to the IOS router

The configuration of the SSL VPN can be accomplished in four steps. These steps are described in the following sections.

Step 1: Setting Up an SSL VPN Gateway

In SSL VPNs, the Cisco IOS router acts as a proxy between the SSL-enabled VPN client and the resources on the private network. Before an SSL VPN tunnel can be established, you need to allocate a public IP address or host name to terminate the VPN sessions. The VPN users point their browser to this configured IP address or host name and start the SSL negotiation process. An IOS SSL VPN gateway can be configured by issuing the **webvpn gateway** command followed by a gateway name. This gateway only has local significance, and it is used to map the gateway configuration to the SSL VPN context, discussed in the next step.

Using SDM, the SSL VPN gateway can be defined by choosing **Configuration** > **VPN** > **SSL VPN** > **SSL VPN Gateways** > **Add**. You can define the following six parameters:

- **Gateway name:** This is used to define a service instance that is mapped to the SSL VPN context to terminate user sessions. You can use any name you like to make this gateway connection meaningful.

- **IP address:** This is used to terminate the SSL VPN connections to a Cisco IOS router. This can be either a unique public IP address or an existing IP address from one of the interfaces. In a small deployment, you can certainly use the IP address of the Internet-facing interface. However, for medium to large SSL VPN deployment, you should use a dedicated IP address for VPN termination.

- **Port:** This is used to proxy traffic. By default, the port number is TCP 443. However, if you want your SSL VPN to terminate on a different port, you can specify a port between 1024 and 65535.

- **Host name:** This is an optional parameter generally used in the scenarios where load balancers are deployed to share loads among multiple SSL VPN devices. The host name defined here is mapped to the virtual IP address of the load balancer.

- **Trustpoint:** This provides a drop-down menu where you can select an existing certificate. This certificate must be SSL enabled because it is used to negotiate an encrypted session with the client browser.

- **HTTP port:** This is used if the redirected HTTP Traffic check box is selected. By default, if SSL VPN users access the IOS router on TCP port 80, their sessions are automatically redirected to secure HTTP (TCP port 443). It is useful for not-so-technology-savvy users who usually specify HTTP as the protocol in their browser URL rather than using HTTPS as the protocol. If this option is configured, their HTTP sessions are automatically redirected as HTTPS.

The SSL VPN gateway definition is not active until the **Enable Gateway** check box is selected. After it is enabled, SDM pushes the **inservice** command to the Cisco IOS router to active this gateway.

NOTE	You cannot enable an SSL VPN gateway until you configure an IP address for terminating user sessions.

As shown in Figure 6-3, the gateway name is SecureMeGW and the IP address for SSL VPN termination is 209.165.200.225. The router is configured using the default SSL port (TCP 443) and is set up to use SecureMeTrustpoint for the SSL certificate. All traffic destined to port 80 will be redirected to the SSL VPN port. The **Enable Gateway** check box is selected to activate this gateway.

Figure 6-3 *SSL VPN Gateway Configuration in SDM*

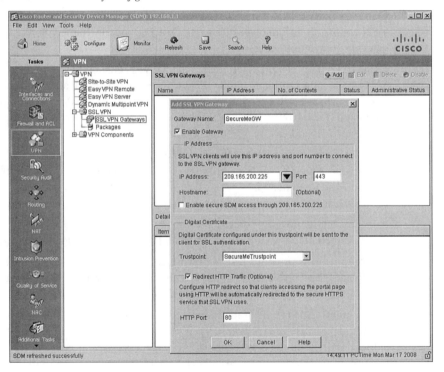

Example 6-13 shows the relevant configuration that SDM pushes to the IOS router when the SSL VPN gateway is defined.

Example 6-13   *Setting Up an SSL VPN Gateway*

```
Chicago(config)# webvpn gateway SecureMeGW
Chicago(config-webvpn-gateway)# ip address 209.165.200.225 port 443
Chicago(config-webvpn-gateway)# http-redirect port 80
Chicago(config-webvpn-gateway)# ssl trustpoint SecureMeTrustpoint
Chicago(config-webvpn-gateway)# inservice
Chicago(config-webvpn)# end
```

Step 2: Setting Up an SSL VPN Context

After setting up the SSL VPN gateway, you must define an SSL VPN context. The actual user sessions are established to the SSL VPN context using the IP address definition of the SSL VPN gateway. Additionally, you can apply all the policies to limit a user or a group of users. An authentication server that is mapped to the context performs the actual user authentication here. After a user is authenticated, any configured policies are applied to the user's session. Step 4 discusses user and group policies in detail.

Using SDM, the SSL VPN context can be defined by choosing **Configure > VPN > SSL VPN > Edit SSL VPN > Add**. You can define the following parameters:

- **Name:** This is used to define an instance that is mapped to the SSL VPN context to terminate user sessions.

- **Associated gateway:** This maps the previously defined SSL VPN gateway to this context. SDM even allows you to create an SSL VPN gateway if you missed the earlier step.

- **Domain:** This identifies a domain in case multiple contexts share the same SSL VPN gateway address. For example, if you have one public IP address to be used by many different contexts, you can segregate each context connection by using a different domain name. Having a meaningful name for domains makes them easier to manage. Do not confuse the domain name mentioned here with the fully qualified domain name (FQDN).

- **Authentication list:** This is used to specify the authentication method used for this context. Before you can map a AAA authentication list in a context, you need to define it first. Consult the section "Setting Up User Authentication," earlier in this chapter, for details.

- **Authentication domain:** This is used to append a domain name to the username before user credentials are sent to the authentication server. This feature is useful if two different organizations or departments use the same authentication server and you want to distinguish usernames based on a domain name. The domain name you define here must match the domain name on the authentication server. Typically, this feature is not used unless you are sharing an authentication server among many enterprises or domains.

- **Maximum number of users:** This is used to limit the number of users that can use the SSL VPN services. It is useful if you are load-balancing SSL VPN connections across a number of devices and do not want to overburden a specific IOS router with the number of SSL VPN sessions. If you do not specify this limit, the router restricts the number of maximum users to 1000.

- **VRF name:** This is used to map a context to an internal virtual routing and forwarding (VRF) instance. This feature is generally used by service providers that want to provide SSL VPN services to their end customers and prefer to segregate data traffic from one customer to another.

- **Default group policy (optional):** This is used to apply a policy group as the default policy to a context. A policy group defines the permissions that are applied to a group of users. It also defines the presentation of the portal that users get after successfully logging in. You have to create a policy group first, before you can apply it as a default group policy here. The policy group is covered in the next configuration step.

The SSL VPN context definition is not active until the **Enable Context** check box is selected. After it is enabled, SDM pushes the **inservice** command to the Cisco IOS router to activate this gateway. As shown in Figure 6-4, the context name is SecureMeContext, and it is associated with the SecureMeGW gateway. The domain name is securemeinc. The authentication list name is sslvpn, and the maximum number of users is set to 100. The **Enable Context** check box is selected to activate this gateway.

Figure 6-4 *SSL VPN Context Configuration in SDM*

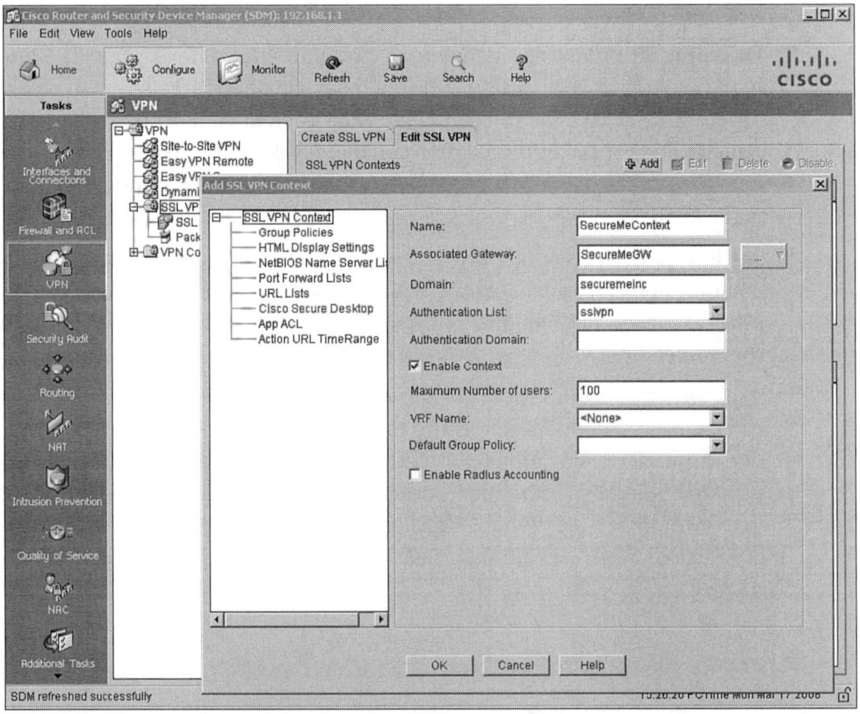

Example 6-14 shows the relevant configuration that SDM pushes to the IOS router when the SSL VPN gateway is defined.

Example 6-14 *Setting Up an SSL VPN Gateway*

```
Chicago(config)# webvpn context SecureMeContext
Chicago(config-webvpn-context)# aaa authentication list sslvpn
Chicago(config-webvpn-context)# gateway SecureMeGW domain securemeinc
Chicago(config-webvpn-context)# inservice
Chicago(config-webvpn-context)# max-users 100
Chicago(config-webvpn-context)# end
Chicago#
```

Step 3: Configuring SSL VPN Look and Feel

Figure 6-5 shows the default SSL VPN page when a connection is made to the IOS router from a web browser. The title of the page is SSLVPN Service, and the Cisco Systems logo is displayed in the upper-left corner of the web page. The initial page prompts the user for user authentication credentials. The default login message is Welcome to Cisco Systems SSLVPN Service. You can customize the initial SSL VPN login page based on the security policies of your organization. Cisco IOS routers also allow you to customize the user web portal based on configured group policy.

Figure 6-5 *Default SSL VPN Page*

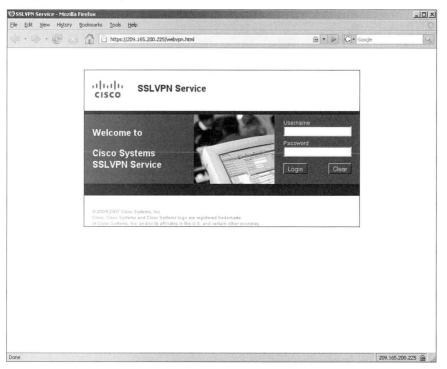

Customizing Login Page

Figure 6-6 shows the customized login page for SecureMe. The title of the login page has been changed to SecureMe SSL VPN Service, and the login message has been changed to Welcome to SecureMe Inc. Network. The primary and secondary title colors are changed to #808080 (dark gray) and #c0c0c0 (light gray), respectively. Additionally, the primary and secondary title text colors are set to white and black, respectively. The logo is replaced with the SecureMe image.

NOTE　　The SSL VPN portal customization functionality in the Cisco ASA offers many more options and features than the portal customization functionality in the Cisco IOS router.

Figure 6-6　*Customized SSL VPN Page*

These changes are configured by choosing **Configure > VPN > SSL VPN > Edit SSL VPN > Edit > HTML Display Settings**, as shown in Figure 6-7.

Figure 6-7   *SDM Configuration Page*

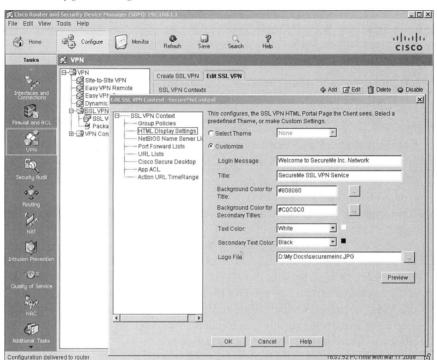

If you prefer not to customize the initial login page, SDM offers a number of preconfigured themes that you can select from the drop-down menu.

Example 6-15 shows the corresponding Cisco IOS router configuration for customization.

Example 6-15   *Customizing the SSL VPN Login Page*

```
Chicago(config)# webvpn context SecureMeContext
Chicago(config-webvpn-context)# login-message "Welcome to SecureMe Inc. Network"
Chicago(config-webvpn-context)# title "SecureMe SSL VPN Service"
Chicago(config-webvpn-context)# secondary-color #C0C0C0
Chicago(config-webvpn-context)# title-color #808080
Chicago(config-webvpn-context)# logo file securemeinc.JPG
Chicago(config-webvpn-context)# text-color white
Chicago(config-webvpn-context)# secondary-text-color black
Chicago(config-webvpn-context)# exit
```

NOTE   You can upload a customized logo file in flash. The accepted formats are JPEG, GIF, and PNG.

Although the current version of SDM does not allow you to configure a login photo, the Cisco IOS CLI does. If you prefer to change the login photo from the default to a customized one, the command is **login-photo** under the SSL VPN context configuration, as shown in Example 6-16.

Example 6-16 *Configuring a Login Photo*

```
Chicago(config)# webvpn context SecureMeContext
Chicago(config-webvpn-context)#login-photo Secureme.png
```

Customizing a Web Portal Page

After users are authenticated, the Cisco IOS router presents them with the web portal page. The contents of the web portal page can be defined by the SSL VPN administrator. However, users are allowed to save their personal bookmarks, or links, on the portal page. The content of their bookmarks are saved locally on the router's flash under flash:/webvpn/ *<context_name>*/*<user_name>*.xml. For example, if a user, called sslvpnuser, connects to SecureMeContext context and creates personal bookmarks, the router stores his bookmark information at flash:/webvpn/SecureMeContext/sslvpnuser.xml. After a user has been authenticated, the IOS router looks up the XML file based on the username and the SSL VPN context name that was used for his authentication. The bookmarks that are defined in the XML file are shown to the user under personal bookmarks. If the user adds, deletes, or modifies the contents, the file is automatically updated on the router's flash. Figure 6-8 illustrates a customized web portal for a user.

Figure 6-8 *SSL VPN User Web Portal Customization*

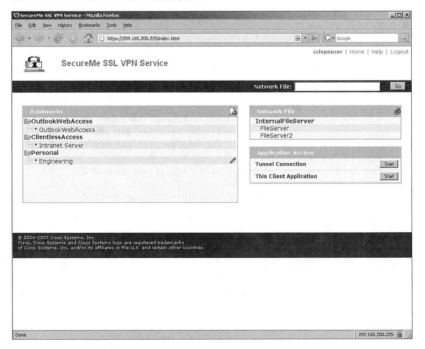

Step 4: Configuring SSL VPN Group Policies

A group policy is a set of common parameters that an SSL VPN user inherits during tunnel negotiations. You can define multiple group policies in a context; however, only one group policy can be designated as the default policy, and only one group policy can be applied to a user. If you need to satisfy requirements for different sets of users, you can define multiple group policies to meet those requirements. You can leverage a RADIUS server to pass the group policy when the user authentication is successful. This is achieved by mapping the webvpn:user-vpn-group vendor-specific attribute to the user definition in the RADIUS server. If the IOS router does not receive this attribute, it applies the default group policy parameters to user sessions.

As mentioned earlier, only one group policy can be designated as the default group policy. The designation is achieved by using the **default-group-policy** command followed by the group policy name. The default group policy is applied to the users if

- Only one group policy is defined in a context, and consequently that policy must be set as the default group policy.

- Multiple group policies are defined in a context, and a policy is not pushed through the RADIUS server. In this case, the default group policy is applied for those users who do not receive a designated policy.

A group policy can be defined by choosing **Configure > VPN > SSL VPN > Edit SSL VPN > Edit > Group Policies > Add**. A new window opens, as shown in Figure 6-9. On the General tab, specify the policy name and indicate whether it is designated as the default group policy. In Figure 6-9, the policy name is SecureMeDefaultPolicy, and it is set as the default group policy for this context.

Figure 6-9 *Defining the Default Group Policy in SDM*

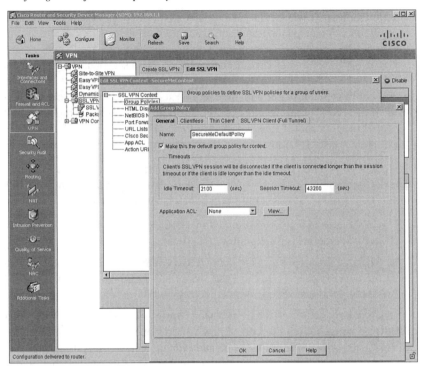

Example 6-17 shows the corresponding Cisco IOS router configuration for customization.

Example 6-17 *Customizing the SSL VPN Login Page*

```
Chicago(config)# webvpn context SecureMeContext
Chicago(config-webvpn-context)# policy group SecureMeDefaultPolicy
Chicago(config-webvpn-policy)# exit
Chicago(config-webvpn-context)# default-group-policy SecureMeDefaultPolicy
```

Table 6-4 lists all the SSL VPN attributes that can be mapped to a group policy.

Table 6-4 *Configurable SSL VPN Group Policy Attributes*

Attribute	Purpose
acl	Applies a WebVPN ACL for traffic filtering.
banner	Creates a banner that is displayed to user connections.
cifs-url-list	Applies the CIFS list to a policy.
citrix	Configures Citrix parameters.
filter	Filters HTML content, such as Java and images, from the SSL VPN sessions.

Table 6-4   *Configurable SSL VPN Group Policy Attributes (Continued)*

Attribute	Purpose
functions	Enables NetBIOS and SVC features.
	NetBIOS features include file access, file browsing, and file entry.
	SVC features includes tunnel mode support—enabled or required.
hide-url-bar	Hides the URL bar from the web portal. Users are limited to accessing the servers listed on the portal.
mask-urls	Maps the port-forwarding list to the group.
nbns-list	Configures the name to be shown on the SSL VPN page for the port-forwarding applet.
port-forward	Maps the port-forwarding list to the group.
sso-server	Defines the single sign-on server to a group.
svc	SSL VPN Client (SVC) configuration parameters.
timeout	Timeout values for SSL VPN sessions. You can configure idle and session timeout values in seconds. The default values are 2100 and 43200 seconds, respectively.
url-list	Maps the URL-mangling list to the group.

These attributes are discussed throughout this chapter.

Advanced SSL VPN Features

Cisco IOS routers provide many advanced SSL VPN features to suit your VPN implementations:

- Clientless SSL VPNs
- Thin client SSL VPNs
- AnyConnect SSL VPNs
- E-mail proxy
- Windows file sharing

The sections that follow cover these features in more detail.

Configuring Clientless SSL VPNs

As mentioned in Chapter 3, "SSL VPN Design Considerations," Chapter 4, "Cisco SSL VPN Family of Products," and Chapter 5, "SSL VPNs on Cisco ASA," remote users can use SSL VPNs to browse their internal websites and Outlook Web Access. A Cisco IOS router terminates the HTTPS connections on its public interface and then forwards the HTTP or HTTPS requests to the internal web server. The response from the web server is then encapsulated into HTTPS and forwarded to the client. This feature uses only an Internet browser to access corporate resources. Thus, this mode is referred to as clientless SSL VPNs. Figure 6-10 illustrates this mode. The following sequence of events takes place when UserA tries to connect to a web server located at 192.168.1.100:

1 UserA initiates an HTTP request to the web server, which is located on the other side of the SSL VPN tunnel. The user request is encapsulated into the SSL tunnel and is then forwarded to the IOS router.

2 The IOS router deencapsulates the traffic and initiates a connection to the server on behalf of the web client.

3 The response from the server is sent to the router.

4 The router, in turn, encapsulates and sends the response to UserA.

Figure 6-10 *HTTP Requests Using Clientless SSL VPN*

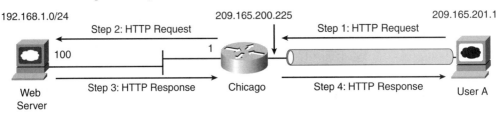

192.168.1.0/24	209.165.200.225	209.165.201.1

Step 2: HTTP Request   Step 1: HTTP Request

100   1

Step 3: HTTP Response   Chicago   Step 4: HTTP Response

Web Server   User A

NOTE   If you frequently use Java and ActiveX coding on a web page, a Cisco IOS router might not be able to rewrite web pages that embed that content. You can enable the port-forwarding option to tunnel HTTP traffic directly to the web server. Additionally, a Cisco IOS router does not perform content transformation of non-HTTP-based URLs, such as ftp:// or telnet://.

The IOS SSL VPN gateway does not allow SSL VPN communication with websites that present expired certificates during session negotiations.

Configure the SSL VPN clientless services by choosing **Configure > VPN > SSL VPN > Edit SSL VPN > SecureMeContext > Edit > URL Lists > Add**. You can specify a URL list name that is then mapped to the group policy. Additionally, you can specify a URL heading that appears on the main portal page after a successful user authentication. A URL heading groups similar links to multiple servers under one heading for easier web navigation. You can click the **Add** option to add specific URLs to the web and Outlook Web Access e-mail servers. The SDM prompts you to provide the following information:

- **URL label:** This is a static bookmark entry that appears in the portal page when the user logs in. This label provides an easy-to-remember name to an internal web or e-mail server link. For example, if you have an intranet server located at http://intranet.securemeinc.com, you can provide a bookmark to this link as "Intranet server" for easier navigation. This way, users who access the web server frequently can access it without having to specify the URL every time.

- **URL link:** This is the actual link that is identified by the label.

In Figure 6-11, a URL list name (bookmark) is defined as ListForClientlessUsers with a heading name of ClientlessAccess. Under this list name, an internal server is mapped with a label called Intranet Server. This server is located at http://intranet.securemeinc.com.

Figure 6-11 *URL List (Bookmark) for Web Servers*

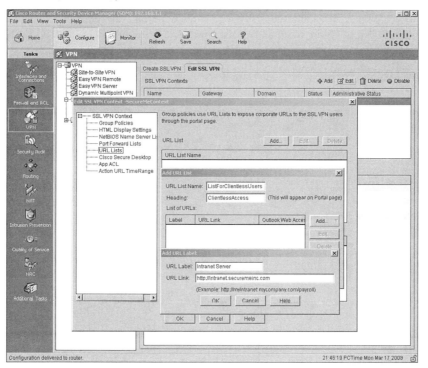

Example 6-18 shows the complete CLI configuration of a clientless SSL VPN.

Example 6-18 *Defining Web Servers for a Clientless SSL VPN*

```
Chicago(config)# webvpn context SecureMeContext
Chicago(config-webvpn-context)# url-list "ListForClientlessUsers"
Chicago(config-webvpn-url)# url-text "IntranetServer" url-value "http://
  intranet.securemeinc.com"
Chicago(config-webvpn-url)# heading "ClientlessAccess"
```

NOTE   If you define a URL list using the fully qualified domain names (FQDN) of the servers, make sure that you define the Domain Name System (DNS) server on the Cisco IOS router so that it can resolve those names before initiating a connection on behalf of the clientless computers. To define a DNS server on a Cisco IOS router, use the **ip name-server** command. For example, to define a DNS server located at 192.168.1.10, use the following command:

```
ip name-server 192.168.1.10
```

Under SDM, it can be configured by choosing **Configuration > Additional tasks > DNS**.

To display the name of an Outlook Web Access e-mail server, select **email** when defining a new server. SDM automatically selects the Outlook Web Access check box during server definition. In Figure 6-12, a URL list name is defined as WebOutlook with a heading name of OutlookWebAccess. Under this list name, an internal server is mapped with a label called OutlookWebAccess. This server is located at http://email.securemeinc.com.

Figure 6-12 *URL List for Outlook Server*

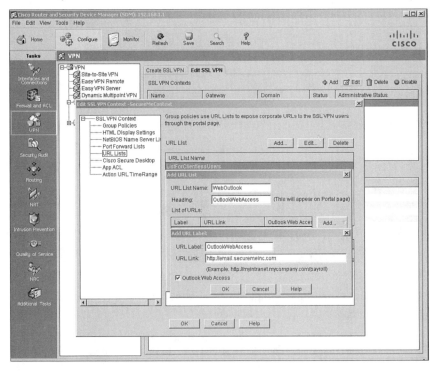

Example 6-19 shows the corresponding CLI configuration.

Example 6-19   *Defining Outlook Server*

```
Chicago(config)# webvpn context SecureMeContext
Chicago(config-webvpn-context)# url-list "WebOutlook"
Chicago(config-webvpn-context)# url-text "OutlookWebAccess" url-value "http://
  email.securemeinc.com/exchange"
Chicago(config-webvpn-context)# heading "OutlookWebAccess
```

After defining the URL list names for the internal servers, the next step is to map those
definitions to the appropriate group policies. This is achieved by choosing **Configure >
VPN > SSL VPN > Edit SSL VPN > SecureMeContext > Edit > Group Policies >
SecureMeDefaultPolicy > Edit > Clientless tab** and selecting the previously defined URL
list names. As shown in Figure 6-13, WebOutlook and ListForClientlessUsers are enabled
under SecureMeDefaultPolicy.

Figure 6-13   *Mapping a URL List to a Group*

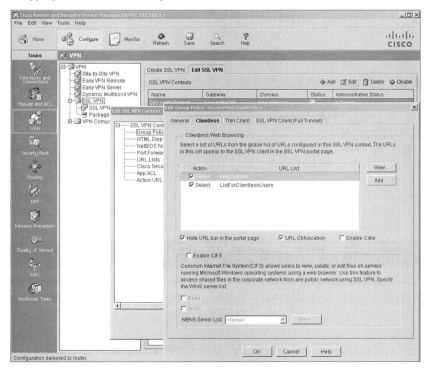

Example 6-20 shows the corresponding configuration in the CLI.

Example 6-20 *Mapping a URL List to a Group*

```
Chicago(config)# webvpn context SecureMeContext
Chicago(config-webvpn-context)# policy group SecureMeDefaultPolicy
Chicago(config-webvpn-policy)# url-list WebOutlook
Chicago(config-webvpn-policy)# url-list ListForClientlessUsers
Chicago(config-webvpn-policy)# hide-url-bar
```

In Figure 6-13, notice that the **Hide URL bar in the portal page** check box is also selected. Using this option, the URL bar is hidden so that users cannot enter a URL of their choice. This enhances SSL VPN security if you do not want your users to enter URLs other than what is listed as the bookmark on their portal page. In Figure 6-14, the clientless portal page is shown after a successful user authentication.

Figure 6-14 *Web Portal Displaying URL Lists (Bookmarks)*

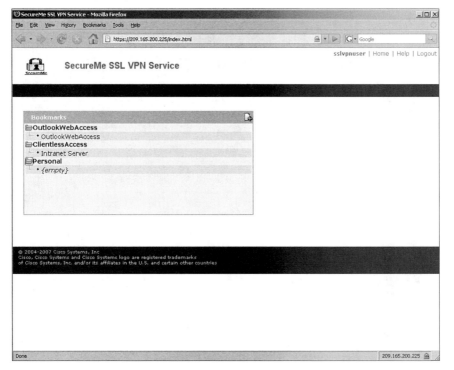

Windows File Sharing

Cisco IOS routers support network file sharing through Common Internet File System (CIFS). Using CIFS, users can access their file shares located on the file servers, as illustrated in Figure 6-15. Users can download, upload, delete, or rename the files under the shared directories, but only if the file system permissions allow them to perform those actions.

Figure 6-15 *CIFS Browsing on the IOS SSL VPN Gateway*

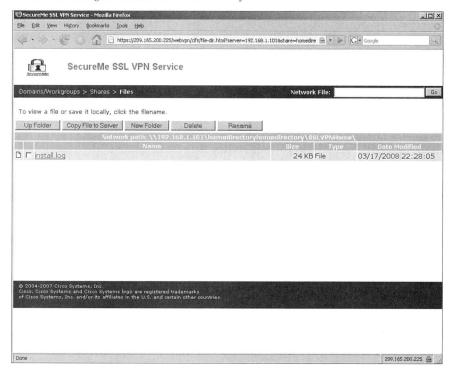

Administrators can either create CIFS bookmarks or allow users to specify the NetBIOS name or the IP address of the server in the Network File link. As depicted in Figure 6-16, the logged-in user specifies **\\192.168.1.101\homedirectory** in the Network File link.

Figure 6-16 *CIFS Support on Cisco IOS Routers*

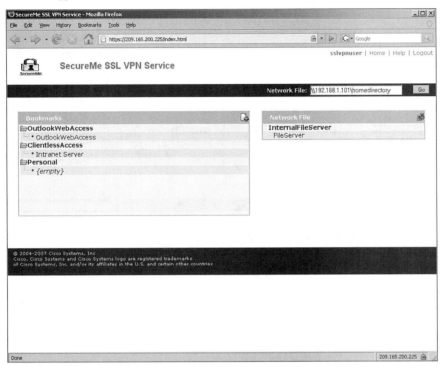

NOTE	Actions such as read, write, delete, and rename files and folders depend on the configured SSL VPN functions.

The configuration of CIFS requires the use of a NetBIOS Name Server (NBNS), also known as Windows Internet Naming Server (WINS). When an SSL VPN user queries to browse the network, the Cisco IOS router contacts the WINS server and acquires the list of available domains, workgroups, and workstations. In SDM, you can specify an NBNS by choosing **Configure > VPN > SSL VPN > Edit SSL VPN > SecureMeContext > Edit > NetBIOS Name Server List > Add**. You can create a list name that is then mapped to the group policy. Click **Add** and specify the IP address of the NBNS for CIFS name resolution. The **master** keyword specifies that the configured NBNS server acts as the master browser in addition to being a WINS server. The **timeout** value instructs an IOS router to wait for the configured number of seconds (default is 2 seconds) before sending another query to the next server. The **retry** option is used to specify the number of times a Cisco IOS router has to go through the list of the configured NBNS servers. The default retries is 2, and it ranges from 0 to 10.

Figure 6-17 illustrates the configuration of an NBNS server. The NBNS list name is NBNS-Server, while the server is located at 192.168.1.40 and acts as a master browser and a WINS server. The **timeout** and **retry** values are set to their defaults.

Figure 6-17 *CIFS Support on a Cisco IOS Router Through SDM*

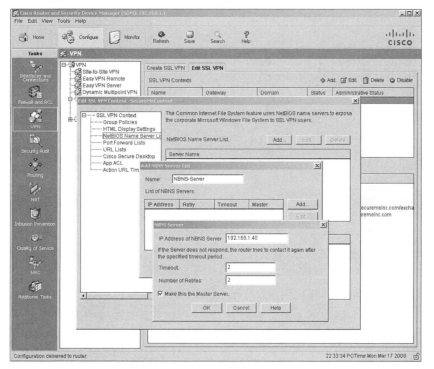

NOTE   You can specify up to three WINS servers in the current version.

Example 6-21 shows the SDM-generated configuration.

Example 6-21 *CIFS-NBNS Server Configuration*

```
Chicago(config)# webvpn context SecureMeContext
Chicago(config-webvpn-context)# nbns-list NBNS-Server
Chicago(config-webvpn-nbnslist)#  nbns-server 192.168.1.40 master
```

A Cisco IOS router does not enable CIFS functionality until the **functions** parameter is set up to allow file browsing, file access, and/or file entry. This is achieved by choosing **Configure > VPN > SSL VPN > Edit SSL VPN > SecureMeContext > Edit > Group Policies > SecureMeDefaultPolicy > Edit > Clientless tab**. Select the **Enable CIFS** option and select the **Read** and **Write** check boxes. Under NBNS Server List, select the NBNS-Server list defined earlier. Click **OK** when the mapping is complete. This is illustrated in Figure 6-18. The contents of NBNS-List are also shown.

Figure 6-18 *Mapping an NBNS List to a Group Policy*

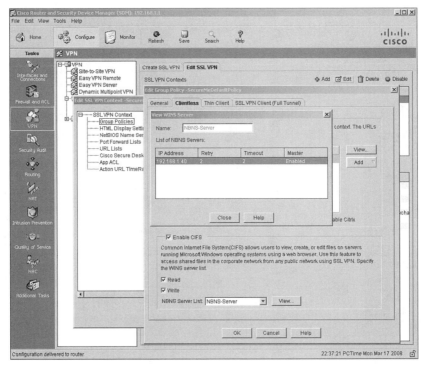

The configuration in Example 6-22 sets up a Cisco IOS router with a user group policy named SecureMeDefaultPolicy, which allows users to browse, access, and enter file information using the **functions** attribute.

Example 6-22 *Configuration of WINS Mapping to a Group Policy*

```
Chicago(config)# webvpn context SecureMeContext
Chicago(config-webvpn-context)# policy group SecureMeDefaultPolicy
Chicago(config-webvpn-policy)# functions file-access
Chicago(config-webvpn-policy)# functions file-entry
Chicago(config-webvpn-policy)# functions file-browse
Chicago(config-webvpn-policy)# nbns-list NBNS-Server
```

The current version of SDM, version 2.5, does not allow you to configure a list of CIFS servers on the web portal page. For example, if a file server is frequently used by the SSL VPN users, you can configure a link on the portal page for that server. This way, users do not have to enter the IP address of the NetBIOS name of the server manually. In Example 6-23, a CIFS URL list called InternalFileServer is defined. The heading of the server is defined as InternalFileServer. The URL text is defined as FileServer with a configured value of //192.168.1.101.

Example 6-23 *Defining a CIFS Server on a Web Portal*

```
Chicago(config)# webvpn context SecureMeContext
Chicago(config-webvpn-context)# cifs-url-list "InternalFileServer"
Chicago(config-webvpn-context)# heading "InternalFileServer"
Chicago(config-webvpn-context)# url-text "FileServer" url-value "//192.168.1.101"
```

After a CIFS server is defined, you must link it to the user group policy named SecureMeDefaultPolicy by using the **cifs-url-list** command, as shown in Example 6-24.

Example 6-24 *Linking the CIFS Server to a Group Policy*

```
Chicago(config)# webvpn context SecureMeContext
Chicago(config-webvpn-context)# policy group SecureMeDefaultPolicy
Chicago(config-webvpn-policy)# cifs-url-list "InternalFileServer"
```

Configuring Application ACL

Network administrators can restrict their clientless SSL VPN users to access certain application servers by configuring the application access control lists (ACL). They can filter traffic such as Hypertext Transfer Protocol (HTTP), HTTPS, FTP, and Common Internet File System (CIFS), to name a few. These ACLs affect only the clientless SSL VPN traffic. An application ACL is configured by choosing **Configure > VPN > SSL VPN > Edit SSL VPN > SecureMeContext > Edit > App ACL**. Click **Add**, specify an ACL name, and then select **Add** to define a new application ACL. You can either deny or permit specific entries for each access control entry (ACE). From SDM, you can define a URL-based ACL, whereas from the CLI you can also define an address and service-type ACL. These ACL types are defined as follows:

- **Filter on URL:** A URL-based web ACL is used to filter out SSL VPN packets if they contain a URL such as http:// or ftp://.

- **Filter on address and service:** An address- and service-based web ACL is used to filter out SSL VPN packets if they use TCP encapsulation based on the IP address and a Layer 4 port number.

If you prefer to add a URL-based entry to filter out SSL VPN traffic, select **Filter on URL** and specify a complete URL. For example, if you want all clientless users to restrict web traffic to payroll.securemeinc.com, create an application ACL and deny traffic destined to http://payroll.securemeinc.com. After you define an ACL to deny traffic, be sure to create another entry to allow traffic to other websites. As shown in Figure 6-19, a new ACL called FilterWebServer denies traffic destined to http://payroll.securemeinc.com.

Figure 6-19 *Defining an Application ACL*

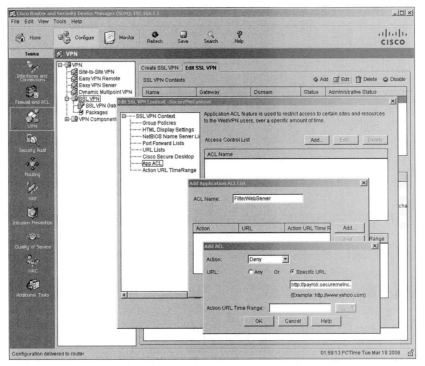

Example 6-25 shows the SDM-generated configuration for an application ACL.

Example 6-25 *Defining an Application ACL*

```
Chicago(config)# webvpn context SecureMeContext
Chicago(config-webvpn-context)# acl FilterWebServer
Chicago(config-webvpn-acl)# deny url http://payroll.securemeinc.com
```

After an application ACL is configured, the next step is to link it to a group policy. Choose **Configure > VPN > SSL VPN > Edit SSL VPN > SecureMeContext > Edit > Group Policies > SecureMeDefaultPolicy > Edit > General tab** and select the configured ACL, FilterWebServer, from the Application ACL drop-down menu, as shown in Figure 6-20.

Figure 6-20 *Mapping an Application ACL to a Group Policy*

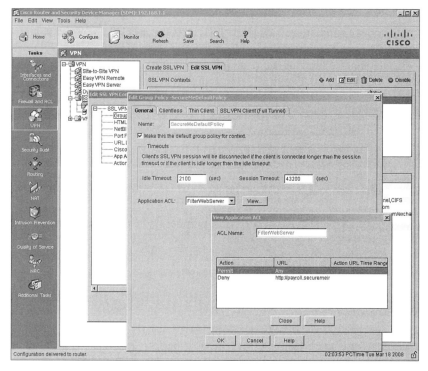

Example 6-26 shows the SDM-generated configuration for mapping an application ACL to a group policy.

Example 6-26 *Mapping an Application ACL to a Group Policy*

```
Chicago(config)# webvpn context SecureMeContext
Chicago(config-webvpn-context)# policy group SecureMeDefaultPolicy
Chicago(config-webvpn-policy)# acl FilterWebServer
```

CAUTION   Application ACLs ensure that SSL VPN traffic denied by the ACLs will not pass through the router. However, they will not block a user from accessing the resources outside the SSL VPN tunnel.

Thin Client SSL VPNs

Thin clients are also known as port forwarding. Using this feature, SSL VPN sessions use application port forwarding to access the TCP-based corporate resources. Thus, clients access the internal servers over the known and fixed TCP ports such as Telnet, SSH, Terminal Services, and Simple Mail Transfer Protocol (SMTP).

To use this feature, the authenticated SSL VPN users click the **Start** button next to Thin Client Application under the Application Access heading. It launches a Java applet on the client computer showing the IP address or the host name and the port number that can be used for the session. Figure 6-21 illustrates the Java applet launched on the client computer.

Figure 6-21 *Port-Forwarding Applet*

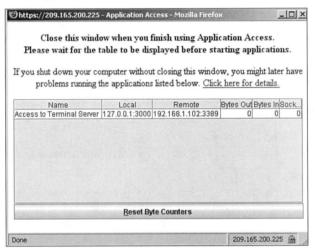

The port-forwarding feature requires you to install Sun Microsystems' Java Runtime Environment (JRE) and configure applications on the end user's PC. If users are establishing the SSL VPN tunnel from public computers, such as Internet kiosks or web cafés, they might not be able to use this feature. The installation of Sun's JRE requires administrative rights on the client computer.

NOTE   As discussed in Chapter 5, Cisco ASA supports a new feature called smart tunnels that are used to forward application-specific traffic. Smart tunnels are currently not offered in the Cisco IOS SSL VPN gateways.

Because most of the network applications use host names versus an IP address to connect, port forwarding modifies the HOSTS file on the client computer. It resolves the host name using one of the loopback addresses in the range from 127.0.0.2 to 127.0.0.254.

If the HOSTS file cannot be modified, the host listens on 127.0.0.1 and the configured local port. When the session is terminated, the application port mapping is restored to the default.

NOTE   Certain security applications such as Cisco Security Agent (CSA) detect the modifications of the HOST and other files. You might be asked to acknowledge these modifications.

Configuration of a thin client SSL VPN is a two-step process:

Step 1   Defining port-forwarding lists

Step 2   Mapping port-forwarding lists to a group policy

Step 1: Defining Port-Forwarding Lists

In this step, you have to define a list of servers and the application that you want to access through the SSL VPN. The port-forwarding list is defined by choosing **Configure > VPN > SSL VPN > Edit SSL VPN > SecureMeContext > Edit > Port Forward Lists > Add**. Specify a name for this port-forwarding list. This list name has only local significance, and it is used to map the port-forwarding attributes to a group policy, discussed in the next step. To define a specific application for thin clients, click **Add** and specify the following attributes:

- Server IP address.
- Server port on which service is listening.
- Port on client PC. You should use a local port between 1024 and 65535 to avoid conflicts with existing network services.
- Description.

As shown in Figure 6-22, a port-forwarding list called TerminalServer is defined. A server, located at 192.168.1.102 and listening on port 3389, is added in this list. SDM, by default, specifies a local port of 3000 for this connection. The administrator has added a description of Access to Terminal Server.

Figure 6-22 *Defining a Port-Forwarding List*

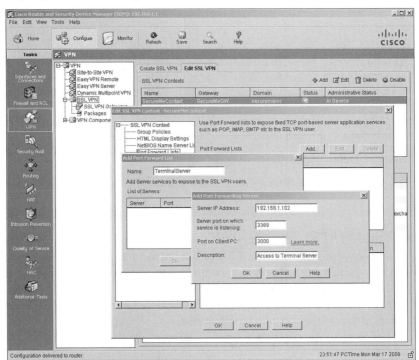

CAUTION   In the current software release, a compatibility issue exists if you use 3des-sha1 aes-sha1
as the encryption type. The Java port-forwarding applet does not download properly with
this encryption setting.

Example 6-27 shows the corresponding configuration.

Example 6-27 *Defining a Port-Forwarding List*

```
Chicago(config)# webvpn context SecureMeContext
Chicago(config-webvpn-context)# port-forward TerminalServer
Chicago(config-webvpn-context)# local-port 3000 remote-server 192.168.1.102 remote-
  port 3389 description "Access to Terminal Server"
```

Step 2: Mapping Port-Forwarding Lists to a Group Policy

The port-forwarding list is mapped to a group policy by choosing **Configure** > **VPN** > **SSL**
VPN > **Edit SSL VPN** > **SecureMeContext** > **Edit** > **Group Policies** >

SecureMeDefaultPolicy > Edit > Thin Client tab. From the Port Forward List drop-down menu, select the list defined in Step 1. If you prefer to view the content of the list before applying the policy, click the **View** button. Activate the thin client SSL VPN by selecting the **Enable Thin Client (Port Forwarding)** check box. As shown in Figure 6-23, a port-forwarding list of TerminalServer is selected and enabled for the SecureMeDefaultPolicy context. The contents of this list are also shown. The administrator has also selected the **Automatically Download Applet** check box so that port forwarding is automatically launched when a user establishes the SSL VPN session.

Figure 6-23 *Mapping of a Port-Forwarding List*

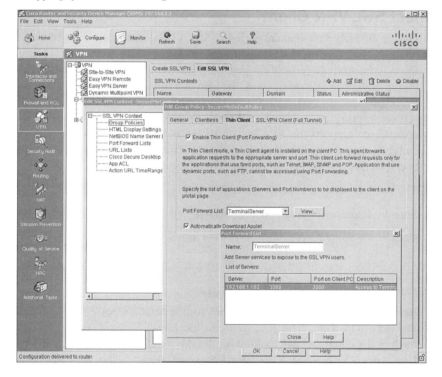

Example 6-28 shows the CLI-related configuration.

Example 6-28 *Port-Forwarding List Mapping*

```
Chicago(config)# webvpn context SecureMeContext
Chicago(config-webvpn-context)# policy group SecureMeDefaultPolicy
Chicago(config-webvpn-policy)# port-forward TerminalServer auto-download
```

After a successful user authentication, the applet is launched automatically. After the applet is loaded on the client, the user launches a Remote Desktop connection to establish a connection to the server by using the loopback IP address of 127.0.0.1 and the destination port of 3000. This redirects the connection over the SSL VPN tunnel to the server at 192.168.1.102 on port 3389. Additionally, you can click **Start** under Thin Client Application to start a new applet if the previous one was closed.

NOTE   You should use a local port between 1024 and 65535 to avoid conflicts with existing network services.

AnyConnect SSL VPN Client

During the early development period of SSL VPNs, network administrators needed a VPN client that had benefits that were similar to an IPsec remote access VPN client, but required less administrative overhead for installing and maintaining the IPsec VPN client. To accommodate those requirements, the idea of a full tunnel SSL VPN client emerged. Cisco first introduced the SSL VPN Client (SVC) that was a self-downloading, self-installing, self-configuring, and self-uninstalling VPN. In Release 12.4(15)T and higher versions of code, Cisco supports the AnyConnect VPN Client, which offers all the benefits that are currently available in the Cisco IPsec client. The SSL VPN client leverages the SSL encryption engine that is already present on the client computer.

The configuration of a AnyConnect SSL VPN is a two-step process:

Step 1   Loading the AnyConnect package

Step 2   Defining AnyConnect SSL VPN attributes

Step 1: Loading the AnyConnect Package

Before you define configuration policies for the AnyConnect VPN Client in an IOS router, you have to load the client package in the local flash. You can verify it by issuing the **show flash** or **dir** command and looking for the svc.pkg file. Using SDM, you can choose **Configure > VPN > SSL VPN > Packages** and check whether the Cisco AnyConnect VPN Client software is installed. SDM allows you to

- Download the latest version of AnyConnect Client if you do not already have it. It connects to Cisco.com by prompting you for login credentials. If the login credentials are correct, SDM displays all the posted AnyConnect files in a different browser window.

- Select a preloaded AnyConnect file from flash. Even if you have a preloaded AnyConnect file in flash, you should check the latest version of SVC on the Cisco website. Click **Browse** to select a file from either the router's flash or the workstation running the SDM software.

In Figure 6-24, an svc.pkg file is selected from flash. This file is located at flash:/webvpn. After the file is selected, the last step is to install the file by clicking the **Install** button. The router confirms the process by prompting, "Are you sure you want to install the package?" If you select **Yes**, the router installs the package and displays the message "Cisco SSL VPN client package successfully installed."

Figure 6-24 *Installing the SVC Package*

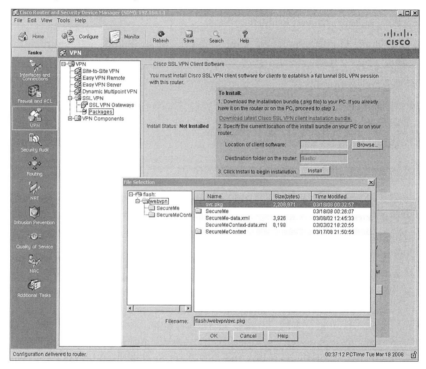

Example 6-29 shows the corresponding command for installing the selected AnyConnect Client package.

Example 6-29 *CLI Output to Install the AnyConnect Client*

```
Chicago(config)# webvpn install svc flash:/webvpn/svc.pkg
```

Step 2: Defining AnyConnect VPN Client Attributes

After loading the AnyConnect package in the router's configuration, SDM allows you to define the client parameters. Before an AnyConnect VPN Client is functional, you have to configure the following attributes:

- Enabling SVC functionality
- Defining a pool of addresses
- Creating a Layer 3 interface

Optionally, you can define other attributes to enhance the functionality of the SSL VPN configuration. They include

- Traffic filtering
- Split tunneling
- DNS and WINS assignment
- Keep SSL VPN client installed

The sections that follow define these options.

Enabling SVC Functionality

The Cisco IOS router allows you to enable AnyConnect VPN Client functionality by using the **functions** command followed by one of two options:

- **svc-enabled:** This option enables SVC functionality on an IOS router. After a user is authenticated, the AnyConnect Client is automatically launched on the user's computer. If the SVC client fails for any reason, the user can still use clientless and thin client SSL VPN modes. The svc-enabled mode is useful if you want to provide backup connectivity to certain critical applications (such as Web, Mail, and Terminal Server) through clientless and thin client modes should SVC fail to work.

- **svc-required:** This option also enables AnyConnect Client functionality in an IOS router. After a user is authenticated, the SVC client is automatically launched on the user's computer. However, if the SVC client fails to load for any reason, the user cannot use clientless or thin client SSL VPN modes. The svc-required mode is useful if you require VPN users to use strictly the full tunnel functionality with no fail-open method.

Using SDM, AnyConnect VPN Client can be enabled by choosing **Configure > VPN > SSL VPN > Edit SSL VPN > SecureMeContext > Group Policies > SecureMeDefaultPolicy > SSL VPN Client (Full Tunnel) tab**. SDM provides a drop-down menu from which you can select whether you want to simply enable the AnyConnect VPN Client or whether you want to require it. Figure 6-25 illustrates that the Cisco IOS router administrator has enabled the AnyConnect Client for SecureMeDefaultPolicy. The client cannot be enabled until you define a pool of addresses, discussed in the next section.

Figure 6-25   *Enabling AnyConnect on a Group Policy*

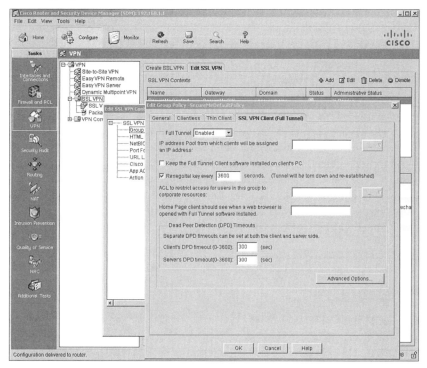

Example 6-30 shows the command-line equivalent of the configuration shown in Figure 6-25.

Example 6-30   *Enabling SVC on a Group Policy*

```
Chicago(config)# webvpn context SecureMeContext
Chicago(config-webvpn-context)# policy group SecureMeDefaultPolicy
Chicago(config-webvpn-policy)# functions svc-enabled
```

The AnyConnect VPN Client requires administrative privileges on the client computer when it is installed. For Windows-based workstations, the SSL VPN client is pushed through ActiveX as the preferred method. If ActiveX installation fails, the SSL VPN client is pushed to the workstations through Java. If installation through Java fails, the client is pushed as an executable as the last option. For non-Windows clients, Java is used as the installation method.

Defining a Pool of Addresses

During the SSL VPN tunnel negotiations, an IP address is assigned to the VPN adapter of the SVC client. The client uses this IP address to access resources on the protected side of the tunnel. The IP address is assigned by configuring an address pool and then linking the pool to a policy group. You can either create a new pool of addresses or select a preconfigured address pool.

The pool of addresses can be defined or selected by choosing **Configure** > **VPN** > **SSL VPN** > **Edit SSL VPN** > **SecureMeContext** > **Group Policies** > **SecureMeDefaultPolicy** > **SSL VPN Client (Full Tunnel) tab**. Under IP Address Pool from Which Clients Will Be Assigned an Address, click the **...** button and choose the appropriate option. To use a preconfigured pool, click **Select an existing IP Pool**. SDM presents you with a list of pools that are already defined in the configuration that you can select for the SSL VPN connections. If you would rather define a new pool of addresses for these SSL VPN connections, select the **Create a new IP Pool** option. You can specify a name for this pool under Pool Name. Click **Add** and define a range of IP addresses by specifying a start and an end IP address. Click **OK** when finished. As illustrated in Figure 6-26, a new pool is defined as sslvpnpool with a start IP address of 192.68.2.2 and an end IP address of 192.168.2.100.

Figure 6-26 *Defining an Address Pool Using SDM*

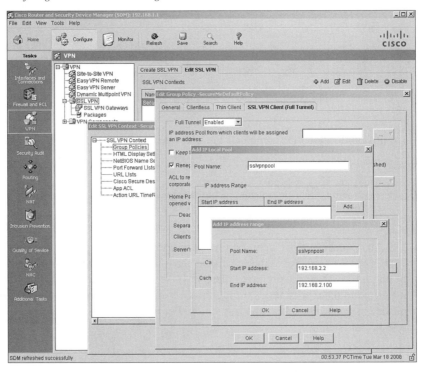

Example 6-31 shows the command-line equivalent of the configuration shown in Figure 6-26.

Example 6-31 *Address Assignment from the Local Pool*

```
Chicago(config)# ip local pool sslvpnpool 192.168.2.2 192.168.2.100
Chicago(config)# webvpn context SecureMeContext
Chicago(config-webvpn-context)# policy group SecureMeDefaultPolicy
Chicago(config-webvpn-policy)# svc address-pool sslvpnpool
```

Creating a Layer 3 Interface

The SSL VPN implementation on Cisco IOS routers requires you to configure an interface in the same network as the pool of addresses. If the configured address pool spans a different network, and you do not have an interface in that particular network, you can create a loopback interface. The IP address must belong to the address pool network. An interface can be defined by choosing **Configure** > **Interfaces and Connections** > **Edit Interface/Connection** > **Add** > **New Logical Interface** > **Loopback.** From the IP address drop-down menu, select **Static IP address** and configure an IP address that belongs to the address pool network. Specify the appropriate subnet mask for this IP address. As shown in Figure 6-27, a static IP address of 192.168.2.1 is configured with a subnet mask of 255.255.255.0.

Figure 6-27 *Creating a Loopback Interface*

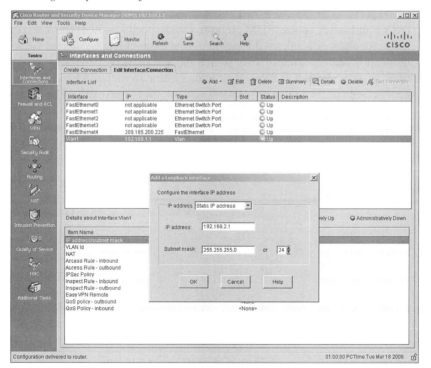

NOTE	If you create a new loopback interface, it must be advertised in your network through a routing protocol.

Example 6-32 shows the command-line equivalent of the configuration shown in Figure 6-27.

Example 6-32 *Defining an Interface*

```
Chicago(config)# interface Loopback1
Chicago(config-if)# ip address 192.168.2.1 255.255.255.0
```

Traffic Filtering

In some cases, you do not want your remote or mobile users to access the entire network resources. For example, if you provide access to contractors but you only allow them to access a web server to complete their tasks, you can create and apply appropriate filters to restrict their access. Traffic filtering is achieved by setting up an access control list (ACL) and then mapping it to the group policy. If you choose **Configure > VPN > SSL VPN > Edit SSL VPN > SecureMeContext > Group Policies > SecureMeDefaultPolicy > SSL VPN Client (Full Tunnel) tab**, you can either define a new ACL or link an existing ACL under the ACL to Restrict Access for Users In This Group to Corporate Resources option. If you prefer to define a new ACL, click the **...** button and select the **Create a new rule (ACL) and select** option. SDM prompts you to specify an ACL name and describe its usage. To add a rule, click **Add** and define the filter attributes, such as the source and destination addresses/networks or source and destination service ports. As shown in Figure 6-28, an ACL, defined as SVC-ACL, allows traffic from the 192.168.2.0 network (local pool) to send traffic to the 192.168.1.0 network (inside network). The network administrator has added a description of "ACL to restrict users to a Terminal Server."

Figure 6-28 *Defining Traffic Filtering*

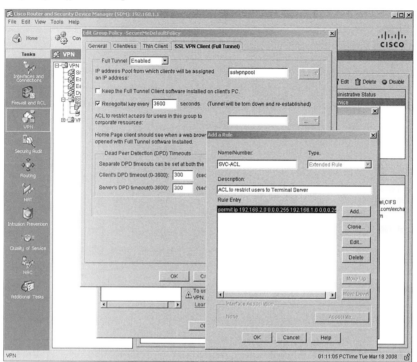

After the ACL is defined, just map the ACL name to the ACL to Restrict Access for Users in This Group to Corporate Resources option. The corresponding CLI format of the Figure 6-28 configuration is shown in Example 6-33.

Example 6-33 *Access List to Filter Traffic Through an SSL VPN*

```
Chicago(config)# ip access-list extended SVC-ACL
Chicago(config-ext-nacl)# remark ACL to restrict users to Terminal Server
Chicago(config-ext-nacl)# permit ip 192.168.2.0 0.0.0.255 192.168.1.0 0.0.0.255
Chicago(config-ext-nacl)# exit
Chicago(config)# webvpn context SecureMeContext
Chicago(config-webvpn-context)# policy group SecureMeDefaultPolicy
Chicago(config-webvpn-policy)# filter tunnel SVC-ACL
```

Split Tunneling

After the tunnel is up, the default behavior of the Cisco VPN client is to encrypt traffic destined to all the IP addresses. This means that if an SSL VPN user wants to browse http://www.cisco.com over the Internet, as illustrated in Figure 6-29, the packets will be encrypted and sent to the Cisco IOS router. After decrypting them, the Cisco IOS router will look at its routing table and forward the packet to the appropriate next-hop IP address in clear text. These steps are reversed when traffic returns from the web server and is destined to the SSL VPN client.

Figure 6-29 *Traffic with No Split Tunneling*

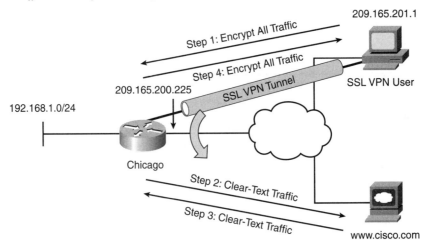

NOTE Remove the traffic filter that was created in the previous section ("Traffic Filtering"). This filter restricts traffic to pass from 192.168.2.0/24 to 192.168.1.0/24.

This behavior might not always be desirable, for the following two reasons:

- Traffic destined to the nonsecure networks traverses the Internet twice: once encrypted and once in clear text.
- A Cisco IOS router handles extra VPN traffic destined to the nonsecure subnet.

With split tunneling, the Cisco IOS router can notify the AnyConnect VPN Client for the secured subnets. The client, using the secured routes, encrypts only those packets that are destined for the networks behind the Cisco router.

CAUTION With split tunneling, the remote workstation is susceptible to hackers who can potentially take control over the computer and possibly direct traffic over the tunnel. To mitigate this behavior, you should have a personal firewall on the SSL VPN client workstations.

Additionally, the Cisco IOS router also supports tunneling all traffic except for a list of networks that require clear-text access. This feature is useful if users require clear-text access to their local LANs and encrypted tunnels to the corporate network.

As mentioned earlier, the SSL VPN gateway provides three modes for split tunneling:

- Tunnel all traffic (no split tunneling)
- Tunnel specific networks (split tunneling)
- Tunnel all but specific networks (exclude split tunneling)

These modes can be configured by choosing **Configure > VPN > SSL VPN > Edit SSL VPN > SecureMeContext > Group Policies > SecureMeDefaultPolicy > SSL VPN Client (Full Tunnel) tab > Advanced Options > Split Tunneling tab**. To enable split tunneling, select **Include Traffic** and click **Add** to define the network for data encryption. To tunnel all traffic except for certain networks (including local network), select **Exclude Traffic** and define the networks to be excluded from data encryption. In Figure 6-30, the 192.168.1.0 network is included for split tunneling.

Figure 6-30 *Split-Tunneling Configuration*

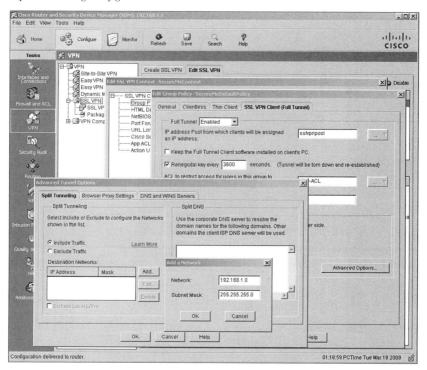

The related split-tunneling configuration is shown in Example 6-34.

Example 6-34 *Split-Tunneling Configuration*

```
Chicago(config)# webvpn context SecureMeContext
Chicago(config-webvpn-context)# policy group SecureMeDefaultPolicy
Chicago(config-webvpn-policy)# svc split include 192.168.1.0 255.255.255.0
```

DNS and WINS Assignment

For SSL VPN clients, you can assign DNS and WINS server IP addresses so that they can browse and access internal sites when their VPN tunnel is established. You can configure these attributes by choosing **Configure > VPN > SSL VPN > Edit SSL VPN > SecureMeContext > Group Policies > SecureMeDefaultPolicy > SSL VPN Client (Full Tunnel) tab > Advanced Options > DNS and WINS Servers tab**. In Figure 6-31, the primary DNS server is defined as 192.168.1.10 and the secondary DNS server is 192.168.1.40, whereas the primary WINS server is 192.168.1.40 and the secondary WINS server is 192.168.1.10. The default domain name to be pushed to the SSL VPN client is securemeinc.com.

Figure 6-31 *Defining DNS and WINS Servers for SSL VPN Clients*

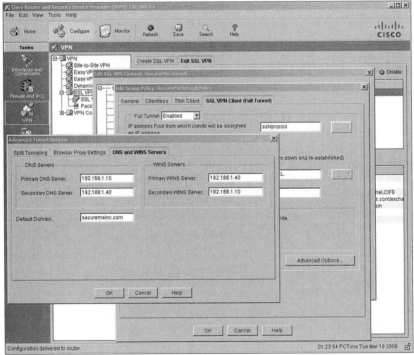

The related split-tunneling configuration is shown in Example 6-35.

Example 6-35 *Defining DNS and WINS Servers for SSL VPN Clients*

```
Chicago(config)# webvpn context SecureMeContext
Chicago(config-webvpn-context)# policy group SecureMeDefaultPolicy
Chicago(config-webvpn-policy)# svc default-domain secureminc.com
Chicago(config-webvpn-policy)# svc dns-server primary 192.168.1.10
Chicago(config-webvpn-policy)# svc dns-server secondary 192.168.1.40
Chicago(config-webvpn-policy)# svc wins-server primary 192.168.1.40
Chicago(config-webvpn-policy)# svc wins-server secondary 192.168.1.10
```

Keep SSL VPN Client Installed

After the SSL VPN client is installed successfully, the Cisco IOS router allows you to keep the client installed on the computer even if the tunnel is disconnected. By default, the client is automatically removed after the users log off and is reinstalled when the tunnel is successfully established. You can configure to keep the client installed by choosing **Configure > VPN > SSL VPN > Edit SSL VPN > SecureMeContext > Group Policies > SecureMeDefaultPolicy > SSL VPN Client (Full Tunnel) tab**, as shown in Figure 6-32.

Figure 6-32 *Configuration of Keep SSL VPN Client Installed*

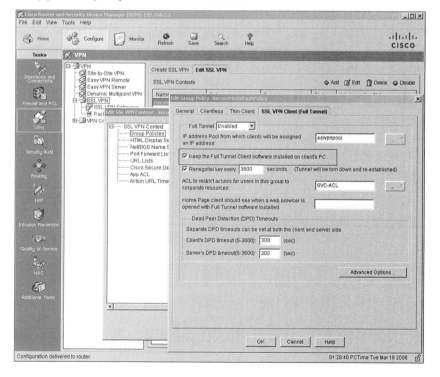

The related CLI configuration is shown in Example 6-36.

Example 6-36 *Configuring Keep the Client Installed*

```
Chicago(config)# webvpn context SecureMeContext
Chicago(config-webvpn-context)# policy group SecureMeDefaultPolicy
Chicago(config-webvpn-policy)# svc keep-client-installed
```

NOTE   You should keep the client on the system. Otherwise, administrative rights are needed to reinstall the client on the computer.

Cisco Secure Desktop

As mentioned in Chapter 5, Cisco Secure Desktop (CSD) provides a secure desktop environment to remote users after validating a number of security parameters on the client workstation. The purpose of CSD is to minimize the risk posed by remote workstations by collecting necessary information from them. If the received information matches the preconfigured criteria, the Cisco IOS router can create a secure environment and optionally apply certain policies and restrictions on the user session. When the user session is disconnected, the secure desktop environment is by default removed. This way, a user who wants to access corporate resources from a hotel workstation or even from an Internet café can create a secure vault that can be used to access corporate resources through clientless, thin client, or even full tunnel mode. When the user is done using the public workstation, the vault is destroyed to ensure that data cannot be accessed by a different user. This includes removing cookies, temporary files, browser history, and even any downloaded content.

CSD is designed to help system administrators enforce security policies for remote users. When a user tries to connect to the SSL VPN gateway, a client component is downloaded and installed on the client workstation. This client component scans the computer and gathers information such as the operating system, installed service pack, antivirus version, and installed personal firewall. This information is sent to the SSL VPN gateway and then matched against predefined criteria. If the user's computer meets the criteria, it is given appropriate access to the internal resources. If the criteria are not met, users are granted either limited or no access. For example, an administrator might require that all remote computers have Windows XP with Service Pack 2 installed. If remote computers meet this condition, the users are allowed to use the SSL VPN solution for their corporate network access; if not, they get no corporate network access.

To identify the location of an SSL VPN client, CSD supports three attributes. For example, you can define a range of IP addresses that belong to your corporate network as Work.

When clients connect from this address range, they are given access based on the defined policies. The supported attributes include

- Issuer or distinguished name in a certificate
- IP address of the client
- Presence of a file and registry key

CSD uses proven industry standards such as Triple Data Encryption Standard (3DES) and Rivest Cipher 4 (RC4) to ensure security of the vault. If the logged-in user has administrative privileges, CSD uses a 3DES encryption algorithm; if the user has lesser privileges, it uses RC4 to encrypt the data.

CSD Components

CSD consists of three components, which are discussed in the sections that follow.

Secure Desktop Manager

Secure Desktop Manager is a GUI-based application that allows administrators to define policies and locations for remote users. It currently supports two modules: Secure Desktop and Cache Cleaner. Secure Desktop Manager can be launched by pointing your browser to https://<*gateway-ip-address*>/csd_admin.html, where the gateway-ip-address is the IP address of the SSL VPN gateway for user connections. The default username to log in to Secure Desktop Manager is admin, and the default password is the enable password of the router.

Secure Desktop

Secure Desktop is a module that creates an encrypted and secure vault in the client computer. It allows users to securely access local resources or even allows users to establish SSL VPN sessions. Files created in this vault are encrypted and cannot be accessed by the applications outside this secure desktop. When a user disconnects a session, the vault can be destroyed.

By using Secure Desktop, users are given appropriate access to the corporate network after their system information is detected. System information includes elements such as operating system and service packs, antivirus version and signatures files, and firewalls. Before granting access, Secure Desktop can also determine whether the client workstation has any keystroke-logging applications installed. However, this system detection is transparent to the end user. Users do not know what type of information is being collected by CSD, and therefore a different set of features are applied based on the criteria defined by an administrator.

Cache Cleaner

Cache Cleaner securely cleans local browser data such as web pages, history information, and cached user credentials. Cache Cleaner is supported not only on the Windows operating systems but also on the Linux and MAC OS X systems.

When Cache Cleaner is launched on a client computer, it closes any existing browser windows and initiates the Cache Cleaner process. It monitors the browser data and when a user logs out of the SSL VPN session, it closes the browser and cleans the cache associated with the SSL VPN session.

NOTE   Cache Cleaner does not protect your computer from downloaded attachments and therefore does not guarantee full system cleanup.

Cache Cleaner monitors only one browser application per SSL VPN session. If the initial session was established through Internet Explorer, only Internet Explorer–specific browser data is cleaned after the user session is terminated. If the user launches Firefox after Cache Cleaner has already started, the Firefox browser data is not wiped out after the user terminates the session.

CSD Requirements

Before you deploy CSD into a production environment, analyze your current system and network architecture first to make sure that they meet the minimum version of supported operating systems and Internet browsers. A list of supported platforms is presented in the sections that follow.

Supported Operating Systems

In the current release of CSD, Secure Desktop is supported strictly in the Windows environment. The supported Windows platforms include

- Windows XP, including options with no service pack, Service Pack 1, and Service Pack 2
- Windows 2000, including options with no service pack, Service Pack 1, Service Pack 2, Service Pack 3, and Service Pack 4
- Windows Me
- Windows 98 Second Edition
- Windows NT Service Pack 6

MAC OS X and Linux-based operating system users can use Cache Cleaner and VPN feature policies on the remote clients.

User Privileges

CSD does not require administrative privileges on the client computer when it is launched. However, the ActiveX installation will fail if you are not logged in as an administrator. Therefore, it is expected that when using Internet cafés, users cannot run either an ActiveX installation or workstations with no administrative rights. For users without administrative rights, the Java installation should succeed.

NOTE   If you are using Microsoft Java Virtual Machine (JVM), the user must have administrative rights. However, for Sun JVM, you do not have to be a local administrator.

Supported Internet Browsers

You can use the following browsers to manage, configure, administer, and use the current version of CSD:

- Internet Explorer 6.*x* and 7.0
- Netscape 7.*x* and 8
- Mozilla 1.7.*x*
- Mozilla Firefox 1.0.*x* through 1.5

CAUTION   If you use Netscape 8 to install Windows Cache Cleaner, it starts Internet Explorer and cleans only the Internet Explorer cache.

Internet Browser Settings

As discussed in the previous section, CSD is installed on the client computer through ActiveX, Java, or an executable file. You must configure the appropriate security settings in your Internet browser to allow those functions. For example, in Internet Explorer, use the guidelines discussed in Table 6-5. These settings are configured by choosing **Tools > Internet Options > Security tab > Internet > Custom Level**.

Table 6-5   *Configurable SSL VPN Group Policy Attributes*

Attribute	Setting
ActiveX controls and plug-ins > Download signed ActiveX controls	Enable
ActiveX controls and plug-ins > Run ActiveX controls and plug-ins	Enable
Downloads > File download	Enable
Scripting > Active scripting	Enable
Scripting > Scripting of Java applets	Enable
Microsoft VM > Java permissions	High, medium, or low safety

CSD Architecture

CSD not only checks certain attributes on the client computer to ensure its compliance but also enhances data security by providing an encrypted vault to authorized users. When a user wants to establish an SSL VPN session and CSD is enabled, the client and the gateway go through a number of steps, as outlined in the list that follows. These steps are illustrated in Figure 6-33.

Step 1   Users request the SSL VPN login page by pointing their browsers to the gateway IP address.

Step 2   User sessions are redirected to a different web page (/start.html) because a secure desktop session has not been created. The gateway tries to install the Secure Desktop client component on the user workstation using ActiveX, Java, or Executable mode.

Step 3   After installing the client component, the system is scanned and necessary information is collected from the client workstation. This information is forwarded to the gateway.

Step 4   The collected information is matched against the policies that are defined in Secure Desktop Manager and are stored in data.xml.

Step 5   A secure desktop cookie is written on the client computer, and the secure vault is created on the hard disk. The web session is redirected to the SSL VPN user login page.

Step 6   The user presents authentication credentials, and if authentication is successful, the clientless SSL VPN session or AnyConnect SSL VPN session is created.

Figure 6-33 *CSD System Architecture*

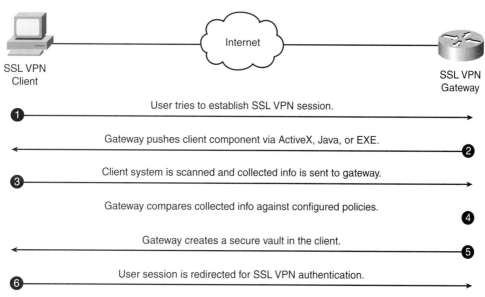

The data.xml file contains CSD-specific configuration information such as

- Location information
- Criteria for SSL VPN features

The SSL VPN features criteria are defined using specially formatted strings that are divided into different classes by a semicolon. Each class is identified by two characters, such as AV for antivirus and FW for personal firewall, followed by an equal sign and a value for that character.

Configuring CSD

CSD is configured using the following three steps:

Step 1 Loading the CSD package

Step 2 Launching the CSD package

Step 3 Defining policies

Step 1: Loading the CSD Package

Like AnyConnect Client, you have to load the CSD package in the local flash of the SSL VPN gateway. If you are not sure whether you have CSD installed on your IOS router, type **show flash** or **dir** and look for the sdesktop.pkg file in the webvpn directory. Using SDM, you can choose **Configure > VPN > SSL VPN > Packages** and check whether the CSD is installed. SDM allows you to

- Download the latest Cisco Secure Desktop (CSD) installation bundle. It connects to Cisco.com by prompting you for login credentials. If the login credentials are correct, SDM displays all the posted CSD files in a different browser window.

- Select a preloaded CSD file from flash. Even if you have a preloaded CSD file in flash, you should check the latest version of CSD at the Cisco website. Click **Browse** to select a file from either the router's flash or the workstation running the SDM software.

In Figure 6-34, an sdesktop.pkg file is selected from flash. This file is located at flash:/webvpn. After the file is selected, the last step is to install this file for the SSL VPN process by clicking the **Install** button. The router confirms the process by prompting "Are you sure you want to install the package?" If you select **Yes**, the router installs the package and displays the message "Cisco Secure Desktop package successfully installed."

Figure 6-34 *Installing the CSD Package*

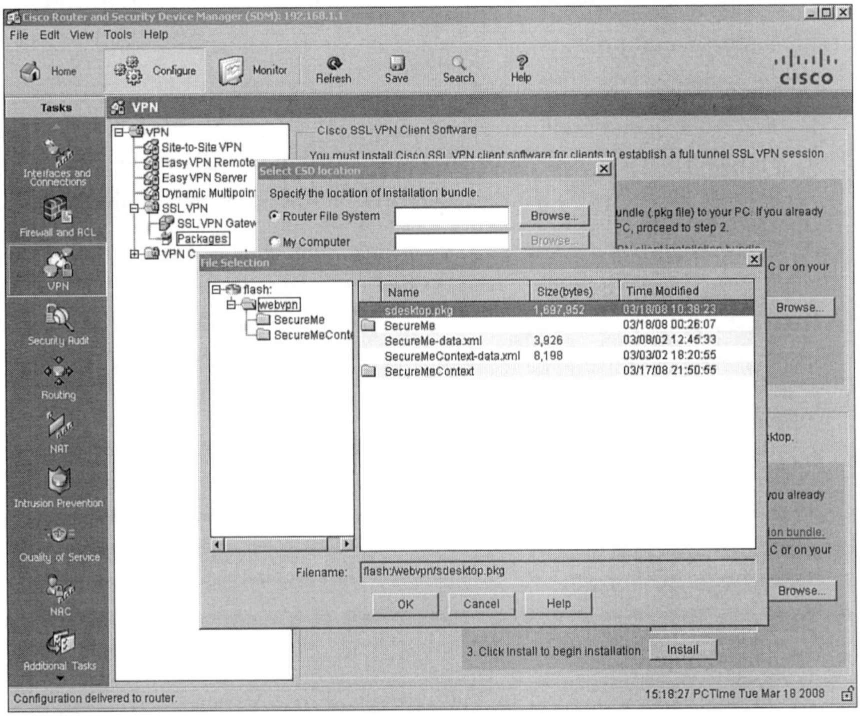

Example 6-37 shows how the CSD package can be installed on an IOS router through the CLI.

Example 6-37 *Installing CSD Through the CLI*

```
Chicago(config)# webvpn install csd flash:/webvpn/sdesktop.pkg
```

Step 2: Launching the CSD Package

After installing the package file, the next task is to enable CSD in the SSL VPN gateway. You can choose **Configure > VPN > SSL VPN > Edit SSL VPN > SecureMeContext > Cisco Secure Desktop** and select the **Enable Cisco Secure Desktop** check box to activate the package. SDM pushes the **csd enable** command to the IOS router.

Next, launch the management application by clicking **Launch Cisco Secure Desktop Admin Application** under **Configure > VPN > SSL VPN > Packages** and under the Cisco Secure Desktop Software option. A new browser window is opened and the administrator is prompted to provide administrative user credentials. The default username is admin, while the default password is the enable password of the router. After being authenticated, SDM displays all the configured contexts and allows you to select the context you want to configure for CSD.

NOTE   In some versions of SDM, after launching the CSD admin application, you receive the error message, The Page Cannot Be Found. In this case, point your browser to https://<*gateway-ip-address*>/csd_admin.html, where gateway-ip-address is the IP address of the SSL VPN gateway.

Step 3: Defining Policies for Windows-Based Clients

After successfully logging in to Secure Desktop Manager, you can define policies that the SSL VPN users must adhere to. If the client's computer matches a certain profile, the client is given access based on the configured policies on the profile. The following sections walk you through the configuration of Secure Desktop Manager in defining the profiles and the respective policies for the SSL VPN users. The following topics are presented:

- Defining Windows locations
- Identifying machines
- Enabling SSL VPN features
- Identifying keystroke loggers
- Defining Secure Desktop general attributes
- Applying Secure Desktop restrictions

- Defining Cache Cleaner policies
- Defining browser bookmarks

Defining Windows Locations

In the supported Windows-based operating systems, you can define the potential locations from where these client computers can connect. For example, if your users connect from the office network, home office network, and even from Internet cafés, you can define a location for each setup and give appropriate access to your users. For users connecting from the office network, you classify those hosts as fairly secure and allow a less restrictive environment. For users connecting from their home offices, you can classify those hosts as somewhat secure and apply more restrictive policies. For users connecting from the Internet cafés, you classify those hosts as least secure and apply the most restrictive policies.

Throughout this chapter, we use three Windows locations to build a configuration. They include

- **OfficeCorpOwned:** This location is defined for those workstations that establish an SSL VPN tunnel from the corporate-owned IP addresses. Additionally, the workstations must have a unique registry setting to identify them as corporate-owned computers. If workstations match this profile, Secure Desktop or Cache Cleaner will not be launched.

- **HomeCorpOwned:** This location is defined for those Windows computers that are corporate owned but are used by people who establish an SSL VPN tunnel from their home offices and whose address does not match the corporate-owned address range. The workstations are classified as corporate owned by identifying a unique registry setting. If workstations match this profile, Secure Desktop is launched.

- **InternetCafe:** This location is defined for those computers that do not match any of the previously described profiles. Cache Cleaner is launched.

These profiles are defined by choosing **Secure Desktop Manager > Windows Location Settings**. Specify a new location name, such as OfficeCorpOwned, under Location Name and click **Add**. If a workstation matches this profile but fails to launch Secure Desktop, specify a fallback VPN feature. The available options for fallback VPN features include web browsing, file access, port forwarding, and full tunneling. As shown in Figure 6-35, a Windows location called HomeCorpOwned is defined, and the default VPN feature policy is set to allow all VPN methods except for full tunnel mode. Click **Save** to save the configuration in the system.

Figure 6-35 *Defining a Windows Location*

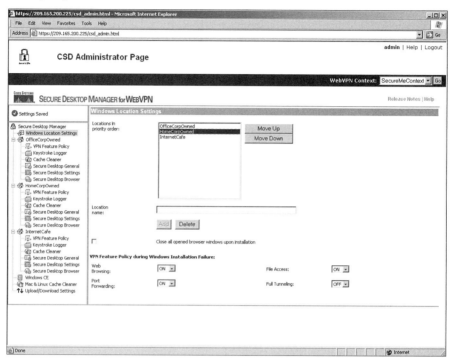

When you have multiple Windows locations defined, CSD matches the client computer in sequential order. If the client computer attributes do not match the first profile, it tries the second profile, and so on until a match is found. If a match is not found, the default VPN feature policy is applied on the user session.

Identifying Machines

After defining the required Windows locations, the next step is to define criteria used to match Windows computers to each profile. CSD supports the following three ways to identify a host:

- **Certificates:** If you use certificates in your environment, you can leverage the subject and the issuer names in the identity certificates to match a specific profile. The subject and issuer names contain a number of subordinate fields such as common name (CN), organization (O), organizational unit (OU), and country , to name a few. You can use one of the subordinate fields in the subject and issuer names to identify computers that match a specific profile.

> **NOTE** To identify computers based on certificates, specify the value of the subordinate fields. For example, to identify computers based on organizational unit (OU), simply specify the value of OU but do not list OU in the names.

- **IP address range:** If you know the IP address space of client computers, use this feature to identify computers to match a profile. You can define one or multiple address spaces to identify computers.

> **NOTE** If the client computer has multiple IP addresses, CSD uses the first identified IP address to match against a profile.

- **File or registry setting:** You can use the location of a file or a specific registry key or value to identify computers. This feature is useful if, for example, you want to determine whether computers are corporate owned by identifying a specific file or registry key.

> **NOTE** If you specify more than one registry key or file location, CSD applies an OR logical operation. For example, if you define the location of a registry key and define the location of a file, one of the locations must be present to identify a host.

As illustrated in Figure 6-36, one identification feature is enabled for the HomeCorpOwned windows location. A registry check is enabled to ensure that the HKEY_LOCAL_MACHINE\ SOFTWARE\McAfee\VirusScan key exists. If clients match this feature, they will be identified as company-owned workstations that create SSL VPN sessions from a home network. For these computers, Secure Desktop is launched.

> **NOTE** If you want to identify a computer by locating a specific file in the system and ensuring the integrity of the file, you can find its checksum. To assist you with calculating the correct checksum of a file, CSD provides the crc32.exe application.

Figure 6-36 *Identifying Windows Machines*

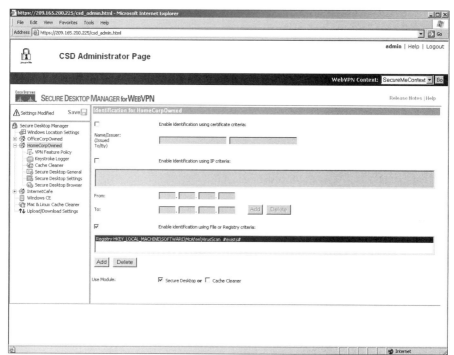

Enabling SSL VPN Features

After matching a computer to one of the predefined Windows locations, you can provide access to the available VPN features such as web browsing, file access, port forwarding, and full tunneling mode. The robust implementation of CSD can detect applications such as antivirus, antispyware, personal firewalls, and service packs before giving access to the VPN features. For each SSL VPN feature attribute, you have three options:

- **ON:** Enable an SSL VPN feature when the client matches this location.

- **OFF:** Disable an SSL VPN feature when the client matches this location. This is the default option for all attributes.

- **ON if criteria are matched:** Enable an SSL VPN feature when the client computers match a Windows location and a set of predefined criteria. If this option is selected, you can click the **...** icon and specify what criteria the SSL VPN users' computers must meet to gain network access. For example, if you require computers to have Cisco Security Agent (CSA) as well as McAfee VirusScan before they can be given SSL VPN access, you must select these criteria after you click the **...** button.

Table 6-6 lists all the currently available criteria that you can define. After a criterion is selected, if the user's computer does not meet that criterion, the SSL VPN functionality will not be available to that user's computer.

NOTE   As discussed in Chapter 5, CSD in the security appliance supports more than 400 products.

Table 6-6   *Available Criteria for System Scan*

Category	Available Options
Antivirus	Avast AntiVirus version 4.0
	AVG AntiVirus version 7.0-7.1
	eTrust AntiVirus version 7.0-2005
	F-Secure AntiVirus 2003 to 2005
	McAfee VirusScan version 8.0 to 10.0, Enterprise version 7.0 to 8.0
	Norton AntiVirus Corporate version 8.0 to 10.0, Professional 2004 to 2006
	Panda AntiVirus Titanium 2004, Platinum 7.0 to 8.0
	PC-Cillin 2003 or 2005
	Trend Micro OfficeScan Corporate AntiVirus 7.0
Antispyware	Microsoft AntiSpyware
	Anonymizer AntiSpyware
	Trend Micro OfficeScan Corporate AntiSpyware 7.0
Firewalls	Cisco Security Agent version 4.0 to 4.5
	Internet Connection Firewall (Windows XP to Windows XP SP2)
	ISS BlackICE PC Protection version 3.6
	McAfee Personal Firewall version 4.0 to 7.0
	Norton Personal Firewall version 2003 to 2006
	PC-Cillin Personal Firewall 2005
	Sygate Personal Firewall version 5.0 to 5.6
	Trend Micro OfficeScan Corporate Firewall 7.0
	ZoneAlarm Personal Firewall version 5.0 to 5.5

Table 6-6   *Available Criteria for System Scan (Continued)*

Category	Available Options
Operating systems	Windows XP (no service pack)
	Windows XP (Service Pack 1)
	Windows XP (Service Pack 2)
	Windows 2000 (no service pack)
	Windows 2000 (Service Pack 1)
	Windows 2000 (Service Pack 2)
	Windows 2000 (Service Pack 3)
	Windows 2000 (Service Pack 4)
	Windows NT Service Pack 6
	Windows Me
	Windows 98
Features*	Secure Desktop
	Cache Cleaner

*If either Secure Desktop or Cache Cleaner option is selected, the presence of these services is required before SSL VPN modes (web browsing, file access, port forwarding, or full tunneling) are allowed.

After all the required options are selected, click **OK** to return to the previous configuration window. CSD displays the configured parameters for each SSL VPN mode. Click **Save** to save the configuration.

As illustrated in Figure 6-37, an administrator has defined the following criteria:

- **Antivirus:** McAfee VirusScan (8.0-10.0, Enterprise 7.0-8.0)
- **Firewall:** Cisco Security Agent (4.0-4.5)
- **OS:** Windows XP SP2

These criteria are defined under full tunneling mode. When all the defined criteria match, the full tunneling client is available for the computers that match HomeCorpOwned as the Windows location.

Figure 6-37 *Defining VPN Feature Policy*

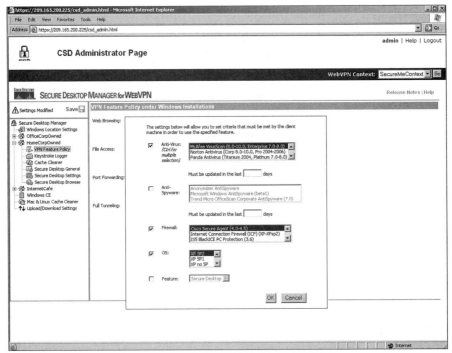

Identifying Keystroke Loggers

The robust implementation of CSD allows you to detect certain software-based keystroke loggers in a workstation and take appropriate actions before allowing a user's computer to create a secure desktop environment. Keystroke loggers usually capture keystrokes without informing the legitimate users of the computer. These applications then send the captured information to a server, generally owned by hackers. If, for example, you have a keystroke logger installed on your computer and you are doing online banking, the keystroke logger can potentially capture your user credentials and pass that information to a hacker who can misuse your personal information for his/her advantage.

To prevent users' computers that have a keystroke logger installed from establishing an SSL VPN tunnel, select **Keystroke Logger** under the name of the location and enable the **Check for keystroke loggers** option. With this option enabled, the system scans and detects a keystroke-logging application on the workstation. If one is detected, the system allows the user to identify whether the application is safe. However, if you do not trust user discretion, you can enable **Force admin control on list of safe modules** and manually identify which keystroke loggers are safe. Applications, such as Corel Paint Shop Pro, usually capture keystrokes to allow users to easily modify data. In that case, an administrator can identify Paint Shop Pro as a safe application.

CSD allows you to define a list of safe keystroke-logger applications under Module Path. When an application is added, it appears under Path of Safe Modules. You can define as many keystroke-logging applications as you want.

NOTE   If Force Admin Control on List of Safe Modules is enabled and contents under Path of Safe Modules are defined and you later disable Force Admin Control on List of Safe Modules, CSD still keeps the content under Path of Safe Modules. It simply deactivates the defined values.

As shown in Figure 6-38, the **Force admin control on list of safe modules** check box is selected and the path to Paint Shop Pro is added under Path of Safe Modules. The complete path shown in this figure is C:\Program Files\Corel\Corel Paint Shop X\.

Figure 6-38 *Example of a Keystroke-Logging Application*

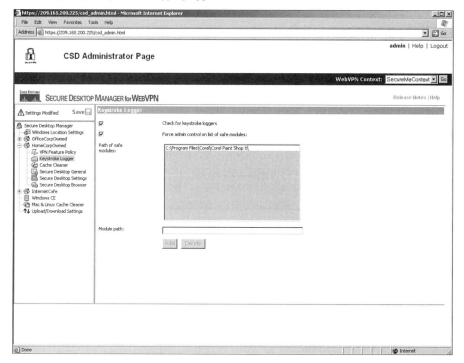

NOTE   If you receive a message that this tab is not available, this means that you do not have either Secure Desktop or Cache Cleaner enabled for that specific Windows location.

Defining Secure Desktop General Attributes

In CSD, you can set up general attributes that are applied to all SSL VPN sessions within a Windows location. For example, if you want to launch Secure Desktop as soon as it loads the package file, you can enable that feature here. The supported Secure Desktop general attributes are as follows:

- **Automatically switch to Secure Desktop after installation:** After CSD is initialized and loaded, the user's desktop is automatically switched to Secure Desktop. This is a recommended option to ensure that users are automatically placed in Secure Desktop without having them manually do it.

- **Enable switching between Secure Desktop and local desktop:** With this option enabled, the user has an option to switch back and forth between Secure Desktop and the local desktop. In many cases, when an application is launched within Secure Desktop, it sends a notification or user prompt on the local desktop. Hence, you should enable this option should you need to switch to local desktop to respond to a prompt.

- **Enable vault reuse (user chooses a password):** For users who use Secure Desktop more often than others, you can enable this option. This option is useful if, for example, home users connect to corporate networks from the same desktop computer. Knowing that their computers are fairly secure at home, you can let them use the same vault. This vault is protected by a password that can be up to 127 characters long.

- **Enable Secure Desktop inactivity timeout:** When this option is enabled, the system automatically closes the secure vault after a specified duration of inactivity. This option is useful for sessions that are left behind when applications are not properly closed. You should enable this option for those Windows locations that are not very secure, such as Internet cafés or untrusted host computers. If users are allowed to access critical or sensitive applications over the SSL VPN tunnel, you can choose to configure a lower timeout value, such as 5 minutes. If users access insensitive data, you can set up a higher timeout, such as 30 minutes.

- **Open following web page after Secure Desktop closes:** As the name suggests, this option requires you to input a URL that you want to launch after Secure Desktop disconnects on a user's computer. This option is useful if you want to redirect user web sessions to a website that lists a company's policies for SSL VPN usage.

- **Suggest application uninstall upon Secure Desktop closing:** With this option enabled, users are prompted and recommended to uninstall Secure Desktop when their session is terminated. This option is useful if you trust all your user computers (that belong to a Windows location) and rely on user discretion to destroy the vault.

- **Force application uninstall upon Secure Desktop closing:** With this option enabled, Secure Desktop is removed when a user session is terminated. This option is useful if you do not trust any user computers (that belong to a Windows location) and do not want to rely on user discretion to destroy the vault.

- **Secure delete:** When Secure Desktop is terminated, CSD converts all data to binary 0s. It then changes all vault space to all 1s and eventually randomized data to 0s and 1s. This entire process is considered one pass. You can change this default setting to run multiple times. After it goes through all the configured passes, it eventually deletes the allocated space that was being used by Secure Desktop.

- **Launch the following application after installation:** You can configure CSD to launch an application after Secure Desktop has been launched. This is useful if you require your users to work on a specific application when they connect through an SSL VPN. The application must reside in the Program Files folder.

As shown in Figure 6-39, the administrator has configured CSD to automatically switch to Secure Desktop after installation and has allowed users to switch their desktops between Secure Desktop and the local desktop. Secure delete is set for ten passes for the HomeCorpOwned Windows location.

Figure 6-39 *Defining Secure Desktop General Attributes*

Applying Secure Desktop Restrictions

In addition to the global parameters that can be configured (discussed in the preceding section), you can apply certain restrictions to Secure Desktop to further enhance the level of security for SSL VPN sessions. You can configure these restrictions under Secure Desktop Setting for a Windows location. These restrictions include

- **Put Secure Desktop in restricted mode:** With this option, you can restrict users to launch the same browser that initiated the Secure Desktop session. For example, if a user launches Secure Desktop using Internet Explorer, the user will be denied the launching of a different browser, such as Firefox, from within Secure Desktop. This option enhances security on the system because features such as Cache Cleaner do not clean the cache if a different browser is launched.

- **Restrict network folder and drive access on Secure Desktop:** Using this option, a user is denied access to network folders and drives. This even includes printers and any network shares that use Server Message Block (SMB) protocols. You should enable this restriction for those Windows locations that are the least secure so that unauthorized or illegitimate users do not access protected network shares or resources.

- **Restrict removable drive access on Secure Desktop:** When this option is enabled, users are restricted access to their portable drives, such as thumb or external hard drives, within the Secure Desktop environment. This restriction is recommended so that users cannot copy sensitive data on a portable drive when accessing data from insecure Windows locations.

- **Restrict registry tools on Secure Desktop:** To restrict users from modifying the system registry within Secure Desktop, you should enable this option.

- **Restrict DOS-CMD tools on Secure Desktop:** If unauthorized users get access to a system running Secure Desktop, they can launch command-line based attacks against corporate resources. You should restrict users to launching only DOS prompts within Secure Desktop to prevent such scenarios.

- **Restrict printing on Secure Desktop:** If illegitimate users get access to a Secure Desktop environment, they can print sensitive data such as software code on a local printer. You should prevent users in the least secure Windows locations from being able to print.

- **Do not encrypt files on network drives:** With this option enabled, users are restricted from saving encrypted files on the network drives. This option is grayed out if Restrict Network Folder and Drive Access on Secure Desktop, mentioned earlier, is enabled.

- **Do not encrypt files on removable drives:** With this option enabled, users are restricted from saving encrypted files on portable drives. This option is grayed out if Restrict Removable Drive Access on Secure Desktop, mentioned earlier, is enabled.

- **Allow email application to work transparently:** With this option enabled, users can access their e-mails while Secure Desktop restricts the deletion of e-mails when the session terminates. This option allows users to save e-mail attachments to the My Documents folder, which can be accessed from Secure Desktop and from the local desktop.

In Figure 6-40, the CSD administrator has enabled all restrictions for the HomeCorpOwned Windows location.

Figure 6-40 *Enabling Secure Desktop Restrictions*

Defining Cache Cleaner Policies

As discussed earlier in this chapter, Cache Cleaner securely removes local browser data such as web pages, history information, and cached user credentials. When Cache Cleaner is launched on a client computer, it closes any existing browser windows and initiates the Cache Cleaner process. It monitors the browser data, and when a user logs out of the SSL VPN session, it closes the browser and cleans the cache associated with the SSL VPN session. Cache Cleaner can be configured under Cache Cleaner of a Windows location.

Cache Cleaner can be launched for any Windows location, if enabled. Table 6-7 lists the options presented to you if Cache Cleaner is enabled for a Windows location.

Table 6-7   *Available Cache Cleaner Options*

Available Option	Option Description
Launch hidden URL after installation	After Cache Cleaner is installed, you might want the system to access a hidden URL. This way, you can track the users and know whether they have successfully installed Cache Cleaner. This is recommended if you want to know how many users use Cache Cleaner.
Show message at the end of successful installation	Using this option, users are shown a message indicating that Cache Cleaner has been successfully installed. This is recommended so that users know that the cache-cleaning process has started on their computers.
Launch cleanup upon inactivity timeout	To start the cache cleanup process after users have been idle for a while, enable this option and specify the timeout value in minutes. If this option is enabled, the default timeout value is 5 minutes.
Launch cleanup upon closing of all browser instances or SSL VPN connection	This option is useful if you want to start the Cache Cleaner when users close all their browser windows.
Disable cancellation of cleaning	By default, when Cache Cleaner is started, users can cancel the process. If you enable this option, users will not be allowed to cancel the cleanup process.
Clean the entire cache in addition to the current session cache (IE only)	If this option is enabled, Cache Cleaner cleans the entire Internet Explorer cache, including the data and files that were generated before CSD was launched.
Secure delete	When Secure Desktop is terminated, CSD converts all cached data to binary 0s. It then changes all cached data to 1 and eventually randomized data to 0s and 1s. This entire process is considered one pass. You can change this default setting to run multiple times. After it goes through all the configured passes, it eventually deletes the allocated space that was being used by Secure Desktop.

In Figure 6-41, the administrator has enabled Launch Hidden URL After Installation and added a hidden URL of http://www.securemeinc.com/cachecleaner.html for the InternetCafe Windows location. All users that match this profile will be shown a message that Cache Cleaner has successfully started. If user sessions are inactive for 10 minutes or if users close all browser windows, Cache Cleaner will start. Additionally, users are restricted from canceling the cache-cleaning process.

Figure 6-41 *Defining Cache Cleaner Policies*

Defining Secure Desktop Browser Settings

Using Secure Desktop, you can present users with a predefined list of browser bookmarks. These bookmarks are generally the most common URLs (or favorite sites) that users connect to after their SSL VPN session is established. These bookmarks are defined under "Secure Desktop Browser" of a Windows location. You can customize these bookmarks under folders or, if there are just a few bookmarks, define them under the parent folder. As illustrated in Figure 6-42, two bookmarks are defined for the InternetCafe Windows location under the parent folder. They include http://internal.securemeinc.com and http://email.securemeinc.com.

Figure 6-42 *Defining Browser Bookmarks*

Defining Policies for Windows CE

CSD provides limited support for Windows CE–based devices. You can configure a VPN feature policy to allow users to browse the web or allow them to access files on a remote server. The Windows CE policies are configured under "Windows CE." Figure 6-43 shows that both web browsing and file access are enabled for Windows CE–based devices.

Defining Policies for the Mac and Linux Cache Cleaner

As mentioned earlier in the chapter, Cache Cleaner is supported not only on Windows operating systems but also on Linux and Mac OS X systems. Additionally, you can define a limited VPN feature policy for these clients. Table 6-8 lists the available features that you can implement for Mac- and Linux-based computers.

Figure 6-43 *Defining Windows CE Policies*

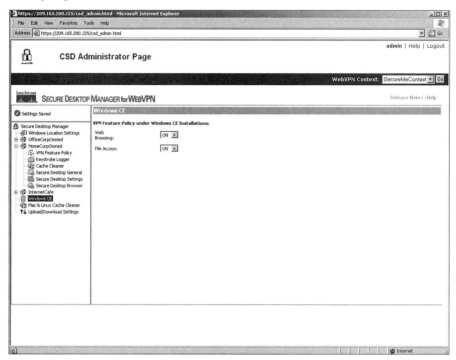

Table 6-8   *Available Cache Cleaner and VPN Feature Policy Options*

Available Option	Option Description
Launch cleanup upon global timeout	To start the cache cleanup process after users have been idle for a while, enable the global option and specify the timeout value in minutes. If this option is enabled, the default global timeout value is 1 minute.
Let user reset timeout	If this option is enabled, users can reset the timeout period.
Launch cleanup upon exiting of browser	This option is useful if you want to start Cache Cleaner when users close all instances of their browsers.
Enable Cancel button of cleaning	With this option enabled, users can cancel the cache cleaner process. We do not recommend enabling this feature to provide enhanced security.
Secure delete	When Secure Desktop is terminated, CSD converts all cached data to binary 0s. It then changes all cached data to 1s and eventually randomized data to 0s and 1s. This entire process is considered one pass. You can change this default setting to run multiple times. After it goes through all the configured passes, it eventually deletes the allocated space that was being used by Secure Desktop.

continues

Table 6-8 *Available Cache Cleaner and VPN Feature Policy Options (Continued)*

Available Option	Option Description
Enable web browsing if Mac or Linux installation fails	This option allows Mac- and Linux-based workstations to use the clientless SSL VPN feature if Cache Cleaner fails to load.
Web browsing	With this VPN feature turned on, Mac- and Linux-based hosts can establish clientless tunnels and browse internal websites.
File access	With this VPN feature turned on, Mac- and Linux-based hosts can establish clientless tunnels and access files on the remote servers through SMB.
Port forwarding	With this VPN feature turned on, Mac- and Linux-based hosts can access internal resources through port forwarding.

In Figure 6-44, the administrator has set up CSD to start Cache Cleaner if there is either inactivity for 5 minutes or if a user closes all instances of a browser. Secure delete is set for two passes, and Mac and Linux users are allowed to browse the web, access files, and forward traffic on preconfigured TCP ports.

Figure 6-44 *Defining Mac and Linux Policies*

Deployment Scenarios

The SSL VPN solution can be deployed in many ways. For ease of understanding, however, the sections that follow cover two design and deployment scenarios:

- Clientless connections with CSD
- AnyConnect Client and external authentication

NOTE   The design scenarios discussed in these sections should be used solely to reinforce learning. They are for reference purposes only.

Clientless Connections with CSD

SecureMe wants to deploy an SSL VPN solution for a group of contractors that access some resources from their laptops. These contractors use a terminal server as well as a web server for browsing, and a Windows file server to save and retrieve their documents. All contractors use Windows-based operating systems on their workstations. SecureMe prefers to create a secure environment before SSL VPN sessions are allowed. Figure 6-45 shows SecureMe's proposed network topology for clientless connections.

Figure 6-45 *SecureMe's Clientless Connection Topology with CSD*

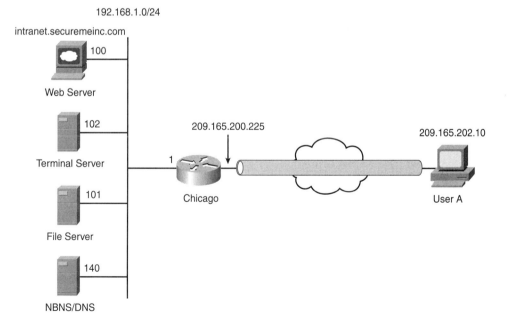

The security requirements for SecureMe are as follows:

- Contractors are not allowed to connect until a secure vault is created.

- A secure vault should only be created if remote workstations have Cisco Security Agent installed.

- Access should be allowed to the internal web server located at intranet.securemeinc.com.

- Access should be allowed to a file server with an IP address of 192.168.1.101.

- Access should be allowed to a terminal server with an IP address of 192.168.1.102.

- Contractors should not to be able to browse or specify any other web server in the SecureMe network.

To achieve SecureMe's requirements, the administrator has proposed that the Cisco IOS router be configured for clientless access. The URL list will be configured to provide access to the web and file servers. Port forwarding will be set up to provide connectivity to the terminal server. CSD will be used to scan a registry key of HKEY_LOCAL_MACHINE\ SOFTWARE\Cisco\CSAgent. If the registry key is present, a secure vault will be created. CSD will also scan the remote workstation for personal firewall Cisco Security Agent 4.5. If a firewall is installed, users will be allowed to browse the web and file server, and will also be allowed to use port forwarding.

The steps to implement the proposed solution are outlined in the sections that follow.

Step 1: User Authentication and DNS

The first step in achieving the listed goals is to define a local database of users who are going to use the SSL VPN service. Follow these instructions to achieve this:

1 Choose **Configure** > **Additional Tasks** > **AAA** and select **Enable AAA**. Choose **Authentication Policies** > **Login** > **Add** and specify a list name of sslvpn. Click **Add** and choose **Local** as the authentication method. Click **OK** when finished.

2 Choose **Configure** > **Additional Tasks** > **Router Access** > **User Accounts/View** > **Add** and configure user accounts on the router by defining the usernames and passwords.

3 Choose **Configure** > **Additional Tasks** > **DNS** > **Edit** and select **Enable DNS based hostname to address translation**. Click **Add** and specify 192.168.1.140 as the IP address of the DNS server.

Step 2: Set Up CSD

The second step in achieving the listed goals is to create a secure environment for remote users as follows:

1 Choose **Configure > VPN > SSL VPN > Packages**, click **Browse** under Cisco Secure Desktop Software, select the CSD file you want to use, and click **Install**.

2 Launch the CSD application and log in to Secure Desktop Manager. After it is launched, click **Windows Location Settings** and specify **Contractors** under Location Name. Click **Add**.

3 Click the newly created Windows location, select the **Enable Identification Using File or Registry Criteria** option, click **Add**, specify **HKEY_LOCAL_MACHINE\SOFTWARE\Cisco\CSAgent** under Path, and click **Exists** as the option. Select **Secure Desktop** under Use Module:.

4 Select the **VPN Feature Policy** option for Contractors and choose **ON If Criteria Are Matched** from the Web Browsing, File Access, and Port Forwarding drop-down menu. Click the **...** button for all these options, and select **Cisco Security Agent (4.0-4.5)** under Firewall.

5 Click **Save** to save these settings.

Step 3: Define Clientless Connections

The last step in achieving the listed goals is to set up clientless connections for remote contractors as follows:

1 Choose **Configure > VPN > SSL VPN > SSL VPN Gateways > Add** to create a gateway. Specify a gateway name of **SecureMeGW**, enable this gateway, and configure **209.165.200.225** as the IP address of this gateway. Select a digital gateway if one is already installed. If you prefer to use a self-signed certificate, select a certificate from the Trustpoint drop-down menu. Click **OK** when finished.

2 Choose **Configure > VPN > SSL VPN > Edit SSL VPN tab**. Click **Add** to create an SSL VPN context. Under Name, specify **SecureMeContext**, select **SecureMeGW** as the associated gateway, specify **securemeinc** as the domain, and select **sslvpn** as the authentication list. Make sure that you select the **Enable Context** check box, and click **OK** when finished.

3 Under SSL VPN Context, choose **URL Lists > Add.** Specify a list name and heading of **InternalServer** and click **Add** to add a website. Under URL Label, configure **InternalWebServer** with a value of **http://intranet.securemeinc.com**. Click **OK** when finished.

4 Under SSL VPN Context, choose **NetBIOS Name Server List > Add**. Specify a list name of **NBNS-Server** and click **Add** to specify an NBNS server located at 192.168.1.140. Select the **Make this the Master Server** check box and click **OK** when finished.

5 Under SSL VPN Context, choose **Port Forward Lists > Add**. Specify a list name of **TerminalServer** and click **Add**. Under Server IP Address, specify **192.168.1.102**; under Server Port On Which Service Is Listening, specify **3389**; under Port on Client PC, configure **3000;** and under Description, specify **Access to Internal Terminal Server**. Click **OK** when finished.

6 Define a group policy to link the URL list, port-forwarding list, and NetBIOS name server list. Choose **Configure > VPN > SSL VPN > Edit SSL VPN > SecureMeContext > Edit > Group Policies > Add.** Under Name, specify **SecureMeDefaultPolicy** and select the **Make this the default group policy for context** check box. Click the **Clientless** tab, select **InternalServer**, and choose **Hide URL bar in the portal page**. Select **Enable CIFS**, choose the **Read** and **Write** options, and select the **NBNS-Server** list from the NBNS Server List drop-down menu. Click **OK** when finished.

7 Click the **Thin Client** tab, select **Enable Thin Client (Port Forwarding)**, and choose **TerminalServer** from the Port Forward List drop-down menu. Click **OK** when finished.

8 Under SSL VPN Context, click **Cisco Secure Desktop** and select the **Enable Cisco Secure Desktop** option. Click **OK** when finished.

9 Distribute **https://209.165.200.225/securemeinc** as the SSL VPN login portal link to the users who will use the SSL VPN service.

AnyConnect Client and External Authentication

SecureMe has recently learned about the full network connectivity method that is offered by the Cisco IOS router through SSL VPN. The company wants to use this feature for its regular employees so that they can work from home and have full access to the internal network. Figure 6-46 shows SecureMe's network topology for AnyConnect Client.

Figure 6-46 *SecureMe's SSL VPN for AnyConnect Clients*

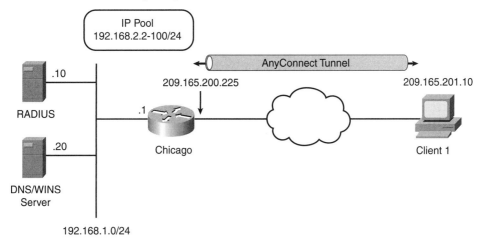

SecureMe's security requirements are as follows:

- Allow full access to the internal network when a user is authenticated.
- Use a RADIUS server as the external database for user lookup.
- Encrypt traffic going over to the 192.168.0.0/16 network; no other traffic should be encrypted.

To achieve SecureMe's requirements, the administrator has proposed that user credentials be checked against the RADIUS database, and if users are successfully authenticated, they will be allowed to establish an SSL VPN tunnel through the AnyConnect Client. After AnyConnect Client is loaded on the workstation, it should remain installed. The administrator will enable split tunneling to encrypt traffic destined to 192.168.0.0/16.

The steps to implement the proposed solution are listed next.

Step 1: Set Up RADIUS for Authentication

The first step is to set up a RADIUS server for user authentication as follows:

1 Choose **Configure > VPN > AAA > AAA Servers and Groups > AAA Servers > Add**. Choose **RADIUS** as the Server Type and configure **192168.1.10** as its IP address. Select **Configure Key** and specify **cisco123** as the New Key. Enter **cisco123** under Confirm Key. Click **OK** when finished.

2   Choose **Configure** > **VPN** > **AAA** > **AAA Servers and Groups** > **AAA Server Groups** > **Add**. Under Group Name, type **InternalRADIUS**, select **RADIUS** under Server Type, and select the previous defined **192.168.1.10** server from the list. Click **OK** when finished.

3   Choose **Configure** > **Additional Tasks** > **AAA** and select the **Enable AAA** option. Choose **Authentication Policies** > **Login** > **Add** and specify a list name of **SSLVPNRADIUS**. Click **Add** and choose **Group radius** as the authentication method. Click **OK** when finished.

Step 2: Install the AnyConnect SSL VPN

The next step is to install the AnyConnect package file on the local flash of the IOS router as follows:

Choose **Configure** > **VPN** > **SSL VPN** > **Packages**, click **Browse** under Cisco SSL VPN Client Software, select the AnyConnect file you want to use, and click **Install**.

Step 3: Configure AnyConnect SSL VPN Properties

The last step necessary to meet the listed requirements is to configure AnyConnect VPN Client on the router for remote users. This deployment scenario assumes that an SSL VPN gateway and context were not defined earlier and creates new ones. Follow these guidelines to achieve the goals:

1   Choose **Configure** > **VPN** > **SSL VPN** > **SSL VPN Gateways** > **Add** to create a gateway. Specify a gateway name of **SecureMeGW**, enable this gateway, and configure **209.165.200.225** as the IP address of this gateway. Select a digital certificate if one has already been installed. If you prefer to use a self-signed certificate, select a certificate from the Trustpoint drop-down menu. Click **OK** when finished.

2   Choose **Configure** > **VPN** > **SSL VPN** > **Edit SSL VPN tab**. Click **Add** to create an SSL VPN context. Under Name, specify **SecureMeContext**, select **SecureMeGW** as the associated gateway, specify **securemeinc** as the domain, and select **sslvpn** as the authentication list. Make sure you select the **Enable Context** check box, and click **OK** when finished.

3   Define a group policy to configure the AnyConnect-specific parameters. Choose **Configure** > **VPN** > **SSL VPN** > **Edit SSL VPN** > **SecureMeContext** > **Edit** > **Group Policies** > **Add**. Under Name, specify **SecureMeDefaultPolicy** and select the **Make this the default group policy for context** check box. Click the SSL VPN Client (Full Tunnel) tab and choose **Enabled** under Full Tunnel.

4   Under IP Address Pool from Which Clients Will Be Assigned an IP Address, click the **...** option and select **Create a new IP Pool**. Under Pool Name, specify **SSLVPNPool**, and then click **Add** to define a range of IP addresses. The Start IP Address is **192.168.2.2** and the End IP Address is **192.168.2.100**. Click **OK** when finished.

5   Choose **Configure > Interfaces and Connections > Edit Interface/Connection > Add > New Logical Interface > Loopback > Static IP address** and specify **192.168.2.1** as the IP address and **255.255.255.0** as the subnet mask.

6   Click **Advanced Options** and, on the Split Tunneling tab, select the **Include Traffic** option. Click **Add** and specify **192.168.0.0** as the network and **255.255.0.0** as the subnet mask. Click **OK** when finished.

7   Click the option for **Servers** in the left pane and configure **192.168.1.20** as the DNS and WINS server addresses.

8   On the DNS and WINS Server tab, specify **192.168.1.20** under Primary DNS Server and Primary WINS Server. The Default Domain is **securemeinc.com**. Click **OK** when finished.

9   The SSL VPN users can now connect to the IOS router using the following URL in your browser: https://209.165.200.225/securemeinc.

Monitoring an SSL VPN in Cisco IOS

This section discusses the monitoring steps that are available to help you run the SSL VPN solution smoothly on the IOS router. To monitor SSL VPN sessions, the first step is to check how many active SSL VPN tunnels are established on the IOS router. You can achieve this by choosing **Monitor > VPN Status > SSL VPN (All Contexts) > SecureMeContext > Users**. The Cisco IOS router shows you all the active VPN sessions for the SecureMeContext context. As shown in Figure 6-47, an active clientless connection is created by a user called sslvpnuser. The user computer's IP address is 209.165.200.230 and the user session was created 27 seconds ago. The applied group policy is SecureMeGroupPolicy. SDM also shows the values of the applied group policies, such as the applied URL, port forwarding, and NBNS list names.

Figure 6-47 *Monitoring SSL VPN Sessions Through SDM*

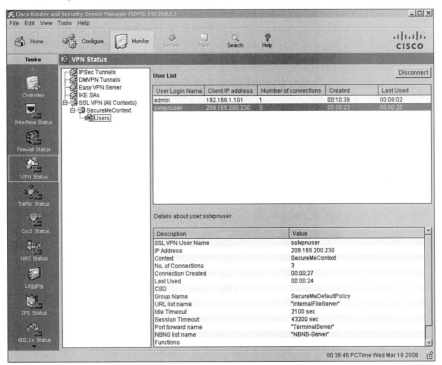

You can also monitor the SSL VPN connections through the CLI. For example, you can type the **show webvpn session user sslvpnuser context securemecontext** command to see most of the information that was shown in Figure 6-47. Example 6-38 shows the output of this command. It shows you not only the SSL VPN session statistics for a user but also provides information on CSD and indicates what policies are applied for that specific session.

Example 6-38 *Output of the* **show webvpn session** *Command*

```
Chicago# show webvpn session user sslvpnuser context SecureMeContext
WebVPN user name = sslvpnuser ; IP address = 209.165.200.230 ; context =
  SecureMeContext
    No of connections: 2
    Created 00:02:04, Last-used 00:02:01
    CSD secure desktop Enabled
    CSD cache cleaner Disabled
    CSD Session Policy
       CSD Web Browsing Disabled
       CSD Port Forwarding Allowed
       CSD Full Tunneling Disabled
       CSD File Access Allowed
    Client Port: 1707
```

Example 6-38 *Output of the* **show webvpn session** *Command (Continued)*

```
Client Port: 1710
User Policy Parameters
  Group name = SecureMeDefaultPolicy
Group Policy Parameters
  url list name = "WebOutlook"
  url list name = "ListForClientlessUsers"
  cifs url list name = "InternalFileServer"
  idle timeout = 2100 sec
  session timeout = 43200 sec
  port forward name = "TerminalServer"
  nbns list name = "NBNS-Server"
  functions =
              hide-urlbar
              file-access
              file-browse
              file-entry
              svc-enabled
              port-forward-auto-download-enabled

  citrix disabled
  address pool name = "sslvpnpool"
  default domain = "securemeinc.com"
  tunnel-mode filter = "SVC-ACL"
  dpd client timeout = 300 sec
  dpd gateway timeout = 300 sec
  keep sslvpn client installed = enabled
  rekey interval = 3600 sec
  rekey method = new-tunnel
  lease duration = 43200 sec
  split include = 192.168.1.0 255.255.255.0
  DNS primary server = 192.168.1.10
  DNS secondary server = 192.168.1.40
  WINS primary server = 192.168.1.40
  WINS secondary server = 192.168.1.10
```

Another useful command for monitoring or even troubleshooting SSL VPN sessions on the Cisco IOS router is the **show webvpn stats detail** command. By using this command, you can gather almost any information you need on user SSL VPN sessions on the router. Whether you are looking for information about bookmarks, port forwarding, AnyConnect Client, or SSL protocol, you can get it with this command, as shown in Example 6-39.

Example 6-39 *Output of the* **show webvpn stats detail** *Command*

```
Chicago# show webvpn stats detail
User session statistics:
    Active user sessions     : 2        AAA pending reqs         : 0
    Peak user sessions       : 7        Peak time                : 2d01h
    Active user TCP conns     : 2        Terminated user sessions : 27
<snip>
    User cleared VPN sessions: 2        Exceeded ctx user limit  : 0
    Exceeded total user limit: 0

Mangling statistics:
    Relative urls            : 0        Absolute urls            : 0
<snip>
    Backend https response   : 0        Chunked encoding requests: 0

HTTP Authentication stats :
    Successful NTLM Auth      : 0        Failed NTLM Auth         : 0
<snip>
    Num Basic Auth sent       : 0        Num NTLM Auth sent       : 0

CIFS statistics:
  SMB related Per Context:
<snip>
    URL List Access OK       : 119      URL List Access Fails    : 0

Socket statistics:
    Sockets in use           : 3        Sock Usr Blocks in use   : 1
    Sock Data Buffers in use : 0        Sock Buf desc in use     : 2
<snip>
    Sock Premature Close     : 7        Sock Pipe Errors         : 69
    Sock Select Timeout Errs : 0

Port Forward statistics:
  Client                              Server
    proc pkts                : 4        proc pkts                : 5
    proc bytes               : 31       proc bytes               : 134
    cef pkts                 : 0        cef pkts                 : 0
    cef bytes                : 0        cef bytes                : 0

WEBVPN Citrix statistics:
Connections serviced : 0

              Server                Client
  Packets in  : 0                   0
<snip>
  Bytes out   : 0                   0

ACL statistics:
    Permit web request       : 0        Deny web request         : 0
<snip>
    Permit with match ACL    : 0        Deny with match ACL      : 0
```

Example 6-39 *Output of the* **show webvpn stats detail** *Command (Continued)*

```
Single Sign On statistics:
    Auth Requests            : 0          Pending Auth Requests   : 0
<snip>
    Connection Errors        : 0          Request Timeouts        : 0
    Unknown Responses        : 0

Tunnel Statistics:
    Active connections       : 0
    Peak connections         : 1          Peak time               : 2d00h
<snip>
```

Summary

This chapter provided details about the SSL VPN functionality in Cisco IOS routers. It began by offering design guidance and then discussed the configuration of SSL VPNs in greater detail. The configurations of clientless, thin client, and AnyConnect Client modes were discussed. The second half of the chapter focused on Cisco Secure Desktop (CSD) and offered guidance in setting up CSD features. This was done to make sure that you have an in-depth knowledge of the Cisco main SSL VPN platform offering. To reinforce learning, two deployment scenarios were presented along with their configurations. The end of the chapter discussed SSL VPN monitoring through SDM as well as the IOS CLI.

This chapter describes Secure Socket Layer (SSL) Virtual Private Network (VPN) provisioning using Cisco Security Manager (CSM).

CHAPTER 7

Management of SSL VPNs

In general, SSL VPN management spans several topics, including the following:

- **SSL VPN policy configuration and provisioning:** This includes all aspects of provisioning and ongoing maintenance of the configuration. For policy configuration and management, you should consider issues such as configuration and provisioning tools (command-line interface [CLI] versus graphical user interface [GUI], single-device manager versus multidevice manager), configuration change control, and role-based administration.

- **SSL VPN user account management:** This includes user database management, user access privilege management, account activity, and resource consumption tracking.

- **Performance management:** Measurement of the system including the central processing unit (CPU), memory usage, throughput, and end-user performance (latency).

- **Monitoring and reporting:** This includes device monitoring (system statistics, fault situation) and SSL VPN event monitoring and reporting.

This chapter focuses on the discussion of SSL VPN policy configuration and provisioning. In Chapter 5, "SSL VPNs on Cisco ASA," and Chapter 6, "SSL VPNs on Cisco IOS Routers," you have learned how to provision and manage a single Cisco SSL VPN device using CLI or single-device managers. This chapter focuses on how to manage multidevice Cisco SSL VPN deployments using a centralized, multidevice security management tool, Cisco Security Manager.

Cisco Security Manager (CSM) is a single, integrated application for managing security across Cisco security devices, including security routers, Cisco Adaptive Security Appliances (ASA), Cisco PIX firewalls, IPS sensors, Cisco IOS IPS, and Cisco Catalyst 6500 series security service modules. CSM is also a Cisco central SSL VPN management tool.

Multidevice Policy Provisioning

Previous chapters have discussed in detail how to configure an SSL VPN on Cisco intermediate session routers (ISR) or ASAs. With CSM, the fundamental SSL VPN configuration steps are the same as those in a single-device manager, with the exception of some differences in the GUI layout. Hence, the following sections do not repeat the configuration details that show you how to configure the SSL VPN features. Instead, the sections focus on the important multidevice provisioning attributes that you need to be aware of when you manage multiple SSL VPN devices.

Device View and Policy View

A central SSL VPN management solution manages multiple SSL VPN appliances that normally fall into two categories:

- A local cluster of SSL VPN appliances
- Geographically dispersed SSL VPN appliances at various "theaters" of a company

In either case, the SSL VPN policy would be very similar among all the SSL VPN appliances in terms of user access privilege policies, users and VPN policy groups, and security policies. The configuration differences are mainly in the network topology–related attributes, such as the IP address of the SSL VPN appliances, the interface names, and the tunnel client IP pool address ranges.

Because of this, you can create a set of generic SSL VPN policies that are general enough for all the SSL VPN appliances and then apply those policies to individual devices with the addition of device-specific attributes.

You have two ways to come up with this generic set of SSL VPN policies:

- Configure a single device first and generalize its policy as a template for other devices.
- Start from abstract level to first define a general policy template. Then, you can later push it down to a group of SSL VPN appliances.

Cisco Security Manager supports both approaches. It provides device, policy, and topology views to help you easily manage your security devices and policies from different perspectives.

Device View

As its name implies, device view provides a device-centric view of your SSL VPN network. Figure 7-1 shows the layout of a device view.

Figure 7-1   *Cisco Security Manager Device View*

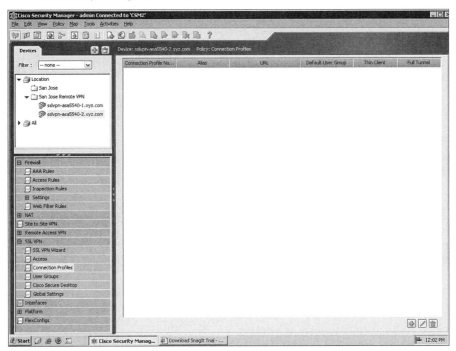

Three main areas are in the device view. The upper-left area lists all the devices and device groups. The lower-left area shows the common policies based on the device selected. The right area is the policy content work area.

The devices can be imported into CSM in multiple ways, as shown in Figure 7-2. For example, you can add a new SSL VPN appliance that already exists on your network given its IP address and secure login credentials, or you can just add a "virtual" device by specifying the device type and target OS version. Given the right device type and OS information, the CSM would be able to load the proper policy templates for you to start the policy configuration.

Figure 7-2 *Device Import*

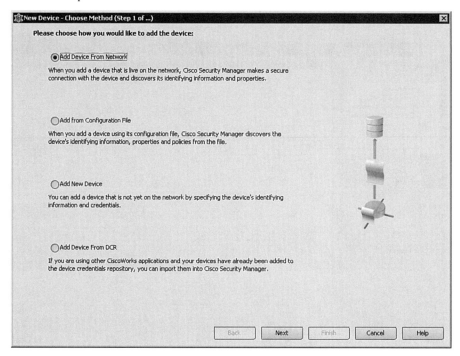

With device view, you can define the SSL VPN policy on one device and later use this policy as a template and share it with other devices that are subject to the same policy.

Figure 7-3 shows an example of sharing policies at the device level. First select a device and right-click it; then choose **Share Device Policies**. CSM provides you a checklist to select which policies to share (see Figure 7-4). The selected SSL VPN policy is saved as a template that can be applied to other devices later.

Figure 7-3   *Sharing Device Policies (1)*

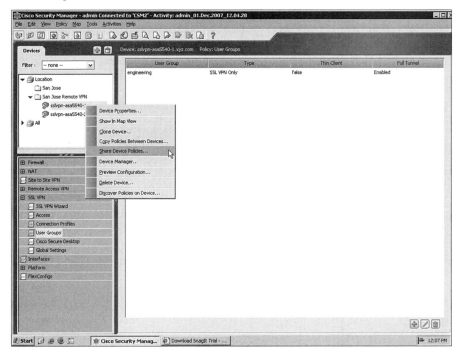

Figure 7-4   *Sharing Device Policies (2)*

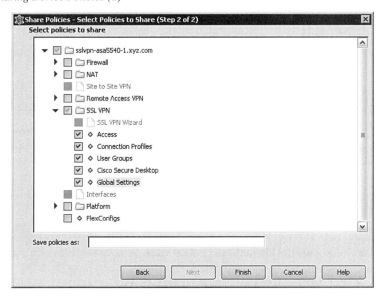

You have mainly two ways to assign defined SSL VPN policies to other devices: in policy view (discussed next) or in device view. In device view, choose **Policy > Copy policies between devices** to copy the predefined policies to other devices that are subject to the same SSL VPN policies. In addition, down to the individual device, CSM also provides granular policy-sharing options. Figure 7-5 shows an example.

Figure 7-5 *Sharing Device Policies (3)*

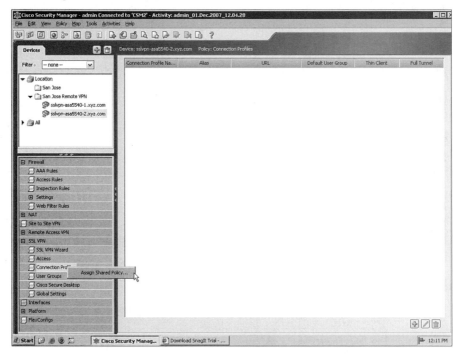

You can share policies and assign or unassign shared policies deep down in the policy tree. For a policy that is currently being shared, a different icon is displayed to differentiate it from unshared policies.

Policy View

The policy view displays the policy-centric view. This is where you can define generic SSL VPN policy templates without worrying about specific device settings. The policy templates can later be assigned to an individual or a group of SSL VPN devices.

Figure 7-6 shows the layout of the policy view. Similar to the device view, the upper-left area displays the list of security policies templates. Clicking **SSL VPN**, you can see all the generic SSL VPN policy templates that are supported by the CSM, for both ASAs and ISRs.

The lower-left area displays the list of previously defined policies. The right area displays the policy content.

Figure 7-6   *Cisco Security Manager Policy View*

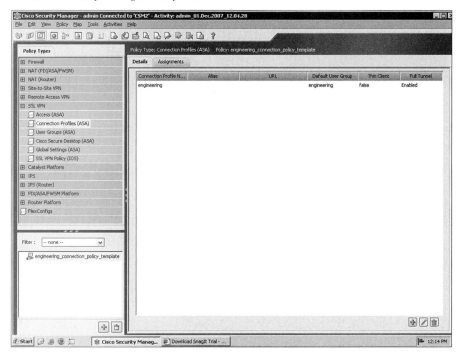

As shown in Figure 7-6, CSM handles ASAs and ISRs differently. For ASAs, the complete SSL VPN policy configuration is divided into five modules, each of which can be applied to ASAs separately. This gives you flexibility in terms of permutation of different modules into different policy sets. For ISRs, all aspects of the policy configuration are bundled together as one template.

After policies are defined, you can assign them to the SSL VPN devices. Figure 7-7 shows an example of how you can assign a defined SSL VPN policy to an SSL VPN device.

Figure 7-7 *Policy Assignment*

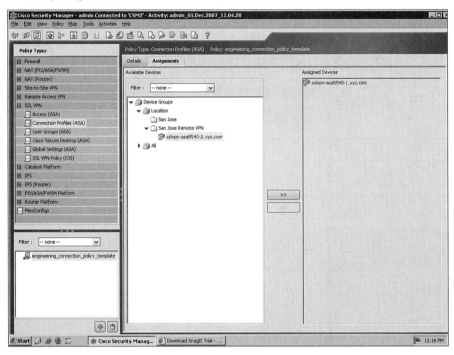

Use of Common Objects for Multidevice Management

We just discussed how to define an SSL VPN policy template and then share it among multiple devices. One question you might have asked by now is this: What about device-dependent attributes, such as interface names and VPN IP pool ranges? These attributes are different from device to device. For example, in a generic SSL VPN policy, the SSL VPN policy template assigns IP addresses to tunnel client users from an IP pool named sslvpn-ip-pool. However, when it comes to each individual device that locates at different parts of the network, sslvpn-ip-pool should have different ranges of IP addresses.

The concept of *objects* is the solution. Objects are the building blocks of CSM security policies. They are logical collections of elements and are reusable by other objects and policies. The use of objects allows you to define the security policy at an abstract level without worrying about network or device-dependent details. For example, you can define the following SSL VPN policy:

All users belonging to the employees group can access an Internet web server called intranet_web_server.

The object intranet_web_server is predefined by the IP address or Domain Name System (DNS) name of that web server. If the IP address of the server is changed in the future, you need only update the object definition. The security policy stays the same.

To apply the objects concept to multidevice policy provisioning, follow these steps:

1 Try to use common generic objects when you define device attributes. For example, use a general "external" interface to define the interface on which you want to enable SSL VPN, instead of very specific Ethernet 0/0, which might not apply to other SSL VPN appliances. The common generic objects defined in a policy template are general enough to apply to all the devices.

2 When you apply the SSL VPN policy template to a specific SSL VPN appliance, you need to transform the common object names to specific device-dependent attributes. We will use the VPN client IP pool scenario just discussed as an example to see how to configure CSM to map common object names to device-dependent attributes.

When you define the SSL VPN policy template, you define a common object sslvpn-ip-pool as the IP pool from which IP addresses are assigned to tunnel client users. This common object can be applied to all the ASAs in the network. To map the sslvpn-ip-pool to device-dependent IP address ranges, select the **Allow Value Override per Device** check box, as shown in Figure 7-8.

Figure 7-8   *Defining Device-Dependent Attributes (1)*

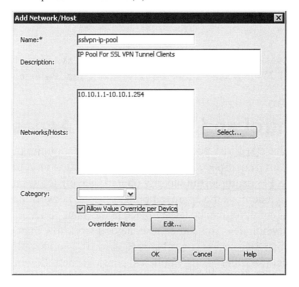

Then click **Edit** to define the IP address ranges for each ASA in the network. Figure 7-9 displays the configuration.

Figure 7-9 *Defining Device-Dependent Attributes (2)*

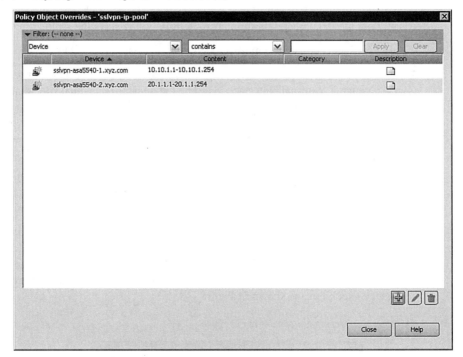

As shown in Figure 7-9, for sslvpn-asa5540-1.xyz.com, the IP range is 10.10.1.1-10.10.1.254; for sslvpn-asa5540-2.xyz.com, the IP range is 20.1.1.1-20.1.1.254.

Workflow Control and Role-Based Access Control

For a centralized security policy management solution, more than one team is often working on different aspects of the policy configuration or at different phases of policy provisioning. For example, the security operation team defines the policies and the network operation team deploys the approved policies to the network devices. Also, multiple management activities can be taking place at the same time, all operating under the same set of security policies. To handle these, a good workflow management process and role-based administrative access control are required. To handle multiple management activities running under the same security policies, consider the following:

- How are administrative roles defined? Who can modify the device configuration? Who can view the changes? Who approves the changes? Who can deploy the changes to the network devices?

- How do you handle multiple changes to a policy?

- Does a policy revision record exist? Is it possible to roll back a policy?

The section that follows discusses how to deploy CSM to handle workflow control and define role-based administration.

Workflow Control

The CSM comes with the following two modes:

- **The workflow mode:** The workflow is for organizations that have a division of responsibility between administrators who can define the security policies and those who administer them. Figure 7-10 shows an example. The security operation group defines the policy. The policy is then approved by the approver. The network operation group then deploys the policy to the security devices.

Figure 7-10 *Example of a Security Policy Provisioning Cycle*

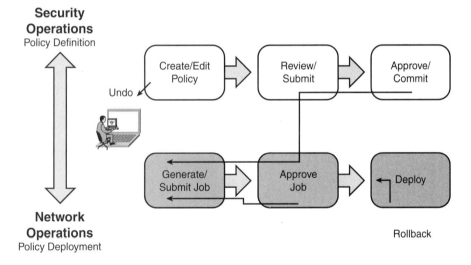

With the workflow mode, CSM provides a formal change-tracking and management system. This is done by using the notion of activity. An activity is a virtual context in which administrators can make changes. Changes are committed only to the database and made public after the activity has been submitted and then approved by an approver with the appropriate permissions. At this stage, the changes can be deployed to the network by creating a deployment job to define the devices to which configurations will be deployed and to define the deployment method to be used.

- **The nonworkflow mode:** This is the default mode of operation. This mode is simpler than the workflow mode. It allows you to define, save, submit, and deploy the policy in one step. The nonworkflow mode is typically for small- to medium-sized organizations.

Figure 7-11 illustrates the difference in the deployment cycle using workflow mode and nonworkflow mode.

Figure 7-11 *Deployment Cycle*

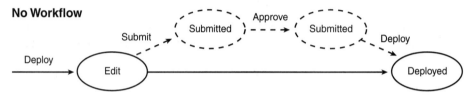

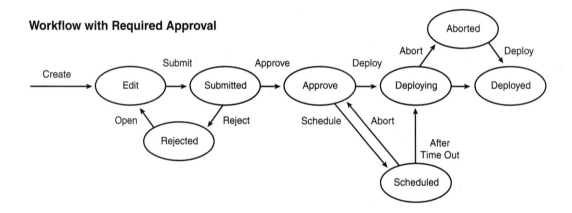

The next section focuses on the workflow mode.

Workflow Mode

As just discussed, workflow mode uses the activity concept to manage configuration changes. Each activity is a private view of the security manager database. The benefits of the activity are as follows:

- Configuration changes are isolated within activities before they are committed.
- The activity concept prevents concurrent modification that affects the same device or policy. This is done by policy locking.

- Activities track changes made in CSM through an audit trail. In this way, the person who made the changes and the changes made can be easily identified.

As shown in Figure 7-11, you need to follow a few steps in the workflow mode:

Step 1 **Enable the workflow mode.** Because the nonworkflow mode is the default mode, you need to turn on the workflow mode. This is done by choosing **Tools > Security Manager Administration > WorkFlow** and enabling the workflow mode. After this step, you see a different set of menus that have a few more options pertaining to workflow activities.

Step 2 **Create an activity.** No new Activities tab shows up on the menu. You need to create a new activity from there before you start a policy change.

Step 3 **Submit the policy.** After the policy work is done, you can submit the policy. In the submit window, you can enter the approver's e-mail address to notify the approver for whom you have just submitted an activity. When you click to submit the policy, the CSM performs an activity validation to verify the policy integrity and deployability.

Step 4 **Approve or reject the policy.** In this stage, the approver can approve or reject the policy change. As shown in Figure 7-12, the policy changes in the approved activities are merged into a "committed" policy, and all the device and policy locks are freed. Also, after the policy is approved, the changes cannot be undone. You need to create another activity for that.

Figure 7-12 *Policy Approval*

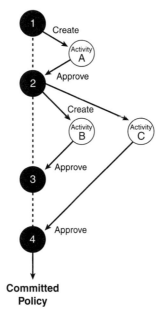

Step 5 **Deploy the policy changes to the devices.** You need to create a deployment job. Choose **Tools > Deployment Manager**. The deployment manager lists all the deployment jobs and their status (for example, deployed, approved, submitted, and failed). Create a new job from there, and select the devices that you would like to deploy. This will send a notification to the approver. After they are approved, you can deploy the policy changes to the physical devices. CSM also gives you an option to view the configuration changes that have been made.

CSM also supports advanced deployment options such as abort, redeploy, and rollback.

Role-Based Administration

Role-based administration is an important concept in the security management of any large network. This is also true for central SSL VPN management. First, with CSM, several teams are working on security management, be it managing different security devices from different teams or managing the same security device from different aspects. Secondly, the single SSL VPN device can be used to support multiple customers or organization units, so it might be required to have multiple administrators, each of which only manages a set of SSL VPN policies.

With role-based administration, the administrative right is determined based on the administrative role that the administrator has as part of the organization. The administrators take assigned roles in CSM based on their roles in the organization. An authentication and authorization process determines the role assignment.

For role-based administration, CSM offers two modes:

* The native mode with built-in predefined roles
* Integration with Cisco Access Control Server (ACS) that provides more granular role definition, including both predefined roles and customizable roles

Native Mode

In the native mode, the following default roles are available with predefined permissions, including view, modify, assign, approve, import, deploy, control, and submit:

* **Help Desk:** Help desk users can view (but not modify) devices, policies, objects, and topology maps.

- **Network Operator:** In addition to viewing permissions, network operators can view CLI commands and CSM administrative settings. Network operators can also modify the configuration archive and issue commands (such as **ping**) to devices.

- **Approver:** In addition to viewing permissions, approvers can approve or reject deployment jobs. They cannot perform deployment.

- **Network Administrator:** Network administrators have complete views and they can modify permissions, except permissions for administrative settings. They can discover devices and the policies configured on these devices, assign policies to devices, and issue commands to devices. Network administrators cannot approve activities or deployment jobs; however, they can deploy jobs that were approved by others.

- **System Administrator:** System administrators have complete access to all CSM permissions, including modification, policy assignment, activity and job approval, discovery, deployment, and issuing commands to devices.

The roles and associated permissions apply globally to all security devices, policies, and objects.

To enable the local authentications and define roles using native mode, simply log in to the CiscoWorks Common Service by connecting to http://<*IP address of CSM*>:1741 and then choosing **Server > Security**.

Cisco Secure ACS Integration Mode

The Cisco Secure ACS integration mode provides more granular administrative permission controls than the native mode. The two main areas are as follows:

- **Application-specific roles:** Cisco Secure ACS allows you to define customized roles that have granular permission down to the policy and object level. For example, you can define an administrative role that is authorized only to view and modify SSL VPN policies, but not other security policies, such as firewall policies or IPS policies. Figure 7-13 and Figure 7-14 show an example of the level of role permission customization you can define in Cisco Secure ACS.

Figure 7-13 *Defining Administrative Roles in Cisco Secure ACS (1)*

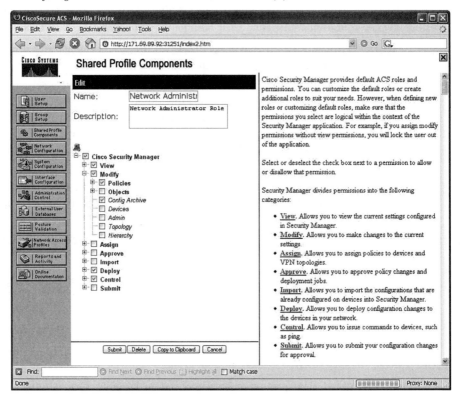

Figure 7-14 *Defining Administrative Roles in Cisco Secure ACS (2)*

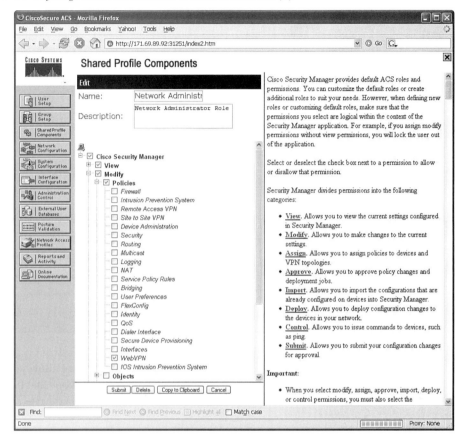

- **Device-specific role assignment:** Cisco Secure ACS uses the concept of Network Device Group, which allows you to put network devices that are subject to the same authentication, authorization, and accounting (AAA) group policy into a device group. The integration with CSM can take advantage of this to apply device group–specific roles. For example, in Cisco Secure ACS, you can define a few security administrators who belong to a group called netadmin_group. Administrators in this group can take on different roles when it comes to different security device groups. Figure 7-15 shows the configuration of this scenario.

Figure 7-15 *Device Group–Based Role Assignment*

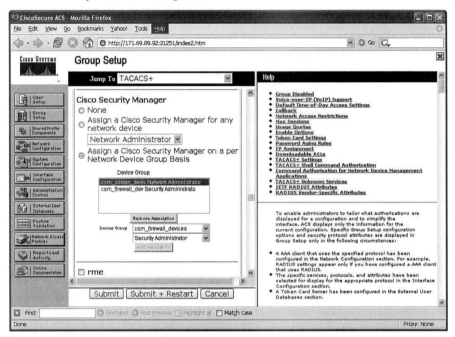

You might find that this is still not granular enough because it does not allow you to drill down to define the permissions for individual SSL VPN policies. We hope that future CSM or Cisco Secure ACS will address this.

Summary

This chapter discusses the multidevice central management of SSL VPN using Cisco Security Manager. Instead of focusing on the specific SSL VPN configuration, which has been covered in the previous chapter, this chapter focuses on the key elements in a multidevice management, including workflow control, common object and policy sharing, and role-based administration. The SSL VPN–specific configuration could change from version to version; these multidevice management concepts should always apply.

References

Cisco Security Manager End User Guide, http://www.cisco.com/en/US/partner/products/ps6498/products_user_guide_list.html.

Cisco Secure ACS Configuration Guide, http://www.cisco.com/en/US/partner/products/sw/secursw/ps2086/products_installation_and_configuration_guides_list.html.

NIST Role-Based Access Control, http://csrc.nist.gov/rbac/.

INDEX

Numerics

3DES, 22

A

AAA (authentication, authorization, accounting),
66
  authentication servers, 66–67
  authorization attributes, 193–195
  servers
    high availability, 68
    resiliency, 67
    scalability, 67
aaa authentication http console command, 105
aaa authentication login sslvpn local command,
227
aaa new-model command, 227
access
  applications
    configuring, 144
    port forwarding, 144–146
    smart tunnels, 147–149
  ASDM, 104–105
  DAPs, 197
    architecture, 190–191
    clientless connections, 209–212
    configuring, 192–197
    records. See *DAPR*
    sequence of events, 191
    troubleshooting, 219–220
  methods, 64–65
  privileges, 68–70
access deny message attribute (ASA group
  policies), 109
Access Method tab (ASDM), 204
acl attribute (group policies), 25
ACLs (Access Control Lists)
  application ACLs
    configuring, 257–259
    defining, 258
    mapping to group policies, 258
  network, 198

web-type
  configuring, 141–143
  DAP records, 199
ACS (Access Control Server) documentation, 67
Action tab (ASDM), 198
activeX relay attribute (ASA group policies), 109
Adaptive Security Appliances. *See* **ASA**
Adaptive Security Device Manager. *See* **ASDM**
address pools, 46–48, 156–158
Advanced Endpoint Assessment module (Host
  Scan), 184, 187–188
AES (Advanced Encryption Standard), 22
alerts protocol, 33
algorithms
  cryptographic, 17
    digital signatures, 24–25
    encryption, 20–24
    hashing, 18
    message authentication code (MAC), 18
    public key infrastructure (PKI), 25–30
    security, 75
  key derivation, 39–41
antispyware endpoint attribute, 196
antispyware host scans, 188
antivirus endpoint attribute, 196
antivirus host scans, 187
AnyConnect client, 86
  attributes, defining, 45, 155
    address pools, 267–269, *156–158*
    client functionality, enabling, 155
    DNS/WINS assignments, 274
    installation, 275–276
    Layer 3 interface, 269
    split tunneling, 271–274
    SVC functionality, 266
    traffic filtering, 270–271, *159*
    tunnel groups, 159
  configuring, 306–307
  CSD and external authentication deployment,
    206
    AnyConnect ASA configuration, 208
    CSD, configuring, 207
    RADIUS servers authentication
      configuration, 207

external authentication deployment scenario, 304
    configuration, 306–307
    installation, 306
    RADIUS server authentication, 305
full tunnel features, 159
    DNS/WINS assignment, 161
    DTLS configuration, 163
    keeping client installed, 162
    split tunneling, 159–160
installing, 85, 153
loading, 264–265
SVC package, 152–155
troubleshooting, 215–216
application ACLs
configuring, 257–259
defining, 258
mapping to group policies, 258
application data protocol, 34
application endpoint attribute, 196
applications
access
    configuring, 144
    port forwarding, 144–146
    smart tunnels, 147–149
role assignment, 327
secure communications, 49
applying
bookmark lists, group policies, 139
Secure Desktop restrictions, 294–295, 179–180
architecture
CSD, 280–281, 168–169
DAPs, 190–191
ASA (Adaptive Security Appliances), 79, 93
AnyConnect client
    attributes, defining, 155–159
    configuring with CSD and external authentication deployment, 208
    full tunnel features, 159–163
    installing, 153
    SVC package, 152–155
clientless SSL VPNs, 114
    application access, 144–149
    bookmarks, 134–140
    client-server plug-ins, 150–151
    enabling on interfaces, 116
    network topology, 114

portal. See portals, clientless SSL VPNs on ASAs
    server locations, 115
    web-type ACLs, 141–143
configuring
    ASDM, 101–105
    digital certificate enrollment, 98–101
    group policies, 107–109
    policies, 106–107
    tunnel groups, 110
    user authentication, 110–114
feature set design considerations, 94
implementation prerequisites
    infrastructure requirements, 97
    Internet browsers, 96–97
    licenses, 95–96
    operating systems, 96–97
monitoring SSL VPNs, 212–215
platform
    history, 87–88
    licenses, 89
    specifications, 88
    supported, 94
troubleshooting SSL VPNs, 215
    AnyConnect clients, 215–216
    clientless SSL VPN issues, 217–218
    CSD, 219
    DAP, 219–220
    SSL negotiations, 215
ASDM (Adaptive Security Device Manager), 86, 101
accessing, 104–105
appliances, configuring, 103–104
configuring, 101
DAP configuration tabs
    Access Method, 204
    Action, 198
    Functions, 200–201
    Network ACL, 198
    Port Forwarding Lists, 202
    URL Lists, 203
    Web-Type ACL, 199
launching, 105
monitoring SSL VPNs, 212–215
uploading, 102
website, 106
asdm image command, 103
asymmetric encryption, 20

attributes

AAA, 193–195

AnyConnect client, 266, 155

address pools, 267–269, 156–158

DNS/WINS assignments, 274

client functionality, enabling, 155

installation, 275–276

Layer 3 interface, 269

split tunneling, 271–274

SVC functionality, 266

traffic filtering, 270–271, 159

tunnel groups, 159

ASA group policies, 108–109

endpoint, 195–197

group policies, 246

Secure Desktop, 292–293, 176–178

authentication, **17**

hashing, 18

message authentication code (MAC), 18

RADIUS servers, 112, 207

servers, 66–67

SSL connections, 37–39

users, 66

AAA servers, 67–68

access privileges, 68–70

authentication servers, 66–67

clientless connections with CSD deployments, 302

configuring, 110–114

IOS routers, 226–228

RADIUS servers, 305

security, 75

authentication, authorization, accounting. *See* **AAA**

B

banner area (clientless SSL VPN portal logon pages), 119

banner attribute (group policies), 25, 108

Basic Host Scan module, 183–185

bookmark list attribute (ASA group policies), 108

bookmarks, configuring

applying bookmark lists to group policies, 139

ASAs, 134–135

file servers, 137

single sign-on, 140

websites, 135–136

browsers

ASA supported, 96–97

Secure Desktop

settings, 167, 182, 279, 297

support, 279

C

CA (certification authority), 230, 28, 99–100

Cache Cleaner, 166, 180–181

Mac/Linux policies, defining, 298–300

policies, defining, 295–296

certification, 28–30

change cipher spec protocols, 34

CIFS (Common Internet File System)

clientless issues, 218

configuring, 254–255

IOS router support, 253–257

servers, 257

cifs-url-list attribute (group policies), 246

CipherSuite, 37

Cisco

ASA 5500 series, 85–87

SAFE VPN IPSec Virtual Private Networks in Depth website, 82

Secure ACS integration mode (CSM), 327, 330

VPN 3000 series concentrator, 85

VPN routers, 86

clientless connections

CSD deployment, 301–302

clientless connections, defining, 303–304

CSD configuration, 303

user authentication, 302

DAP, 209–210

clientless connections, defining, 210–211

DAP configuration, 211–212

clientless SSL VPNs, 8

ASA configuration, 114

application access, 144–149

bookmarks, 134–140

client-server plug-ins, 150–151

enabling on interfaces, 116

network topology, 114

portal customizations. See portals, clientless SSL VPNs

server locations, 115

web-type ACLs, 141–143

configuring, 247–252
  HTTP requests, 248
  on IOS routers, 114
  mapping URL lists to groups, 251
  Outlook servers, defining, 251
  URL lists, 249–250
  web servers, defining, 249
troubleshooting, 217–218
clientless web access. *See* **reverse proxy technology**
client-server plug-ins, configuring, 150–151
clients
  AnyConnect
    attributes, defining, 155–159
    CSD and external authentication deployment, 206–208
    full tunnel features, 159–163
    installing, 153
    SVC package, 152–155
    troubleshooting, 215–216
  loading, 264–265
  port-forwarding, 55, 58
  thin, 259–261
    lists, defining, 261–262
    mapping lists to group policies, 262–264
  tunnel, 58–59
commands
  aaa authentication http console, 105
  aaa authentication login sslvpn group radius, 227
  aaa authentication login sslvpn local, 227
  aaa new-model, 227
  asdm image, 103
  crypto ca authenticate, 99, 230
  crypto ca enroll, 100, 231
  crypto ca import, 101
  crypto ca trustpoint, 101, 230
  crypto key generate rsa, 98, 239
  debug dap trace, 219
  debug menu dap 2, 213
  debug ntdomain 255, 218
  debug webvpn difs 255, 218
  debug webvpn svc, 215
  default-group-policy, 245
  enrollment terminal, 230
  http server enable, 103
  ip radius source-interface, 228

  radius-server host, 228
  service password-encryption, 227–228
  show flash, 233
  show webvpn session user sslvpnuser context securemecontext, 308
  show webvpn stats detail, 309
  ssl trust-point SecureMeTrustPoint outside, 101
  webvpn gateway, 237
Common Internet File System (CIFS) clientless issues, 218
components
  CSD, 165–166, 277–278
  DAP, 191
compulsory tunnel incoming call model (L2TP), 9
concurrent users, 94, 224
confidentiality, 17
configuring
  AnyConnect client, 306–307
    attributes, defining, 155–159
    full tunnel features, 159–163
    SVC package, loading, 154–155
  application access
    ASAs, 144
    port forwarding, 144–146
    smart tunnels, 147–149
  application ACLs, 257–259
  ASA
    ASDM configuration, 101–105
    digital certificate enrollment, 98–101
    group policies, 107–109
    policies, 106–107
    tunnel groups, 110
    user authentication, 110–114
  ASDM, 101–104
  bookmarks
    applying bookmark lists to group policies, 139
    ASAs, 134–135
    file servers, 137
    single sign-on, 140
    websites, 135–136
  CIFS, 254–255
  client-server plug-ins, 150–151
  clientless SSL VPNs, 247–252
    HTTP requests, 248
    mapping URL lists to groups, 251
    Outlook servers, defining, 251

URL lists, *249–250*
web servers, defining, 249
clientless SSL VPNs on ASAs, 114
application access, 144–149
bookmarks, 134–140
client-server plug-ins, 150–151
enabling on interfaces, 116
network topology, 114
portal customizations. See *portals,*
clientless SSL VPNs ASAs
server locations, 115
web-type ACLs, 141–143
clientless SSL VPNs on IOS routers, 114
context, 239–240
CSD, 169, 281
AnyConnect client with CSD and external
authentication, 207
clientless connection deployments, 303
launching CSD package, 283
loading CSD package, 61–62, 169–170
Windows CE policies, defining, 298–300
DAPs, 192–193
AAA authorization attributes, 193–195
access policies, 197–204
clientless connections, 211–212
endpoint attributes, 195–197
DTLS, 163
gateways, 237–238
group policies, 245–247
Host Scan, 184
Advanced Endpoint Assessment, 187–188
Basic Host Scan, 184–185
Endpoint Assessment, 186
IOS routers, 226, 235
context, 239–240
digital certificate enrollment, 229–232
gateways, 237–238
group policies, 245–247
login page, 242–243
network topology, 236
SDM, loading, 232, 234
server locations, 236
web portal page, 244
user authentication, 227–228
login page, 242–243
port forwarding, 144–146
RADIUS server authentication, *207*

smart tunnels, 147–149
SSL connections, 34
authentication/key exchange, 37–39
case study, 43, 46–48
finishing handshake, 41–42
Hello phase, 35–37
key derivation, 39–41
trustpoints, 98, 230
tunnel groups, 110, 159
web portal page, 244
web-type ACLs, 141–143
connections
AnyConnect clients, 215
handshake phase, 33
SSL, configuring, 34
authentication/key exchange, 37–39
case study, 43, 46–48
finishing handshake, 41–42
Hello phase, 35–37
key derivation, 39–41
content area (clientless SSL VPN portal pages),
125
content rewriting, 53
client-side processing, 53
customizable rewriting, 54–55
proxy bypass, 54
selective rewriting, 55
copyright area (clientless SSL VPN portal logon
pages), 122
crypto ca authenticate command, 99, 230
crypto ca enroll command, 100, 231
crypto ca import command, 101
crypto ca trustpoint command, 101, 230
crypto key generate rsa command, 98, 229
cryptographic algorithms, 17
digital signatures, 24–25
encryption, 20
AES, 22
asymmetric, 20
DES/3DES, 22
DH, 23
DSA, 24
RC4, 21
RSA, 24
symmetric, 20
hashing, 18
message authentication code (MAC), 18

public key infrastructure (PKI), 25–26
  certification, 28–30
  digital certificates, 26–28
security, 75
CSD (Cisco Secure Desktop), 164.
  ***See also* Host Scan**
architecture, 168–169, 280–281
attributes, defining, 176–178
browser settings, 182
clientless connections with deployment,
  301–302
    clientless connections, defining, 303–304
    CSD configuration, 303
    user authentication, 302
components, 165
    Cache Cleaner, 278
    Secure Desktop, 277
    Secure Desktop Manager, 277
configuring
    *AnyConnect client with CSD and external
      authentication deployment, 207*
    clientless connection deployments, 303
    launching CSD package, 283
    loading CSD package, 61–62, 169–170
policies, assigning, 174
prelogin sequences, 170
    Cache Cleaner policies, 180–181
    host emulators, 175–176
    keystroke loggers, 175–176
    prelogin policies, defining, 171–173
    Secure Desktop attributes, 176–178
    Secure Desktop browser settings, 182
    Secure Desktop policies, 174
    Secure Desktop restrictions, 179–180
requirements, 166–167, 278–279
restrictions, 179–180
troubleshooting, 219
Windows-based client policies, defining, 283
    browser bookmarks, 297
    Cache Cleaner policies, 295–296
    enabling features, 287–289
    identifying machines, 285–286
    keystroke loggers, 291
    Secure Desktop attributes, 292–293
    Secure Desktop restrictions, 294–295
    Windows locations, 284–285
Windows CE policies, defining, 298–300

CSM (Cisco Security Manager), 86
device imports, 315
device view, 314–318
End User Guide website, 331
multidevice policy provisioning, 314
    device view, 314–318
    objects, 320–321
    policy view, 318–319
policy view, 318–319
role-based administration, 326
    *Cisco Secure ACS integration mode,
      327–330*
    native mode, 326–327
workflow control, 322–324
    nonworkflow mode, 324
    workflow mode, 323–326
customizing
clientless SSL VPN portals, 117–118
    full customization, 129–133
    logon page, 118–122, 127
    logout page, 125
    portal page, 123–125, 129
content rewriting, 54–55
login page, 242–243
web portal page, 244

D

DAPR (DAP records), 191
accessing, 204
actions, 198
functions, 200–201
network ACLs, 198
port-forwarding lists, 202
URL lists, 203
web-type ACLs, 199
DAPs (Dynamic Access Policies), 189
architecture, 190–191
clientless connections, 209–210
    clientless connections, defining, 210–211
    DAP configuration, 211–212
configuring, 192–193
    AAA authorization attributes, 193–195
    access policies, 197–204
    clientless connections, 211–212
    endpoint attributes, 195–197

sequence of events, 191
troubleshooting, 219–220
Data Encryption Standard (DES), **22**
data protection, 76
data theft
prevention, 76–77
threats, 71–72
**Datagram Transport Layer Security (DTLS), 31,
48–49, 163**
debug dap trace command, 219
debug menu dap 2 command, 213
debug ntdomain 255 command, 218
debug webvpn cifs 255 command, 218
debug webvpn svc command, 215
default-group-policy command, 245
default login page, configuring, 242–243
**default post login selection attribute (ASA group
policies), 109**
deployments
AnyConnect client/external authentication, 304
AnyConnect configuration, 306–307
AnyConnect installation, 306
RADIUS server authentication, 305
AnyConnect client with CSD and external
authentication, 206
AnyConnect ASA configuration, 208
CSD, configuring, 207
*RADIUS servers authentication
configuration, 207*
clientless connections with CSD, 301–302
clientless connections, defining, 303–304
CSD configuration, 303
user authentication, 302
clientless connections with DAP, 209–210
clientless connections, defining, 210–211
DAP configuration, 211–212
L2TP, 9
SSL VPN, 8
DES (Data Encryption Standard), 22
designs
access methods, 64–65
ASA feature sets, 94
device placement, 78–79
high availability, 80
implementation scope, 94, 224
infrastructure planning, 94, 224
performance, 81

platform options, 79
router features, 224
router hardware, 224
scalability, 81
security, 70
cryptographic algorithms, 75
data protection, 76
data theft prevention, 76–77
passwords, 75
persistent sessions, 75
preconnect, 75
session timeouts, 75
threats, 71–74, 77
user authentication, 75
user authentication, 66
AAA servers, 67–68
access privileges, 68–70
authentication servers, 66–67
user connectivity, 93, 223
virtualization, 79–80
device view (CSM), 314–318
devices
importing into CSM, 315
placement, 78–79
role assignments, 329
DH (Diffie-Hellman), 23, 60
digital certificates, 26–28
ASA, 98
enrollment, 229–232
CA certificates, obtaining, 99–100, 230
*identity certificates, obtaining, 100–101,
231*
trustpoints, 98, 230
digital signatures, 24–25
DNS (Domain Name System), 161, 274
DSA (Digital Signature Algorithm), 24, 60
**DTLS (Datagram Transport Layer Security), 31,
48–49, 163**
Dynamic Access Policies. *See* **DAPs**

E

encryption, 20
AES, 22
asymmetric, 20
DES/3DES, 22

DH, 23
DSA, 24
RC4, 21
RSA, 24
symmetric, 20
**Endpoint Assessment module (Host Scan), 183,
186**
endpoint attributes (DAP configuration), 195–197
enrolling digital certificates, 8–11
ASAs, 98
CA certificates, obtaining, 99–100, 230
identity certificates, obtaining, 100–101,
231–232
trustpoints, 98, 230
enrollment terminal command, 230

F

file endpoint attribute, 196
file server bookmarks, configuring, 137
**file server browsing attribute (ASA group
policies), 109**
**file server entry attribute (ASA group policies),
109**
filter attribute (group policies), 246
firewalls, 77, 188
**full customization (clientless SSL VPN portals),
129**
logon pages, 129–132
user web portal pages, 132–133
**full tunnel features (ASA AnyConnect clients),
159**
DNS/WINS assignment, 161
DTLS configuration, 163
keeping client installed, 162
split tunneling, 159–160
full tunnel mode, 8
functions attribute (group policies), 247
Functions tab (ASDM), 200–201

G

gateways, configuring, 237–238
generating
identity certificates, 231
RSA key pairs, 98, 229

group policies
address pools, mapping, 158
application ACL mappings, 258
ASA, 107–109
attributes, 246
bookmark lists, applying, 139
CIFS servers, linking, 257
configuring, 245–247
port-forwarding lists, 146, 262–264
smart tunnel lists, 149
WINS mapping, 256

H

handshake protocols, 33–34
authentication/key exchange, 37–39
finishing handshake, 41–42
Hello phase, 35–37
key derivation, 39–41
hardware-based VPN clients, 7
hash-based MAC (HMAC), 18
hashing algorithms, 18
**hidden share access attribute (ASA group
policies), 109**
hide-url-bar attribute (group policies), 247
high availability
AAA servers, 68
deployment designs, 80
history
ASA platform, 87–88
IOS routers, 90
SSL, 30–31
TLS, 31
HMAC (hash-based MAC), 18
**homepage URL attribute (ASA group policies),
109**
host emulators (CSD), 175–176
Host Scan, 182
configuring, 184
Advanced Endpoint Assessment, 187–188
Basic Host Scan, 184–185
Endpoint Assessment, 186
modules, 183
Advanced Endpoint Assessment, 184
Basic Host Scan, 183
Endpoint Assessment, 183

HTTP compression attribute (ASA group policies), 109
HTTP proxy attribute (ASA group policies), 109
HTTP requests
    ASA, 134
    clientless SSL VPNs, 248
http server enable command, 103
HTTPS (HTTP over SSL), 32
    properties, 49
    reverse proxy support, 50–52
        content rewriting, 53–55
        URL mangling, 52

I

identity certificates, 100–101, 231–232
idle timeout attribute (ASA group policies), 108
IETF (Internet Engineering Task Force), 3
IKE (Internet Key Exchange), 6
implementation scope, design considerations, 94, 224
importing devices into CSM, 315
information area (clientless SSL VPN portal logon pages), 121
infrastructure
    planning, 94, 224
    requirements, 97
installing AnyConnect client, 153, 275–276, 306
integrated terminal services access method, 64
Internet browsers
    ASA supported, 96–97
    Secure Desktop settings, 167, 182, 279, 297
Internet Engineering Task Force (IETF), 3
Internet Key Exchange (IKE), 6
Internet Security Association and Key Management Protocol (ISAKMP), 6
IOS routers
    AnyConnect client, 264
        attributes, defining. See AnyConnect
            client, attributes
        loading, 264–265
    application ACLs, configuring, 257–259
    CIFS support, 253–257
    clientless SSL VPNs, 26–31
        configuring, 114
        HTTP requests, 248

        mapping URL lists to groups, 251
        Outlook servers, defining, 251
        URL lists, 249–250
        web servers, defining, 249
    configuring, 226
        digital certificate enrollment, 229–232
        SDM, loading, 232–234
        user authentication, 226–228
    history, 90
    implementation
        concurrent users, 224
        configuring, 226
        licenses, 225
        prerequisites, 225–226
        supported, 224
    licenses, 90–91
    monitoring SSL VPNs, 309–311
    SSL VPN implementation, 235
        context, 239–240
        gateways, configuring, 237–238
        group policies, 245–247
        login page, 242–243
        network topology, 236
        server locations, 236
        web portal page, 244
    thin clients, 259–261
        configuring, 144–146
        lists, defining, 261–262
        mapping lists to group policies, 262–264
ip http access-class command, 234
ip radius source-interface command, 228
IPS (intrusion prevention systems), 77
IPsec, 5–6
    hardware-based VPN clients, 7
    L2TP over IPsec, 11–12
    site-to-site VPN example, 3
    software-based VPN clients, 7
ISAKMP (Internet Security Association and Key Management Protocol), 6

K

key derivation algorithms, 39–41
key exchanges, 37–39
keystroke loggers, 175–176, 291

L

L2TP, 9–10
L2TP over IPsec, 11–12
launching
    ASDM, 105
    CSD packages, 283
Layer 3 interfaces (AnyConnect client), 269
licenses
    ASA, 89, 95–96
    IOS routers, 90–91, 225
linking CIFS servers to group policies, 257
Linux Cache Cleaner, policies, 298–300
loading
    AnyConnect client package, 264–265
    CSD packages, 282–283
    SDM, 232–234
login page (clientless SSL VPN portals), 127
login page, configuring, 242–243
logon page (clientless SSL VPN portals), 118, 121
    banner area, 119
    copyright area, 122
    full customization, 129–132
    information area, 121
    logon area, 121
logout page (clientless SSL VPN portals), 125

M

Mac Cache Cleaner, policies, 298–300
MAC (message authentication code), 18
management
    multidevice policy provisioning, 314
        device view, 314–318
        objects, 320–321
        policy view, 318–319
    role-based administration, 326
        Cisco Secure ACS integration mode, 327, 330
        native mode, 326–327
    workflow control, 322–324
        nonworkflow mode, 324
        workflow mode, 323–326
man-in-the-middle (MITM) attacks, 72

mapping
    application ACLs to group policies, 258
    group policies
        address pools, 158
        port-forwarding lists, 146
        smart tunnel lists, 149
    port-forwarding lists to group policies, 262, 264
    URL lists to groups, 251
    WINS to group policies, 256
mask-urls attribute (group policies), 247
maximum connect time attribute (ASA group policies), 108
MD5 (message digest algorithm 5), 18–19
message authentication code (MAC), 18
message integrity, 17
MMITM (man-in-the-middle) attacks, 72
modules (Host Scan), 183
    Advanced Endpoint Assessment, 184
    Basic Host Scan, 183
    Endpoint Assessment, 183
monitoring SSL VPN sessions
    ASAs, 212–215
    IOS routers, 309–311
multidevice policy provisioning, 314
    device view, 314–318
    objects, 320–321
    policy view, 318–319

N

NAC (Network Admission Control), 77
NAC endpoint attribute, 196
native mode (CSM), 326–327
navigation pane (clientless SSL VPN portal pages), 124
nbns-list attribute (group policies), 247
network ACLs
    ASDM, 198
    DAPs, 198
nonrepudiation, 24
nonworkflow mode (CSM), 324

O

operating system endpoint attribute, 196
operating systems supported
    ASA, 96–97
    CSD, 166
OSI layer placement, 31
Outlook servers, defining, 251

P

password security, 74–75
PCT (Private Communication Technology), 31
performance (design considerations), 81
persistent session security, 75
personal firewall endpoint attribute, 196
PKCS standards website, 60
PKI (public key infrastructure), 25–26
    certification, 28–30
    digital certificates, 26–28
platform options, 79
Point-to-Point Tunneling Protocol (PPTP), 13
policies
    access, 197–204
    ASA, 106–107
    Cache Cleaner, 180–181, 295–296
    CSD, 174
    dynamic access (DAPs)
        architecture, 190–191
        clientless connections, 209–212
        configuring. See DAPs, configuring
        sequence of events, 191
        troubleshooting, 219–220
    group
        address pools, mapping, 158
        application ACL mappings, 258
        ASA, 107–109
        attributes, 246
        bookmark lists, applying, 139
        CIFS servers, linking, 257
        configuring, 245–247
        port-forwarding lists, 41–43, 146
        smart tunnel lists, 149
        WINS mapping, 256
    Mac/Linux Cache Cleaner, 298–300

multidevice provisioning, 314
    device view, 314–318
    objects, 320–321
    policy view, 318–319
prelogin, 171–173
Windows-based clients, 283
    browser bookmarks, 297
    Cache Cleaner policies, 295–296
    enabling features, 287–289
    identifying machines, 285–286
    keystroke loggers, 291
    Secure Desktop attributes, 292–293
    Secure Desktop restrictions, 294–295
    Windows locations, 284–285
Windows CE, 298–300
policy endpoint attribute, 196
policy view (CSM), 318–319
port-forward attribute (group policies), 247
port forwarding. *See* **thin clients**
port forwarding access method, 64
Port Forwarding Lists tab (ASDM), 202
portal customization attribute (ASA group policies), 109
portals
    clientless SSL VPNs, 123
        content area, 125
        displaying, 129
        navigation pane, 124
        title panel, 123
        toolbar, 124
    clientless SSL VPNs on ASAs, 117–118
        full customization, 129–133
        login pages, displaying, 127
        logon page, 118–122
        logout page, 125
        portal page, 123–125, 129
port-forwarding clients, 55, 58
port-forwarding list attribute (ASA group policies), 109
port-forwarding lists
    DAP records, 202
    defining, 145
    mapping to group policies, 146
post login setting attribute (ASA group policies), 109
PPTP (Point-to-Point Tunneling Protocol), 13
preconnect security, 75

prelogin policies, 171–173
prelogin sequences (CSD), 170
    Cache Cleaner policies, 180–181
    host emulators, 175–176
    keystroke loggers, 175–176
    prelogin policies, defining, 171–173
    Secure Desktop
        attributes, 176–178
        browser settings, 182
        policies, assigning, 174
        restrictions, 179–180
prerequisites
    ASA implementations
        infrastructure requirements, 97
        Internet browsers, 96–97
        licenses, 95–96
        operating systems, 96–97
    IOS router implementation, 225–226
Private Communication Technology (PCT), 31
process endpoint attribute, 196
products, 85
    ASA platform, *87–88*
    Cisco
        ASA 5500 series, 85–87
        VPN 3000 series concentrator, 85
        VPN routers, 86
    IOS routers
        clientless SSL VPNS, configuring, 114
        history, 90
        licenses, 90–91
    software-based, 86
protocols
    alerts, 33
    application data, 34
    change cipher, 34
    DTLS, 48–49
    handshake, 33–34
        authentication/key exchange, 37–39
        finishing handshake, 41–42
        Hello phase, 35–37
        key derivation, 39–41
    HTTPS
        properties, 49
        reverse proxy support, 50–55
    IPsec, 5–7
    ISAKMP, 6
    L2TP, 9–10

    L2TP over IPsec, 11–12
    PPTP, 13
    record, 33, 42
    remote access, 4
    site-to-site, 3
    SSL, 30–31
    SSL v2, 30
    SSL v3, 31
    STLP, 31
    TCP/IP, 31
    TLS, 31
proxy bypass feature, 54
public key infrastructure. *See* **PKI**
pure-play SSL VPN appliances, 79

R

RADIUS servers
    authentication, 112, 207
    configuring, 228
    mapping to tunnel groups, 113
    user authentication, 305
radius-server host command, 228
RC4 encryption, 21, 60
record protocols, 33, 42
records (DAP), 191
    accessing, 204
    actions, 198
    functions, 200–201
    network ACLs, 198
    port-forwarding lists, 202
    URL lists, 203
    web-type ACLs, 199
registry endpoint attribute, 196
remote access
    protocols, 4
    technologies
        IPsec, 5–7
        L2TP, 9–10
        L2TP over IPsec, 11–12
        PPTP, 13
        SSL VPN, 7–8
        summary, 14
requirements (Secure Desktop), 166–167, 279
Rescorla, Eric blog, 19
resiliency (AAA servers), 67

resource access
methods, 64–65
privileges, 68–70
restrict access to VLAN attribute (ASA group policies), 108
restrictions (Secure Desktop), 294–295
reverse-proxy access method, 64
reverse-proxy-based web access method, 81
reverse proxy technology, 50–52
content rewriting, 53
client-side processing, 53
customizable rewriting, 54–55
proxy bypass, 54
selective rewriting, 55
URL mangling, 52
role-based administration, 326
Cisco Secure ACS integration mode, 327, 330
native mode, 326–327
routers
features, 224
hardware, 224
IOS
AnyConnect client. See IOS routers, AnyConnect client
application ACLs, configuring, 257–259
CIFS support, 253, 255–257
clientless SSL VPNs, 247–252
configuring, 226–232
digital certificate enrollment, 229–232
licenses, 225
monitoring SSL VPNs, 308–309
SDM, loading, 232, 234
thin clients, 259–264
user authentication, 226–228
IOS implementation, 235
concurrent users, 224
configuring, 226
context, 239–240
gateways, configuring, 237–238
group policies, 245–246
licenses, 225
login page, 242–243
network topology, 236
prerequisites, 225–226
server locations, 236
supported, 224
web portal page, 244

RSA (Ron Rivest, Adi Shamir, and Len Adelman), 24
key pairs, generating, 98, 229
website, 60

S

scalability
AAA servers, 67
design considerations, 81
SCEP (Simple Certificate Enrollment Protocol), 230
Schneier, Bruce blog, 19
SDM (Security Device Manager), 86
context configuration, 240
gateway configuration, 238
loading, 232–234
website, 233
Secure ACS Configuration Guide website, 331
Secure Desktop, 165
architecture, 168–169
attributes, defining, 176–178, 292–293
browser settings, 182
components, 165
configuring
AnyConnect client with CSD and external authentication deployment, 207
loading CSD package, 169–170
policies, assigning, *174*
prelogin sequences, 170
Cache Cleaner policies, 180–181
host emulators, 175–176
keystroke loggers, 175–176
prelogin policies, defining, 171–173
Secure Desktop attributes, 176–178
Secure Desktop browser settings, 182
Secure Desktop policies, 174
Secure Desktop restrictions, 179–180
requirements, 166–167
restrictions, 179–180. 294–295
troubleshooting, 219
Secure Desktop Manager, 165, 277
Secure Hash Algorithm 1 (SHA-1), 18–19
Secure Socket Layer. *See* SSL
Secure Transport Layer Protocol (STLP), 31

SecureMe
  AnyConnect client with CSD and external
    authentication deployment, 206
      AnyConnect ASA configuration, 208
      CSD, configuring, 207
      RADIUS servers authentication
        configuration, 207
  AnyConnect client/external authentication
    deployment scenario, 304
      AnyConnect configuration, 306–307
      AnyConnect installation, 306
      RADIUS server authentication, 305
  clientless connection with CSD deployment
    scenario, 301–302
      clientless connections, defining, 303–304
      CSD configuration, 303
      user authentication, 302
  clientless connections with DAP, 209–210
      clientless connections, defining, 210–211
      DAP configuration, 211–212
security. *See also* **CSM**
  application communication, 49
  authentication, 17
  confidentiality, 17
  cryptographic algorithms, 75
    digital signatures, 24–25
    encryption, 20–24
    hashing, 18
    message authentication code (MAC), 18
    public key infrastructure (PKI), 25–28
    security, 75
  data protection, 76
  data theft prevention, 76–77
  designs, 70
  digital signatures, 24–25
  encryption, 20
    AES, 22
    asymmetric, 20
    DES/3DES, 22
    DH, 23
    DSA, 24
    RC4, 21
    RSA, 24
    symmetric, 20
  hashing, 18
  Message authentication code (MAC), 18
  message integrity, 17

  passwords, 75
  persistent sessions, 75
  preconnect, 75
  public key infrastructure (PKI), 25–26
    certification, 28–30
    digital certificates, 26–28
  session timeouts, 75
  threats, 71
    data thefts, 71–72
    defense technologies, 77
    lack of security on unmanaged computers,
      71
    man-in-the-middle attacks, 72
    password attacks, 74
    split tunneling, 73
    viruses/worms/trojans, 73
    web application attacks, 73
  user authentication, 66, 75
    AAA servers, 67–68
    access privileges, 68–70
    authentication servers, 66–67
  white paper website, 82
Security Device Manager. *See* **SDM**
selection rules (DAPs), 191
selective rewriting, 55
servers
  AAA, 67–68
  authentication, 66–67
  CIFS, 36
  DNS, 161
  file, 137
  Outlook, 251
  RADIUS
    authentication, 112, 207
    configuring, 228
    mapping to tunnel groups, 113
    user authentication, 305
  reverse proxy, 50–52
    content rewriting, 53–55
    URL mangling, 52
  single sign-on, 140
  web, defining, 249
  WINS, 161
service password-encryption command, 227–228
session timeouts, 75
SHA-1 (Secure Hash Algorithm), 18–19
SHA-2 website, 19

show flash command, 233

show webvpn session user sslvpnuser context securemecontext command, 308

show webvpn stats detail command, 309

Simple Certificate Enrollment Protocol (SCEP), 230

simultaneous logins attribute (ASA group policies), 108

single sign-on (SSO) bookmarks, 140

single sign-on server attribute (ASA group policies), 109

site-to-site protocols, 3

smart tunnel attribute (ASA group policies), 109

smart tunnel lists, 147–149

    defining, 148

    mapping to group policies, 149

software-based products, 86

software-based VPN clients, 7

split tunneling, 73, 159–160, 271–274,

SSL (Secure Socket Layer), 30

    connections, configuring, 34

        authentication/key exchange, 37–39

        case study, 43, 46–48

        finishing handshake, 41–42

        Hello phase, 35–37

        key derivation, 39–41

    history, 30–31

    negotiations, troubleshooting, 215

ssl trust-point SecureMeTrustPoint outside command, 101

SSL v2, 30

SSL v3, 31

SSO (single sign-on) bookmarks, 140

sso-server attribute (group policies), 247

STLP (Secure Transport Layer Protocol), 31

storage key attribute (ASA group policies), 109

storage objects attribute (ASA group policies), 109

SVC (SSL VPN Client), 152

svc attribute (group policies), 247

SVC functionality (AnyConnect client), 266

symmetric encryption, 20

T

TCP/IP, 31

technologies

    port-forwarding clients, 55, 58

    remote access

        IPsec, 5–7

        L2TP, 9–10

        L2TP over IPsec, 11–12

        PPTP, 13

        SSL VPN, 7–8

        summary, 14

    reverse proxy, 50–52

        content rewriting, 53–55

        URL mangling, 52

terminal services, 58

thin client mode, 8

thin clients, 259–261

    configuring, 144–146

    lists, defining, 261–262

    mapping lists to group policies, 262–264

threats (security), 71

    data thefts, 71–72

    defense technologies, 77

    lack of security on unmanaged computers, 71

    man-in-the-middle attacks, 72

    password attacks, 74

    split tunneling, 73

    viruses/worms/trojans, 73

    web application attacks, 73

timeout attribute (group policies), 247

title panel (clientless SSL VPN portal pages), 123

TLS (Transport Layer Security), 31

toolbar (clientless SSL VPN portal pages), 124

traffic (AnyConnect clients), 159, 216

traffic filtering (AnyConnect client), 270–271

transaction size attribute (ASA group policies), 109

trojans, 73

troubleshooting

    AnyConnect clients, 215

        connectivity, 215

        traffic, 216

    clientless SSL VPNs, 217–218

    CSD, 219

    DAP, 219–220

    SSL negotiations, 215

SSL VPNs with ASAs, 215
  AnyConnect clients, 215–216
  clientless SSL VPN issues, 217–218
  CSD, 219
  DAP, 219–220
  SSL negotiations, 215
trustpoints, configuring, 98, 230
tunnel client access method, 64, 81
tunnel clients, 58–59
tunnel groups
  ASAs, 110, 159
  RADIUS server mappings, 113
**tunneling protocols attribute (ASA group
  policies), 108**

U

Unified Threat Management (UTM), 79
uploading ASDM, 102
URL entry attribute (ASA group policies), 109
url-list attribute (group policies), 247
URL lists
  DAPs, 203
  mapping to groups, 251
  Outlook servers, 250
  web servers, 249
URL Lists tab (ASDM), 203
URL mangling, 52
**user storage location attribute (ASA group
  policies), 109**
users
  authentication, 66
    AAA servers, 67–68
    access privileges, 68–70
    authentication servers, 66–67
    *clientless connections with CSD
      deployments, 302*
    configuring, 110–114
    IOS routers, 226–228
    RADIUS servers, 305
    security, 75
  connectivity, design considerations, 93, 223
  privileges, 167
  web portal pages (clientless SSL VPN portals),
    132–133
UTM (Unified Threat Management), 79

V

virtualization, 79–80
viruses, 73
voluntary tunnel mode (L2TP), 9

W – Z

web ACL attribute (ASA group policies), 108
web application attacks, 73
web portal page, configuring, 244
web portals (CIFS servers), 257
web servers, defining, 249
websites
  ACS (Access Control Server) documentation,
    67
  AES, 22
  ASDM, 106
  bookmarks, configuring, 135–136
  Cisco SAFE VPN IPSec Virtual Private
    Networks in Depth, 82
  cryptanalysis of SHA-1/MD5, 19
  CSM End User Guide, 331
  Diffie-Hellman introduction, 60
  DSA introduction, 60
  hardware modules, 224
  PKCS standards, 60
  RC4, 60
  RSA, 60
  Secure ACS Configuration Guide, 331
  security white paper, 82
  SDM, 233
  SHA-2, 19
web-type ACLs
  ASDM, 199
  configuring, 141–143
  DAP records, 199
webvpn gateway command, 237
Windows-based clients, policies, 283
  browser bookmarks, 297
  Cache Cleaner policies, 295–296
  enabling features, 287–289
  identifying machines, 285–286
  keystroke loggers, 291
  Secure Desktop
    attributes, 292–293
    restrictions, 294–295
  Windows locations, 284–285

Windows CE policies, defining, 298–300
Windows terminal services, 58
WINS (Windows Internet Naming Service), 161
>   assigning, 274
>   mapping to group policies, 256
Wireless TLS (WTLS), 31
workflow control, 322–324
>   nonworkflow mode, 324
>   workflow mode, 323–326
workflow mode (CSM), 323–326
worms, 73

Safari Library
Subscribe Now!
http://safari.ciscopress.com/library

Safari's entire technology collection is now available with no restrictions. Imagine the value of being able to search and access thousands of books, videos, and articles from leading technology authors whenever you wish.

EXPLORE TOPICS MORE FULLY

Gain a more robust understanding of related issues by using Safari as your research tool. With Safari Library you can leverage the knowledge of the world's technology gurus. For one flat, monthly fee, you'll have unrestricted access to a reference collection offered nowhere else in the world—all at your fingertips.

With a Safari Library subscription, you'll get the following premium services:

- **Immediate access to the newest, cutting-edge books**—Approximately eighty new titles are added per month in conjunction with, or in advance of, their print publication.

- **Chapter downloads**—Download five chapters per month so you can work offline when you need to.

- **Rough Cuts**—A service that provides online access to prepublication information on advanced technologies. Content is updated as the author writes the book. You can also download Rough Cuts for offline reference

- **Videos**—Premier design and development videos from training and e-learning expert lynda.com and other publishers you trust.

- **Cut and paste code**—Cut and paste code directly from Safari. Save time. Eliminate errors.

- **Save up to 35% on print books**—Safari Subscribers receive a discount of up to 35% on publishers' print books.

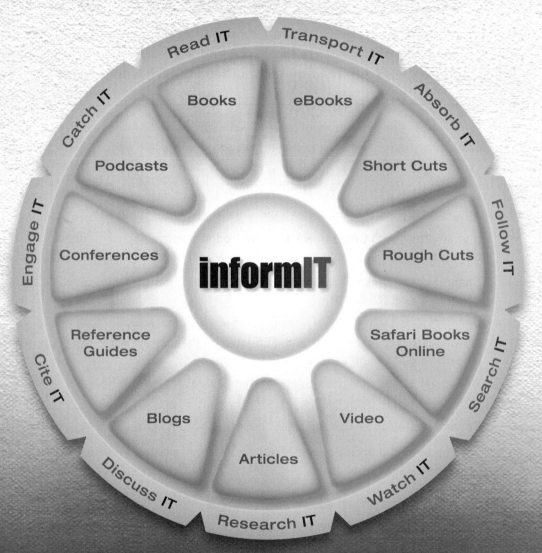